THE AUSTRALIAN SCIENCE FACILITIES PROGRAM:

A STUDY OF ITS INFLUENCE ON

SCIENCE EDUCATION IN AUSTRALIAN SCHOOLS

by

JOHN G. AINLEY

4783217

This study constitutes one of a series of evaluation studies sponsored financially by the Schools Commission and was conducted independently by the Australian Council for Educational Research

The Australian Council for Educational Research Limited
Frederick Street, Hawthorn, Victoria.

1978

Published by
The Australian Council for Educational Research Limited,
Frederick Street, Hawthorn, Victoria 3122.
December 1978.

Printed and bound by
Globe Press Pty Ltd,
430 George Street, Fitzroy, Victoria 3065.

National Library of Australia Cataloguing-in-Publication data.

Ainley, John G.
   The Australian Science Facilities Program : a study of its influence on science education in Australian schools.

   (ACER research monograph; no.2)
   Bibliography
   ISBN 0 85563 187 2

   1. Federal aid to education - Australia. 2. Science - Study and teaching (Secondary) - Australia - Finance. I. Title. (Series: Australian Council for Educational Research. Research monograph; no.2)

379.1212'0994

Copyright © ACER 1978

No part of this publication may be reproduced in any form without the permission of the publisher.

Table of Contents

	Page
Acknowledgments	(x)

Chapter 1   The Australian Science Facilities Program in Context   1
    The General Significance of the Program   1
    The Background to the Proposal   3
    The Needs of Science Education   12

Chapter 2   Evaluating the Science Facilities Program   21
    A Framework for the Evaluation   21
    Studies Related to the Provision of Science Facilities   29
    A Plan for the Evaluation   39

Chapter 3   Conducting the Evaluation   43
    The Survey of School Science Facilities   43
    The School Visits   52
    The Student Questionnaire   55
    Systemic Effects and Administration   66

Chapter 4   Systemic Features of the Science Facilities Program   67
    General Organization   67
    The Non-Government School Program   76
    The Government School Program   85
    Summary   94

Chapter 5   Concomitant Developments in Educational Systems   97
    Laboratory Assistants   97
    Curriculum Development   98
    The Supply of Apparatus   102
    The Design of Science Rooms   110

Chapter 6   Rooms for Teaching Science   121
    Looking at Science Facilities   121
    The Availability of Science Rooms for Science Lessons   123
    The Provision of Science Rooms in Schools   133
    The Quality of Science Rooms   141
    Access to Science Rooms   144
    Summary   147

		Page
Chapter 7	Making Use of Science Rooms	149
	Facilitating Effective Use of Rooms	149
	The Supply of Apparatus	150
	Laboratory Assistants in Schools	153
	Facilities as an Impediment to Practical Work	156
	Differences Between States in Teaching Science	158
Chapter 8	The Impact of Facilities on Science Teaching and Learning	163
	The Views of Non-Government School Principals	163
	Student Views about Studying Science	165
	Science Facilities and Science Learning: A Between-Class Analysis	167
	Correlations Involving School Facilities	173
	The Location of Science Rooms	175
	Conclusions	176
Chapter 9	A Closer Look at Some Schools	179
	Background to the Visits	179
	The Context of the School Visits	181
	Ruraton High School	183
	Riverside High School	188
	Petrin High School	191
	Casterbridge High School	194
	Western College	198
	The Schools : A Resumé	200
Chapter 10	Teacher Retention and Student Enrolments	203
	Introduction	203
	Science Teachers in Australian Schools	203
	Factors Associated with High Stability of Staff	207
	Teachers' Attitudes to Science Teaching	210
	Student Enrolments in Science Subjects	211
Chapter 11	In Retrospect	221
	The Provision of Science Facilities	222
	The Influence of the Science Facilities Program	226
	The Origins of the Program	229
	The Administration of the Program	230
	A Concluding Comment	233

		Page
References		235
Appendix A	A Summary of Questions About the Australian Science Facilities Program	251
Appendix B	The School Questionnaire	253
Appendix C	Details of Sampling and Weighting	271
Appendix D	Letters to Schools	275
Appendix E	The Student Questionnaire	285
Appendix F	Items Used in Scales from the Student Questionnaire	291
Appendix G	Measures of Science Facilities	295
Appendix H	Expenditure Under the Australian Science Facilities Program	297
Appendix I	Teacher Attitude to Science Teaching Scale	299

Tables

		Page
Table 1.1	Percentage of Science Rooms not Considered to be Satisfactory in 1961	13
Table 1.2	Science Staff in Secondary Schools in 1961	14
Table 1.3	Percentage of Science Classes Held in Satisfactory Laboratories in 1964	15
Table 3.1	Questionnaires Returned from Each State and School System	50
Table 3.2	Number of Questionnaires Returned by State and Date	51
Table 3.3	Factor Analysis of the Student Questionnaire Views of Science Classrooms (Section A)	63
Table 3.4	Factor Analysis of the Student Questionnaire Views of Science Classrooms (Section B)	64
Table 3.5	Scale Statistics for the Student Questionnaire Views of Science Classrooms	65
Table 4.1	Total Funds Made Available Under the Science Facilities Program	75
Table 4.2	Per Pupil Allocations of the Science Facilities Program	76
Table 4.3	Percentage of Science Facilities Program Funds Spent on Apparatus - Non-Government Schools	80
Table 4.4	Science Building and Equipment Programs Government Schools 1964-1971	88
Table 4.5	Estimated Building Costs	90
Table 4.6	Laboratory Costs in Government and Non-Government Schools	91
Table 4.7	Percentage of Science Facilities Program Used for the Provision of Apparatus in Government Schools	92
Table 4.8	Percentage of Available Funds Expended 1964-65 (Government Schools)	94
Table 5.1	The Usefulness of Certain Items of Equipment Supplied to Schools - 1967	103
Table 5.2	Usefulness of Certain Items of Apparatus - 1975	104
Table 5.3	Preferred Method of Allocating Apparatus Teachers Comments in 1967	105
Table 5.4	Issues Related to the Use of Apparatus Teachers Comments in 1967	105
Table 5.5	Types of Science Rooms in Australian Schools	113
Table 6.1	Factor Analysis of Responses to the Questionnaire : Science Facilities in Australian Schools	122
Table 6.2	Science Rooms Built or Renovated since 1964 in Schools Established before 1964	123
Table 6.3	Correlations between Various Indices of Need for Science Rooms	124

		Page
Table 6.4	Availability of Science Rooms in Secondary Schools	126
Table 6.5	Availability of Dual Purpose Science Rooms in Secondary Schools	127
Table 6.6	Room Availability for School Systems in Each State in 1975	127
Table 6.7	Dual Purpose Room Availability for School Systems in Each State in 1975	128
Table 6.8	Mean Values of Room Availability and Dual Purpose Room Availability by School Location for Government Schools in 1975	129
Table 6.9	Clusters of Schools with Similar Provision of Science Rooms	132
Table 6.10	Mean Number of Hours per Week per Class Allocated to Teaching Science in 1975 (Science Students Only)	135
Table 6.11	Mean Number of Hours per Week per Class Allocated to Teaching Science at Year 8 in City and Country Schools in 1975	135
Table 6.12	Percentage of Students in Year 10 who did not Study Science in 1975	136
Table 6.13	Mean Number of Hours per Week Allocated to Science, per Pupil in 1975	137
Table 6.14	Mean Values of the Science Enrolment Index for School Systems in Each State in 1975	137
Table 6.15	Science Rooms and Dual Purpose Science Rooms per 1000 Students by State and School System in 1975	139
Table 6.16	Science Rooms and Dual Purpose Rooms per 1000 Students by School Location in 1975	140
Table 6.17	Different Ratings of Similar Rooms - Melbourne Schools	142
Table 6.18	Mean Ratings of Science Room Quality by Science Teachers	142
Table 6.19	Percentage of Schools Where Rooms Rated as a Significant Impediment to Practical Work	143
Table 6.20	Percentage of Science Lessons held in Non-Science Rooms in 1975	145
Table 6.21	The Use of Rooms Provided Under the Science Facilities Program	146
Table 7.1	Percentage of Schools with Frequent Deficiencies in Apparatus	150
Table 7.2	Correlations Between Various Measures of the Adequacy of Apparatus	151
Table 7.3	Lack of Basic Apparatus Regarded as a Problem in Practical Work	152

		Page
Table 7.4	Correlations Between Measures Related to the Provision of Ancillary Staff	154
Table 7.5	Laboratory Assistants per 1000 Students	154
Table 7.6	Percentages of Schools in which Aspects of Assistance Rated as a Significant Impediment to Practical Work	155
Table 7.7	Aspects of Facilities Least and Most Frequently Regarded as Impediments to Practical Work	157
Table 7.8	Group Size for Practical Work in Year 9	158
Table 7.9	Percentage Experimental Work in Year 9	159
Table 7.10	Number of Laboratory Exercises in BSCS Biology	160
Table 8.1	The Views of Non-Government School Principals about Improved Facilities for Science	164
Table 8.2	Between and Within Class Variation in Responses to the Student Questionnaire	166
Table 8.3	The Impact of Science Facilities on the Science Learning Environment : Between Classes Regression Analyses	170
Table 8.4	The Association between Facility Measures and Environment Indices (coefficient of Contribution)	171
Table 8.5	The Impact of Science Facilities on Activities in Learning Science : Between Classes Regression Analyses	172
Table 8.6	Correlation Coefficients Between Facility Measures and Descriptions of Learning (School Facilities)	174
Table 8.7	The Association Between Reports of Science Learning and the Location of Science Rooms	175
Table 10.1	Percentage of Science Teachers with a Completed Tertiary Qualification in Science	204
Table 10.2	Percentage of Science Teachers in 1975 who were Female	205
Table 10.3	Number of Years Teaching Experience of Science Teachers	206
Table 10.4	Number of Years at Present School	207
Table 10.5	Teachers Attitudes to Teaching Science	211
Table 10.6	Enrolments in Science Subjects from 1964 to 1975 in Victoria	213
Table 10.7	Enrolments in Science Subjects from 1964 to 1975 in Western Australia	214
Table 10.8	Percentage of Year 12 Students Enrolled in Science Subjects	215
Table 10.9	A Between States Analysis of the Association Between Time Allocation to Science and the Science Enrolment Index	220

Figures

		Page
Figure 2.1	Expectations of the Australian Science Facilities Program	25
Figure 3.1	A Science Room Built with Funds from the Science Facilities Program	58
Figure 3.2	An Activity Based Science Lesson	58
Figure 4.1	Allocation of Funds Under the Science Facilities Program	69
Figure 4.2	Procedure Leading to an Offer of Assistance	78
Figure 5.1	A Single Purpose Laboratory Designed for Chemistry Practical Work	115
Figure 5.2	A Dual Purpose Room based on Fixed Benches	115
Figure 5.3	An Island Bench Science Room	116
Figure 5.4	A Science Room with all the Services at the Perimeter of the Room	116
Figure 5.5	A Science Room with Peripheral Services in which the desks have been arranged for discussion groups	117
Figure 5.6	A Science Room with Separate Laboratory Work Areas at the Edge of the Room	117
Figure 5.7	A Science Room incorporating Pillars and Movable Tables	118
Figure 5.8	A Science Room with Elongated Pillars and Movable Benches	118
Figure 6.1	AID Analysis to Determine the Distribution of the Availability of Science Rooms in Australian Secondary Schools	131
Figure 10.1	AID Analysis of Teacher Mobility	209
Figure 10.2	AID Analysis of Science Enrolments	217
Figure 10.3	The Association between Science Enrolments and Time Allocated to Science	220

Acknowledgments

Many people have helped me with this study. I wish to thank them for that help.

I am grateful to the members of my advisory committee for the comments they offered on my early proposals for the study, my interpretation of data, and my draft versions of the report. The members of the advisory committee were Dr T.W. Field, Mr E.D. Gardiner, Mr I.M. Hall, Dr J.P. Keeves, Professor Kwong Lee Dow, Professor L.D. Mackay, Mr D.G. Morgan, Mr R. O'Sullivan, and Professor R. Selby Smith who was the chairman.

I spent a great deal of time discussing the project with Dr J.P. Keeves, Professor Kwong Lee Dow, and Mr J.M. Owen. I thank them for their encouragement, sound advice and constructive criticism.

I gratefully acknowledge the co-operation of each State Education Department for the assistance they provided. In particular I should mention Mr F. Jones (ACT), Mrs R.B. Roberts (NSW), Mr I.M. Hall (Vic), Mr G. Robins (Qld), Dr E. Best and Dr J.M. Mayfield (SA), Mr K. Betjeman (WA) and Mr G. Fish (Tas). Thanks are also due to the officials of the Science Facilities Section of the Commonwealth Department of Education who helped me with access to files in that department.

Science teachers in a large number of schools throughout Australia took time to complete questionnaires, talk to me, and allow me access to their classes. For this I am most grateful.

For the duration of this project I was seconded from the Melbourne State College. I wish to thank the administration of that college for making it possible for me to undertake this study.

Finally, I wish to thank the clerical, library, research and typing staff of the Australian Council for Educational Research for their help with various aspects of the project.

John G. Ainley

CHAPTER ONE

THE AUSTRALIAN SCIENCE FACILITIES PROGRAM

IN CONTEXT

The General Significance of the Program

On 12 November 1963 the Prime Minister, R.G. Menzies, delivered an election policy speech on behalf of the Liberal Party. In that speech, just a little less than three weeks prior to the Federal election prematurely called for 30 November, special assistance for science teaching was promised. Menzies announced that, if returned to government, his party would

> make available £5 million per annum for the provision of building and equipment facilities for science teaching in secondary schools. (Menzies, 1963 : 22)

The money ($10 million) was intended 'to meet the special needs for improved science teaching' and was to be available to both government and non-government schools on the basis of school population. So began the Australian Science Facilities Program.

Enabling legislation[1] was passed by Parliament in May 1964 so that finance was available from 1 July of that year. In ensuing years successive Acts of Parliament[2] amended and extended the original Program. When it concluded on 30 June 1975 a little more than $123 million had been provided for or committed to secondary schools. Even though there were small differences between the successive Acts the provisions made under them have been considered to constitute a continuing Program. In recent times this has been known as the Australian Science Facilities Program though it has often been referred to as the 'Federal Science Grant' or the 'Commonwealth Science Scheme'.

The original announcement of the proposal for science aid in late 1963 was unexpected. However its enduring consequences have been considerable. Not all of those consequences have been confined to the precincts of science education though those which were provide the focus of this report.

---

1 The States Grants (Secondary Schools Science Laboratories and Technical Training) Act 1964.

2 The States Grants (Secondary Schools Science Laboratories) Acts 1965, 1967, 1968, 1971.

Studies by Gill (1965), Smart (1975) and Tomlinson (1976) have shown the formative influence of political factors upon the genesis and development of the Program. These studies also suggested that the Program had an effect upon subsequent developments in the financial provision for schooling in Australia.

The Science Facilities Program was the first direct involvement by the Commonwealth Government in secondary education. Smart (1974) and Tomlinson (1976) have demonstrated that this program provided a precedent for the School Libraries Program.[3] Tomlinson (1976) extended his analysis so that the Science Facilities Program was seen in context as the first of a series of Commonwealth government initiatives which culminated in per capita grants to non-government schools and unconditional grants to the States for capital expenditure on primary and secondary schools. As a result of these programs the complex relations between State and Commonwealth governments within the federal system were altered. Tannock (1976:30) considered that because the States became so dependent upon the Commonwealth they surrendered some of their autonomy in the formation of education policies.

In addition to proving a significant turning point in Commonwealth-State relations the Science Facilities Program had important ramifications for the relationship between Church and Government in the financing of education. Money was allocated to non-government schools, and it was the fact that this occurred which helped to re-kindle the embers of a debate over the role of Church and State in education. Subsequent programs extended the assistance available to non-government schools. Tomlinson (1976) showed that this was part of a re-examination of policy by the Liberal Party in government. A similar study of the evolution of Australian Labor Party policy is not available. Yet it is apparent that the "aid according to needs" policy was developed as a response to the issue of aid to non-government schools which was consistent with the more general principle of equal educational opportunity (Fitzgerald and Mathews, 1975; Spaull, 1974).

Not only political parties were forced to re-examine the question of financial assistance to non-government schools. Gill (1965) presented evidence which demonstrated that non-catholic churches were impelled to clarify their attitude towards government assistance. Initially some were reluctant to accept the assistance offered under the Australian Science

---

[3] The States Grants (Secondary Schools Libraries) Acts 1968, 1971.

Facilities Program. By the time the Science Facilities Program terminated "the tradition of separation of denominational schools from public funds had been destroyed" (Tannock, 1976:30).

In the course of a study of the development of education policy in the Liberal Party, Tomlinson (1976) concluded that the announcement of the Science Facilities Program had had considerable impact.

> ... Menzies achieved in a single unexpected statement a resolution of the state aid argument, the creation of a new role for the Commonwealth in providing for schools, and a reversal of the firm Liberal policy that section 96 grants should be made only at the specific requests of the States. After that statement .... the Commonwealth became involved in cumulative but separable and specific programs of assistance to schools, government and independent, within the States. (Tomlinson, 1976: 284).

The Background to the Proposal

Political Exigencies

Gill (1965) has presented convincing evidence of the political advantage which the announcement of aid for science facilities created. Such a scheme simultaneously met the demands of those arguing for assistance to non-government schools, those who supported greater assistance from the Commonwealth government for government schools, and those who pleaded the special case for science. Yet it was sufficiently specific, and so directed to a perceived national need, that it did not offend greatly the opponents of Commonwealth involvement in secondary or primary education. Moreover the proposition was one which, when raised through the New South Wales branch of the Australian Labor Party earlier that year, had created dissension in the Opposition party (Gill, 1965).

Constitutional Interpretation

Particular proposals such as the Science Facilities Program assume significance only when they are a response to more lasting developments. Smart (1975) and Tomlinson (1976) both examined the complex of factors which preceded Menzies' announcement on 12 November, 1963. Smart (1975) added to the short term political exigencies a consideration of long term and medium term developments. A changed view of constitutional power was the principal long term development. In education, as in other areas of government, constitutional amendments,[4] judicial challenges culminating in the Uniform Tax Decisions,[5] and the greater financial resources of the Commonwealth, led to a growth of the powers of the Commonwealth government. Tomlinson (1976) examined in detail the constitutional power of the Commonwealth government to provide funds for education. He argued that there was no legal limitation upon the capacity of the Commonwealth government to fund educational activities through Section 96 grants.[6] Menzies had recognized this in a speech as Opposition leader in 1945 (Menzies, CPD 1945: 4618)[7]. All that was required for the Liberal Party to act under this provision was a circumstance in which such an action could be accommodated within the traditional but changing principle of federalism. These long term developments in constitutional interpretation rendered it possible for the Commonwealth government to provide funds directly for secondary education.

Commonwealth Aid to Government Schools

The influences which Smart (1975) classified as 'medium term' emerged in the late fifties and early sixties. He categorized them as belonging to three clusters of demands. The Science Facilities Program was a response to the confluence of these three sets of demands. The triad of demands included arguments in support of Federal aid to education, supplications requesting government aid to non-government schools, and requests for

---

4 For example Section 51 (xxiiiA) which provides for benefits to be made available to students by the Commonwealth Government.

5 These arose in 1942 and 1957 from, inter alia, the States Grants (Income Tax Reimbursement) Act, 1942, the Income Tax (Assessment) Act, 1942, and the Income Tax Act of 1942. As a result the Commonwealth government became undoubtedly the major taxing power. (Tomlinson, 1976:9)

6 Section 96 at the Constitition of the Commonwealth of Australia provides the Commonwealth with the power to provide financial assistance to the States.

> 96 During the period of ten years after the establishment of the Commonwealth and thereafter until Parliament otherwise provides, the Parliament may grant financial assistance to any State on such terms and conditions as the Parliament thinks fit.

For a discussion of the relevance of this section to educational finance see Tomlinson (1976:3)

7 The notation CPD has been used to indicate a speech made in the Commonwealth Parliament. The year and page number in the Commonwealth Parliamentary Debates are indicated.

special assistance for the teaching of science. Rising costs of schooling were at the root of all three elements of the triad. In government and non-government schools the post-war population 'bulge'[8] exacerbated the strain created by the 'trend' of students to remain longer at school. This created difficulties often considered to be of 'crisis' proportions (Fitzgerald, 1970) in government school systems. State governments had limited financial resources from which to meet the increased cost of staffing, accommodation and sophisticated equipment. The argument that these problems could only be alleviated by Federal aid for education was advanced by a number of groups. Smart (1975: 87) cites the role of national parent and teacher organizations in lobbying State and Commonwealth ministers, conducting national education conferences and campaigning to raise Federal aid to schools as an election issue. Within the Commonwealth Parliament the Opposition often demanded that the Commonwealth Government should become more involved in education. Most influential, in the view of Smart (1975: 88) was a statement, prepared by the Australian Education Council, which drew attention to the need for additional funds to be made available to the States for education. The Australian Education Council included among its members the Directors General of Education from each State, and carried authority which ensured that its deliberations would be carefully considered.

Government Aid to Non-Government Schools

Similarly in non-government schools rising costs which were attributable to demographic changes and greater per capita costs (Bourke, 1969) prompted Roman Catholic school authorities to intensify their efforts to secure financial assistance. The problems of Roman Catholic schools were increased because expanding requirements for staff had to be met by increasing the proportion of non-religious staff in these schools (Bourke, 1969). Parent organizations and the church hierarchy both argued strongly for the introduction of government assistance to church schools. The arguments were presented to Commonwealth and State governments. The desirability of assisting non-government schools became an important political issue. At times the debate was bitter. It was always intense. However, the demand for aid came from some non-Catholic schools also. Smart (1975: 76) noted the changed attitude of the Headmasters' Conference towards

---

[8] The term 'bulge' refers to the transient increase in the population of successive age groups of people born after World War II. The 'trend' of students remaining longer at school is a more lasting phenomenen. These terms are used by Layard, King and Moser (1969).

government assistance. This association of the headmasters of prestigious Independent schools agreed, in the late fifties, to attempt to persuade school councils of the need for government assistance. Caution restrained them to argue only for the acceptance of capital grants which would not compromise their independence. After the payment of staff salaries, the next most expensive cost to schools was the provision of accommodation. Science accommodation was particularly expensive because it involved expensive plumbing, gas fittings and electrical work. Grants for buildings were specifically mentioned by the Headmasters' Conference as an area of special need (Smart, 1975: 77). On behalf of Roman Catholic schools the Archbishop of Sydney had specifically mentioned assistance with science buildings as one of five points presented to the Premier of New South Wales in 1962 (Smart, 1975: 85). Thus demands for Commonwealth assistance to education were made on behalf of Government, Catholic, and Independent schools[9].

The Special Plea for Science

The third of the medium term influences which Smart (1975) saw as leading to the Science Facilities Program was a conglomerate of various arguments which supported special assistance for science teaching. It now appears possible to recognize this third element of the triad as different from the other two. They were general requests for Commonwealth assistance to government and non-government schools respectively. As such they were 'initiating' factors through which the attention of the Commonwealth was drawn to the difficulties in schools. The plea for science was more specific. Hence the case for science aid was a 'formative' factor which guided the Commonwealth's response to the demands placed before it. Pressure for science assistance was formative in two ways. Firstly, it influenced the decision to aid science teaching rather than other facets of the school curriculum. Secondly the nature of the case helped shape the way in which aid to science was given. For these reasons it is necessary to examine the case presented for aid to science in some detail.

Various elements were present in the special pleas for assistance to science education. The pressures for special aid to science teaching have often been seen as exclusively concerned with the supply of technical manpower. The successful launching by the Soviet Union of a satellite in space was just one example of a number of developments which increased

---

[9] Throughout this Report the term Independent, as first suggested by Gordon (1957), has been used to refer to non-catholic, non-government schools. The problems associated with its use are recognized but it is a convenient term.

awareness of the importance of technology. Certainly a large number of voices argued in terms of the need to increase the available technological skill and manpower. Without an expanded scientific workforce, it was argued, the viability of competitive modern industry was threatened. However, the rather more muted argument based upon the belief that science was a necessary constituent of a general education cannot be ignored. This was recognizable as the basis of some arguments for an improvement in the arrangements made for teaching science. Both utilitarian and liberal views of science education were used to argue for improved conditions for school science.

In 1957 the Australian Academy of Science (1957) presented a report on scientific and technical manpower supply to the Prime Minister. This report expressed concern that the economic development of Australia was being hindered by a shortage of skilled scientific manpower. In addition to proposing that this was a serious problem the Academy attributed much of its cause to schools and in particular to the shortage of qualified science teachers.

> The trouble begins at the secondary school where there is insufficient encouragement for the student to take up a scientific career. There is a grave shortage of competent teachers of science and mathematics: this must be overcome speedily if Australia's industrial stability is not to be threatened.
>
> (Australian Academy of Science, 1957: 3)

In the very month that the Academy of Science presented its report to the Prime Minister another committee reported on its deliberations. The Committee on Australian Universities (1957) although not directly concerned with secondary schools, did place special stress on the need to improve scientific and technical education. In doing this it reinforced the comments of the Academy of Science about the supply of qualified science teachers. Neither the Academy nor the Committee on university education made any comment about science facilities in secondary schools. Both of the reports emphasized the utilitarian view of science education: science was related to the improvement of material comfort.

The endeavours of the Industrial Fund were a response to the problems identified in these Reports. Modelled on the Industrial Fund for the Advancement of Science in England (Merrilees, 1958), it was founded in 1959. Its purpose was to use the financial resources of industry to provide assistance for building school science laboratories. Beneficiaries of the Fund were all non-government boys schools. This was a policy copied from that of the Industrial Fund in the United Kingdom (Merrilees, 1958). There is evidence that the administrators of the Fund considered that these schools were the most likely source of potential scientists (Smart, 1972). Schools were invited to apply for assistance after they were rated on two criteria. A priority rating considered the extent to which they produced science students in tertiary education. A needs rating assessed the degree to which the school laboratories satisfied the standards specified by the Industrial Fund (Smart, 1972). By 1963 the Fund had dispersed over £600,000 in assisting some 35 schools (Smart, 1975). All of these schools were boys schools, all were members of the Headmasters' Conference and all were schools considered to produce a large proportion of potential scientists. Few Catholic schools received assistance. Studies by Smart (1972, 1975) and Tomlinson (1976) suggest that the operation of the Industrial Fund was an important influence on the decision to announce a government funded Science Facilities Program. It appears that it focussed attention on the comments made by other bodies about the state of science teaching, provided an indication of a form of assistance which could be made to schools, and even suggested a method of operation for such a Program. Menzies (1970: 95) acknowledged the debt which the conception of the Science Facilities Program owed to the Industrial Fund. In Britain the Industrial Fund had hoped that its efforts would stimulate government action to provide better science facilities in maintained schools. Menzies indicated, in a speech at Scotch College in Melbourne during early 1964, that he was aware of this and did not intend to neglect government schools.[10] Smart (1972, 1975) has demonstrated that many of the procedures used in the non-government school section of the Science Facilities Program were similar to those used by the Industrial Fund. The notion of 'needs' as the number of science rooms for science periods taught was one aspect which continued. In addition such a connection with a Fund concerned with schools likely to produce scientists may have directed the Science Facilities Program towards the needs of upper school science in its early years. Thus the Industrial Fund was a formative influence in two ways. Firstly, its existence directed attention to the needs of science education. Secondly, its priorities and administrative procedures shaped those which were followed by the Science Facilities Program.

---

10 Interview with Professor R. Selby Smith, 10 February 1977.

The Australian Science Teachers Association (ASTA) drew its members from a wider spectrum of schools than those assisted by the Industrial Fund. Many of its members came from non-government schools which did not belong to the Headmasters' Conference. Others were science teachers in government schools. As an organization it was helped by a number of commercial firms (Richards, 1957) and it had suggested ways in which industry could assist science teaching (Berndt, 1957). The first article in the first issue of its journal (ASTA, 1955) drew attention to the shortage of trained scientists in Australia as did the leading article in its second issue (Richardson, 1955). One session of the sixth conference of ASTA was devoted to the role of the science teacher in expanding technical and scientific manpower. The chairman (Olsen, 1956: 19) not only asserted that decisions against scientific careers were made in science classrooms but also recognized the non-vocational role of science teaching. The point was admirably amplified by Schonell.

> The secondary schools are prime educators in science for its own sake and no claims of technology must ever be allowed to distort their educating mission; but more important, perhaps, they must teach those who are not to be scientists ... to think about science, to appraise its results, and recognize its limitations. (Schonell, 1956:21).

Contributing papers (Kevin, 1956; Merrilees, 1956; Pfitzner, 1956) expressed the same important point: science teaching had dual responsibilities and one should not be subordinate to the other. Pfitzner (1956) widened the debate to include a criticism of the simplistic notion of manpower planning which, he said, ignored both detailed consideration of the demand for manpower and the multipurpose nature of society. Science teachers were cautioned by Pfitzner (1956) against becoming too zealous in encouraging able students to scientific careers. Science teachers continued to express their responsibility to those who did not become scientists in debates about science curricula (Anders, 1959; Hughes, 1963; Keeves, 1959). A statement agreed upon by the members of the eleventh conference of ASTA (1962) detailed the changes and development in pupils which it was hoped to foster through science teaching. It clearly assumed that science was to be regarded as a component of general education rather than a specific vocational preparation. Hence in the view of members of ASTA the liberal education purposes of science teaching were important. In addition to this extra perspective on the problems of teaching science ASTA members were aware of the need for Commonwealth funding. Merrilees (1956) as President of the Science Teachers Association of Western Australia argued that because the amounts involved were beyond the resources of State governments Commonwealth assistance should be sought. He argued that ASTA should press for greater funding of education in general and science education in particular. In its campaign to improve the provision for science education in 1964, ASTA prepared a statement of the needs of science education (ASTA, 1964). As this document provides a succinct statement of conditions for science teaching it will be considered later in this chapter. ASTA was thus involved in arguments about the future of science teaching. It recognized that additional funds would need to be provided by the Commonwealth government, it argued that science teaching needed additional assistance and its members argued for a liberal view of science education which leavened the pre-occupation of other groups with utilitarian purposes of science teaching.

In New South Wales the Secondary Teachers' Association and the New South Wales Teachers' Federation jointly sponsored a New Deal for School Science Conference in November 1961 (Cull, 1962). It was followed by a School Science Convention the next year (New South Wales Teachers' Federation, 1962). These conferences were significant in several ways. They involved collaboration between a general teachers union and science teachers. The support of non scientists was obtained. Parents' and teachers' organizations, trades unions, professional associations and academics all supported the conferences (New South Wales Teachers' Federation, 1961 a). The conference in 1961 had the support of the Director General of Education (Cull, 1962). Yet the most important aspect of the Conference was the political acumen with which it was organized and through which it sought to have its deliberations implemented. State and Commonwealth members of parliament were invited to attend the conference. Subsequently a deputation presented the decisions of the conference to the Premier. All delegates were asked to secure the support of their organizations for the conference decisions and to write to the Premier. The problems of science teaching and the conference decisions continued to be publicized through an illustrated pamphlet (New South Wales Teachers Federation, 1962).

Several main resolutions were carried by the conference. They were addressed to the recruitment and training of science teachers, the conditions of rooms and equipment, the problems of class size and the lack of laboratory assistants, the need to revise the junior science syllabus, and the necessity for Federal financial assistance to primary and secondary education (New South Wales Teachers' Federation, 1961 a).

Broader purposes than the creation and development of technical manpower were envisaged by most participants in the conference. The mimeographed letter sent to potential participants stated :

> you are in a better position than most people to appreciate the importance of a sound training in science as part of a balanced secondary education.
>
> (New South Wales Teachers' Federation, 1961 b)

In its preamble the conference papers stressed the same theme. One background paper (Cull, 1961) placed the role of science education in national development in a different perspective. Having acknowledged the need for a country to develop its scientific potential it elaborated that this meant that all concerned with the application of scientific knowledge

> from the highest policy makers to the man in the street whose opinions and whose voice must influence policy decisions, should have some experience in and understand the background of scientific work.
>
> (Cull, 1961: 3)

Only schools, he argued, could provide the necessary background in science, and only if they were given better conditions.

It has been noted already that the first political group to propose a science facilities program was the New South Wales branch of the Australian Labor Party at its June, 1963 conference. This form of assistance had been requested from the State government by the Roman Catholic Archbishop of Sydney (Gill, 1965). It was requested as one of five points in that submission. That it was given precedence above the other four requests suggests that the New Deal for School Science Conference may have exerted some influence. In addition to the more general publicity and pressure group activity which resulted, some conference participants were in especially influential positions. Trades Unions were involved in the conference as were a number of leading political figures in the Australian Labor Party.

Hence in the period before 1963 the two aspects of the special plea for science assistance were interwoven. The utilitarian view of science education saw it as a contribution to industrial development. The liberal view argued for the place of science in a general education. In the arguments presented by various interest groups each was detectable. The first was predominant in the work of the Industrial Fund, the second in the activity of science teachers and general education groups. Both of these views led to a desire to improve science teaching. Each interest group drew attention to similar problems in science teaching. When Menzies introduced the States Grants (Science Laboratories and Technical Training) Act 1964 he was cognizant of both points of view.

> There are two ends to be served. The first is to raise the general level of education in a society which is becoming increasingly dependent on the scientific use of resources. The second is the special education necessary for those young people who are to take up scientific and technical careers of all sorts, and who must come forward in increasing numbers, and must have an ever deeper understanding of science both theoretical and applied.
> (Menzies, CPD 1964: 1640).

The Needs of Science Education

Facilities for Science Teaching

The claim that science education required assistance is supported by evidence which was available at the time and also by evidence which has since become available. A study was conducted by the ACER of the provision for science teaching in non-government schools in 1958 (ACER, 1958). This coincided with the time when consideration was being given to establishing the Industrial Fund. Its two main conclusions were that funds were needed on an extensive scale and that maximum benefit would have resulted if the funds were concentrated on girls schools. The first conclusion was based on the cost of providing suitable accommodation and modern equipment in all non-government schools. The second was based upon an analysis of data which showed that only nine percent of the girls in the third last year of school studied science courses in their final year. The corresponding figure for boys was 31 percent.

The Industrial Fund did not act on this second conclusion. Its members preferred to concentrate their resources on schools which were traditional sources of science specialists. Seven years later a report requested by ASTA suggested that the facilities for teaching physical science in girls' schools were still poor (Carter, 1965). The report conceded some recent improvement in such schools but raised other problems. Discrimination in scientific employment, the influence of occupational stereotypes, the fact

Table 1.1   Percentage of Science Rooms Not Considered to be Satisfactory in 1961

State	Rooms Without Lab. Benches		Unsatisfactory Rooms used in Practical Work	
	Government	Non-Government	Government	Non-Government
New South Wales	42	24	87	68
Victoria	19	24	86	61
Queensland	33	12	86	71
South Australia	16	24	53	49
Western Australia	43	14	93	74
Tasmania	21	21	51	57
Australia	29	24	80	63

Source: Keeves (1966)

that donations from parent groups tended to favour domestic arts and the lack of female science teachers were mentioned as possible factors discouraging girls from pursuing scientific careers.

In 1961 ASTA conducted a survey of the conditions for science education in schools throughout Australia (Keeves, 1966). As only 45 percent of the questionnaires, sent to every secondary school in Australia, were returned there was the possibility of bias in the results. The response was 51 percent for Government schools, 29 percent for Catholic schools, and 51 percent for Independent schools. Though the results quoted underestimate the contribution of Catholic schools the picture they revealed was alarming. One quarter of the rooms used principally for teaching science were equipped with only desks or tables. The greater detail provided in Table 1.1 is an indication that variations existed between States in this regard. Schools in New South Wales and Western Australia appear to have been particularly poorly provided. The Table also records the percentage of those rooms used for practical work which satisfied certain criteria.[11]   It appears that government schools had

---
11 These standards were as follows:
   (a) Bench space: 2.5 feet per student.
   (b) Taps and sinks: 2 per room in Biology and Physics and 1 per 4 students in Chemistry and Science.
   (c) Gas outlets: 1 per 2 students.
   (d) Power points: 1 per 2 students in Physics and Biology and 2 per room in Chemistry and Science.
   (e) Fume cupboards: 1 per room in Chemistry.

Table 1.2   Science Staff in Secondary Schools in 1961

State	Laboratory Assistants per school Government	Laboratory Assistants per school Non-Government	Percentage of Science Teachers without Tertiary Science Qualifications (All Schools)
New South Wales	-	0.5	49
Victoria	0.07	0.18	32
Queensland	-	0.03	36
South Australia	0.25	0.05	40
Western Australia	-	0.06	27
Tasmania	0.22	0.17	31
Australia	0.07	0.10	37

Source: Keeves (1966)

poorer science rooms than non-government schools and that there were differences between States: for example Tasmania and South Australia seemed better provided than Queensland. Other evidence (Keeves, 1966) suggests that girls schools were not as well provided with science facilities as boys schools. In addition to there being many science rooms which were poorly equipped, there were very few schools which had any laboratory assistants. Table 1.2 records the numbers of laboratory assistants in schools in 1961. Science teachers considered the apparatus available to be rather better than the science rooms. Eighty percent of schools considered the expendable[12] apparatus which they possessed as either sufficient or involving only minor shortages. The same comment was made by 82 percent of schools about their minor[13] apparatus but only 69 percent regarded the supply of major[14] apparatus as adequate.

The survey also collected information about the qualifications of science teachers. It found that 30 percent had no tertiary qualifications in science or related fields. There was some variation between States as can be seen in Table 1.2 but a breakdown by school system was not reported. Unfortunately the different rate of response from each school system would have distorted the aggregate figures.

---

12 Expendable apparatus referred to items such as test tubes, beakers and stock reagents.

13 Minor apparatus referred to items such as bunsen burners, stands and magnets.

14 Major apparatus referred to items such as balances, electrical meters and microscopes.

Table 1.3   Percentage of Science Classes Held in 'Satisfactory' Laboratories in 1964

State	Non-Government Catholic	Non-Government Independent
New South Wales	20	56
Victoria	24	45
Queensland	26	20
South Australia	27	19
Western Australia	26	53
Tasmania	44	56
Mean (All Non-Government schools)		33

Source: Commonwealth Department of Education   File Number 68/52 (101)

Other information confirms the view that school science was being taught under poor conditions. One of the first actions taken by the Commonwealth government, when administering the Science Facilities Program, was to obtain data about the science facilities available in non-government schools. Information was obtained from a questionnaire sent to all non-government schools. From this it was estimated that only 33 percent of science lessons in these schools were held in satisfactory rooms (CDE, File 68/52 (101))[15]. It can be seen in Table 1.3 that differences existed between States and school systems. Roman Catholic schools were generally less able to accommodate their science classes in science rooms than were other non-government schools. Comparable figures for government schools existed, only for Western Australia. In that State, in 1964, 32 percent of science periods in Senior High Schools, and 28 percent of science periods in High Schools, were not held in science rooms. (CDE, File 64/1006).

Science Curricula

The needs of science education at this time were not confined to rooms and apparatus. ASTA prepared a comprehensive statement of needs for the council of the Australian and New Zealand Association for the Advancement of Science (ANZAAS) in January 1964 (ASTA, 1964). This statement argued that needs other than rooms and equipment should be considered. While it acknowledged the need for functional laboratories and sufficient simple apparatus, it asserted that there was a danger in concentrating efforts on one aspect of the problem. Providing laboratories alone would be unlikely to provide an effective answer to the problems of science education.

---
15   This notation has been used to refer to files held by the Commonwealth Department of Education.

Like the New Deal for Science conference it drew attention to the need to develop new courses, and to improve the expertise of science teachers. It also argued that adequate numbers of ancillary staff would be needed for facilities to be fully utilized. ASTA concluded that the problems of science education should be studied by a Federal organization. Consequently it recommended the establishment of an independent Australian Science Education Foundation (Stanhope, 1964).

It was intended that the Foundation would be involved in the development of courses, the design of apparatus and rooms, and even giving advice on how best to spend the annual science grant of $5 million. The suggestion was supported by the ANZAAS Council (Stanhope, 1964). ASTA sought support for the establishment of the proposed Foundation from the Commonwealth government, the Industrial Fund and the Australian Academy of Science (ASTA, undated). Its formation was often discussed in the ASTA Journal (Bassett, 1965; Tisher, 1965; Yaxley, 1964), and in 1967 the Federal Council (ASTA, 1967) reasserted the need to establish a national foundation concerned with curriculum development in science. The foundation was never formed. Eventually the Commonwealth government provided substantial assistance through the Australian Council for Educational Research for an Australian Science Education Project to produce curriculum materials (Owen, 1977).

The desire to revise science curricula was evident at the time the Science Facilities Program commenced. It was another facet of the general concern with the state of science education. One issue was whether science in the lower secondary school ought to be taught as a combined or integrated study rather than as a set of separate disciplines (Anders, 1959; Keeves, 1959; Stanhope, 1959). At that time General Science was only firmly established as a subject for most junior secondary students in Victoria and Tasmania (Stanhope, 1961). Science is now taught as a single subject to most students in years 7 to 10 throughout Australia (Shepherd, 1970).

Other aspects of lower secondary school science also received attention. Content was considered dated and poorly organized with the result that major principles were not clearly developed (Stanhope, 1965). The Science course introduced in New South Wales as part of the Wyndham Scheme in 1962 was an early response to curriculum problems. It emphasized the need to make science more modern and better organized around 'big ideas' (Barker, 1963). An important feature of the course was a comprehensive textbook (Messel et al, 1964). Claiming to be integrated, but in practice treating each science discipline separately, this book was a compendium of the information around which the course was structured. While the role of experiments in this course was greater than previously had been the case, it was not as important as in other new courses.

A changed approach to teaching science was manifest in another development which began at a similar time. In October 1963 the Science Standing Committee of the Victorian Universities and Schools Examination Board (VUSEB) convened a conference on lower secondary school science (VUSEB, 1963). At this conference the invited participants considered overseas developments in science curricula, principles which ought to be followed, and action to follow the conference. Specific comment was made that a concentration on revising content and preparing text books would not be sufficient: consideration needed to be given to appropriate methods of teaching science. As a result of this conference a series of changes were made to the lower school science syllabus from 1966 onwards (VUSEB, 1966: 320). More importantly in 1966 the Junior Secondary Science Project (JSSP) commenced (Dale, 1966). Through this project curriculum materials for use in the new science syllabuses were developed. Ramsey (1972) claims that limited financial resources restricted the scope of JSSP. However by 1969 a number of units for use in years 7 and 8 had been developed. Moreover it was of special significance in the development of science education. Its origins coincided with the commencement of the Science Facilities Program, its direction focussed attention upon matters other than content, and it was a direct precursor to the Australian Science Education Project (ASEP) (Ramsey, 1972). Subsequently other curriculum materials developed reflected some of the approach adopted in JSSP. (Western Australia, 1972).

Senior science curricula also changed during the sixties. Stanhope (1967) considered that there were four different approaches to curriculum change in Australian senior science courses.

1. The traditional method of eclectic additions to and deletions from the content of an existing course.
2. The adoption of a course developed in another country, usually the United States, as occurred with PSSC Physics in Victoria and CHEM STUDY Chemistry in Queensland, Tasmania, and Western Australia.

3. The adaptation and modification of an overseas course as was done in producing an Australian adaptation of the BSCS Biology materials.

4. The local development of new courses, albeit with some overseas influence, as in the Victorian 'structural view' Chemistry and New South Wales Senior Science courses.

Several of these innovations resulted from decisions taken in the period during which the Science Facilities Program was introduced.

In November 1963, the Biology Standing Committee of the Schools Board of Victoria established a committee to evaluate the BSCS Biology programs (Morgan, 1963). Pilot programs were conducted in some Victorian schools in 1964 and as a result it was decided to adapt the BSCS materials for use in Victoria (Morgan, 1964). A parallel development occurred in South Australia where some BSCS text materials were used (Best, 1967). Consequently that State became involved in the Victorian trials and adaptation procedures (Morgan, 1964). Adaptation, rather than adoption, was decided on because the original United States materials had been built around American organisms and designed for a different position in the School program. Extensive changes were made to content but not to approach. The course stressed the teaching of Biology as enquiry (Schwab, 1962). It involved an approach in which each topic began with observations, where statements of uncertainty featured, and where laboratory work was intended to be investigatory, special attention being given to training in scientific thinking (Morgan, 1967: 7). After an extensive trial in Victorian schools in 1966 the BSCS materials were produced under the sponsorship of the Australian Academy of Science (Stanhope, 1967). They were introduced in Victoria and South Australia in 1967 and subsequently in every Australian State (Morgan, 1970).

It was also in 1963 that the Physics Standing Committee of the Schools Board of Victoria decided to adopt the PSSC Physics materials. Since this involved direct adoption with minor modifications the time delay before the materials were introduced was shorter: schools were using them in Year 11 in 1965. It should be noted however that this was nine years after the PSSC project had begun in the USA (Lee Dow, 1971). The PSSC Materials were subsequently used in Queensland schools in 1969 and strongly influenced the Western Australian Physics course which started in 1968 (Stanhope, 1967). The other widely adopted overseas course was CHEM STUDY. It arose a little later being tried in Western Australia in 1966 prior to its use from 1968 onward. Queensland tried the material in 1966 (Dettrick, 1966) and introduced it in 1967 (Stanhope, 1967).

The Victorian Year 12 Chemistry course which was first taught in 1966 resulted from a project begun in 1963 (Lee Dow, 1971). This differed from the BSCS adaptation and the PSSC and CHEM STUDY adoption in that it was entirely locally developed. Cognizance was taken of overseas courses, particularly the American Chemical Bond Approach material, but it was essentially locally developed for local circumstances. It also differed from the previously mentioned courses in not emphasizing a particular approach to teaching. It was essentially a complete restructuring and revising of content. The group who wrote the material said that they:

> unanimously endorsed the principle that there is no one way to teach Chemistry well. (Heffernan et al, 1964: 5)

The other locally developed curriculum to originate in this period was the senior Science course in New South Wales. As part of the Wyndham scheme which began in 1962 this course was first taught to Year 11 in 1966. Like the lower secondary school science course it was offered at four levels, level 3 providing a senior science course for non-specialists. Unlike the senior science courses in other States it encompassed all the major science disciplines within the one course (Stanhope, 1967). It was organized around an encyclopaedic textbook (Messel et al, 1966) and became a centre of controversy in New South Wales (Lee Dow, 1971: 59). In a similar fashion to the Victorian Chemistry course it did not emphasize teaching science as enquiry to the extent of the overseas adoptions or adaptations. It appears that the limited funds available for curriculum development in Australia at this time restricted the possibility of developing that type of course. Hence, the choice was between adopting an overseas course which was enquiry based or locally developing a course which was not.

The thorough adaptation of BSCS was possible through the financial support of the Australian Academy of Science. Until the advent of ASEP little Commonwealth government support was available for curriculum development in science. Stanhope concluded that:

> ... greater benefit would accrue to science teaching in Australia if some of the $10 million provided annually by the Federal government wholly for material facilities were diverted to financing curriculum development by (such) modern methods. (Stanhope, 1967: 13)

A Matter of Choice

It is apparent that the needs of science education in the early sixties were rather more extensive than a lack of adequate material facilities. There was a shortage of qualified teachers, a lack of laboratory assistance and a need to develop new curricula. These deficiencies in science education were interrelated: by breaking the cycle at one point it was hoped to stimulate action in other areas[16]. Certainly it had been suggested that what schools could offer was limited by the facilities available. Removing this one barrier, it was hoped, would be tantamount to removing a limiting step in the improvement of science education. More importantly perhaps, the provision of material facilities was more amenable to Commonwealth government action. Such an action would partly satisfy the demands for general Commonwealth assistance to government and non-government schools. It also ensured that such assistance would be immediate and visible. The delay between starting a curriculum project and implementing it in schools would have been several years. Even when introduced it would not have been such a visible contribution as suites of science rooms. The complexities in the issue of science teacher supply were even greater. This problem depended upon the general teaching salary scales and the availability of scientifically trained people. It was therefore beyond the reach of immediate Commonwealth action. At the time the Science Facilities Program was introduced the Commonwealth government was constrained by tradition from a direct involvement in primary and secondary education. The provision of material facilities was a safe way to commence.

Notwithstanding this caveat the view taken in this report is that which was expressed by the Commonwealth's Advisory Committee on Standards for Science Facilities in Secondary Schools (1976).[17] This was that the Program would have been more effective had greater attention been given to such matters as ancillary staff, in-service education, and curriculum revision. That these needs were ignored probably limited the potential impact of the Program on science teaching.

---

16 Interview with Professor R. Selby Smith, 18 May 1976.

17 Where this Committee is subsequently mentioned a short title will be used: The Commonwealth Standards Committee.

CHAPTER TWO

EVALUATING THE SCIENCE FACILITIES PROGRAM

A Framework for the Evaluation

The Science Facilities Program differed from many educational initiatives taken by the Commonwealth Government during the sixties and seventies. It was not based upon recommendations made in a report to the Government. As a result it began operating with neither data which would have indicated areas of need, nor an investigation which would have clarified objectives. The necessary data and the explication of objectives came as the Program progressed. Writing generally of social programs Maling-Keepes(1978) identified as one characteristic a 'planning stage' which involved some assessment of the basis of the program in terms of needs it would attempt to meet, likely attitudes and other resources of clients, and the development of knowledge required for subsequent planning. In the Science Facilities Program this stage was rather truncated so that the objectives of the scheme were not clear at the beginning. Clarification of the goals of the Program was therefore an important prelude to the evaluation. Guidance came from statements of intention and expectation made by those involved with the Program and also from a consideration of criticisms which were made.

General Statements of Intention

Chapter One explored the multifarious influences which led to and shaped the Science Facilities Program. Many of these influences were only marginally related to science education. Even among those which were directly concerned with science teaching no single cause could be identified. As a consequence no unique purpose was clear. Through the provision of funds it was hoped that a range of benefits would flow to science education. Certainly a primary purpose was to improve the quality and abundance of science teaching facilities. However this primary purpose was usually seen as an intermediate step in the quest of other goals. Unfortunately the definitions of some of these subsequent goals are more elusive.

Among the statements of Commonwealth Ministers of Education and the Department of Education were references to the process of science education and to the outcomes of science education. Often one or the other were assumed to be the result of improved facilities and sometimes it was made explicit that the outcomes and the process were related in sequence to the provision of facilities. However the terms which were used to describe anticipated or alleged results of the Program were often global and rarely elaborated. In addition, because the Program operated for some twelve years, differences in terminology and even in aims resulted from changing circumstances. For these reasons it is hard to discern precise goals for the Program.

In November 1975 the Commonwealth Department of Education prepared a resumé of its activities for the new Minister. Of the Science Facilities Program it said that it had

> begun in 1964 in order to improve the quality of science education in Australian secondary schools through the provision of adequate science facilities. (CDE, File 1972/1547)

Of necessity the resumé was terse. Yet in indicating that the provision of facilities was seen as a means of improving the quality of science education it was rather similar to a Ministerial statement in 1971.

> The expenditure of these funds has improved markedly the quality of science teaching facilities available to students and has, without doubt, contributed to the improvement in the quality of teaching of science subjects. (Fairbairn, CPD 1971 : 2665)

When the scheme began in the sixties similar intentions were expressed in different terminology. In introducing the States Grants (Science Laboratories and Technical Training) Bill 1964 Menzies indicated his expectations.

> I believe that the new grants are going to have a stimulating effect on the teaching of science in schools throughout the country. Emphasis on the significance of this is hardly necessary.
> (Menzies, CPD 1964 : 1639)

Similarly the first Minister responsible for Commonwealth activities in education wrote that good facilities at the disposal of good teachers would enhance effective teaching.

> The effective teaching of any subject is primarily
> dependent on the existence of knowledgeable and
> inspiring teachers. But in the case of science,
> the skill of the teacher is greatly enhanced by the
> existence of modern laboratories adequately
> equipped with apparatus. (Gorton, 1966 : 1)

The replacement of the term 'effective teaching' by the more vague 'quality of education' would appear to reflect a change over time. In part the change has been one of fashion in educational terminology, but it also reflects a change in science teaching and science curricula. The change was in the direction of less reliance upon the teacher as an overt instructor. However both terms are abstruse. The operational definitions of these terms was left to the professional consultants who were members of the Commonwealth Standards Committee. Politicians were usually satisfied to extend the terms by suggesting relationships with subsequent objectives.

One example of an extension of these expectations to alleged or anticipated outcomes was contained in the continuation of Fairbairn's remarks which were quoted previously.

> As a result, young people are better prepared in
> science than would otherwise have been the case.
> (Fairbairn, CPD 1971 : 2665)

Unfortunately this extension was not sufficiently specific to clarify the alleged benefits of the Program. Neither the way in which young people were 'better prepared' nor the purpose for which they were 'better prepared' was explained. Menzies was a little more specific when he reflected on the Science Facilities Program.

> Each provision was, of course, directed to the
> need for improved science teaching in the secon-
> dary schools, a need which had been made quite
> clear by the too-high failure rate in first year
> at the universities, and to the urgent need, in
> a growing technological age for the encouragement
> and improvement of technical training.
> (Menzies, 1970 : 94)

Improved science teaching thus would be recognizable by its fruits. When introducing the States Grants (Science Laboratories and Technical Training) Bill 1964 he extended his remarks about stimulating teaching to outcomes. The two purposes mentioned in the quotation[1] in Chapter One were a wider

---

1 See page 12

understanding of science in the general community and a deeper understanding among an increased number of science specialists (Menzies, CPD 1964 : 1640). Gorton echoed these sentiments.

> For the individual, a good general education cannot be complete without some knowledge both of science and of the humanities and, for a modern nation, the efficient development of its industries and utilization of its resources cannot take place without there being a increasing number of people with a special knowledge of science (Gorton, 1966 : 1).

Intended outcomes of the Program were not always expressed in relation to the process of science education. When introducing the States Grants (Science Laboratories) Bill 1968 the Minister claimed support for the provision because of the social utilitarian benefits which could accrue from a concentration upon the production of skilled science specialists.

> These grants for the construction and equipping of science laboratories represent one part of what can be regarded as an overall government programme to upgrade scientific skills in Australia. The government recognizes that if Australia is to develop as we wish and if we are to make the greatest use of our own resources we need a greater number of well trained scientists and technologists.
> If we are to maintain and improve our position in the modern scientific age it is clear that the government must give attention to the standards of training ...
> It was clear that students entering universities would not be able to make the maximum use of the increased facilities being provided unless adequate facilities were provided for their training at school.
> (Fraser, CPD 1968 : 515)

Three Levels of Impact

There appear to be, implicit in these statements, three levels at which the Science Facilities Program was expected to have an impact on schools. The first level of impact was the most direct: science teaching facilities would be more abundant and of better quality. This raises questions concerning the perceptions of the recipients as to the quality of the facilities provided and whether at the conclusion of the Program schools had adequate provision. It also raises questions as to the relative abundance of facilities in different types of schools, and of the access of students in schools to those facilities.

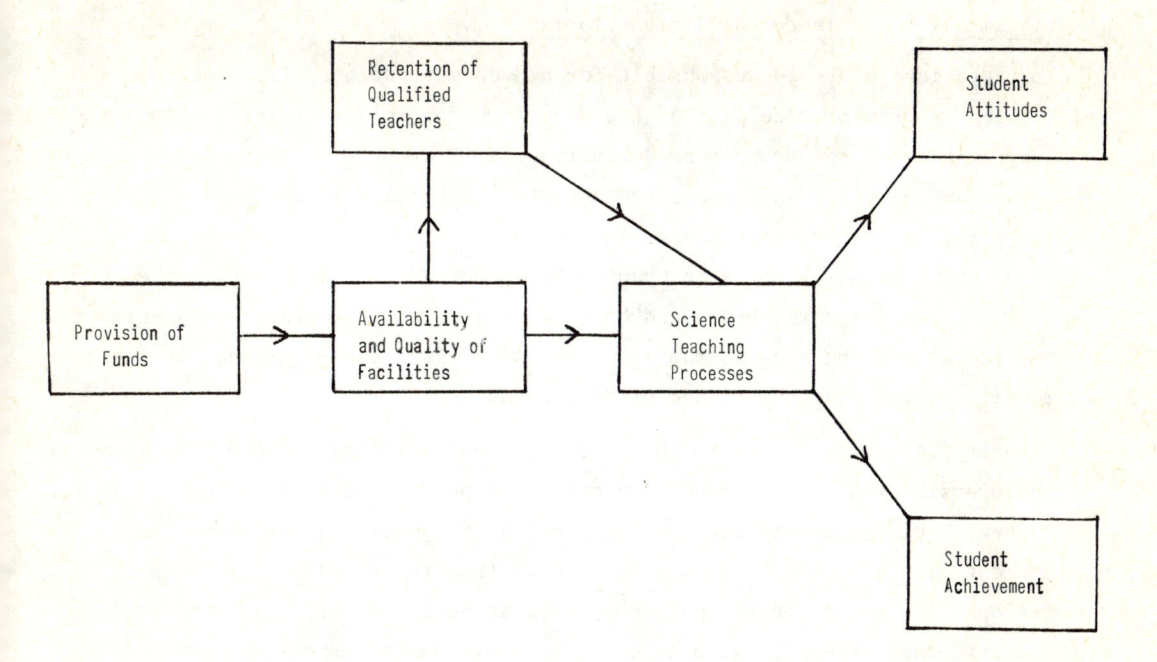

Figure 2.1   Expectations of the Australian Science Facilities Program

    The second level of intended impact was upon the science teaching process. Better facilities were expected to affect the quality of science education. No attempt was made by the politicians responsible for the program to elaborate the meaning of that global term. Statements of what the new buildings and apparatus were intended to facilitate were left to the professional consultants of the Commonwealth Standards Committee and the State Education Departments.

    Thirdly, it was hoped that the provision of better facilities would result in changes in several outcomes of science education on secondary school students. Often these were expressed in terms of a utilitarian view of science education. It was hoped that more students would pursue scientific careers, more would become interested in science and that the level of skill and understanding in science would be enhanced. Sometimes the liberal view of science education was invoked. It was hoped to quicken the interest in, and widen the understanding of science among non-specialists. Especially at this third level the expectations were wide and often given varied emphasis. It was not a single purpose Program at all. The various expectations of the Science Facilities Program have been represented in Figure 2.1.

Criticisms of the Science Facilities Program

The expectations of those responsible for and committed to the Science Facilities Program provide part of the framework for this evaluation. Comments made by critics of the Program are also important for they balanced some of the grand expectations and even suggested other important issues. Particularly in its early stage the Science Facilities Program attracted considerable public comment. As suggested in Chapter One, much of the debate about the Program concerned Federal-State and Church-State relations. The issues which most directly concern the Program as a science program can be grouped in three categories; equity, authority and effectiveness.

Equity in the provision to government and non-government schools, became a controversial issue after 1966. In the election of that year an undertaking was given to alter the ratio of the allocations to government and non-government schools (Holt, 1966 : 7). Until then the total sum had been partitioned in proportion to the school population in each system. From July 1967 onward the per capita allocation to non-government schools was to be double that for government schools. It was a point which drew frequent comment from the Opposition. Consider, as an example, the debate in 1971 when the Opposition moved that the Bill be withdrawn and redrafted so that the per capita grants for government and non-government schools were identical.

> When the States Grants (Science Laboratories) Bill was introduced originally, the formula used was based on the enrolment in secondary schools - roughly on the ratio of 3 to 1. After the first triennium the amount going to private schools was doubled, so that it has been in the ratio of 3 to 2. This Bill provides for $26m for State Schools and $17m for private schools over the 4 years. The previous ratios, when expressed as a per capita amount per pupil, show what has happened. The science grants for State schools represented $10.58 per pupil. For Catholic schools it was $23.16 per pupil. For the other private schools it was $24.08. No matter where one turns, the accusation is being made against the Government that what it is doing in education favours the affluent.
> (Beazley, CPD 1971 : 2814)

The rejoinder from the government to this accusation of unfairness was twofold. It drew attention to other schemes of Commonwealth assistance to the States such as that for technical training and it argued that States were expected to provide science facilities for government schools from other resources.

> There is no particular reason why funds being made
> available to schools for a particular purpose
> should be broken up in the same way between the
> two categories of schools, government and independ-
> ent, because it is relevant to bear in mind that
> government schools are financed almost entirely by
> government funds from the States, a significant
> proportion of which comes indirectly from the
> Commonwealth.
>
> (Fraser, CPD 1968: 988)

Opposition spokesmen (Beazley, CPD 1971: 2815) regarded the inclusion of technical training grants as spurious because they were largely applied to post secondary further education. As such the facilities provided were used by former students of government and non-government schools alike. The capacity of the States to use general revenue to provide science facilities in addition to those funded by the Science Facilities Program was a more complex issue. As mentioned in several debates the relative 'needs' of various school systems were unknown. Some argued that the initial need was greater among government schools (Cairns, J., CPD 1968: 974) while others seemed to imply that non-government schools had been equally or more poorly provided with science facilities when the Program began (Cairns, K., CPD 1968: 984). In relation to this issue of equity it is important to determine the extent to which schools in various States and systems have been brought to a satisfactory level of provision.

The second area of criticism concerned the authority for determining priorities in educational spending. Smart (1975) produced evidence that some State governments and State Education Departments regarded the Science Facilities Program as having placed constraints on their scope for determining educational policies. They argued that they were better placed than the Commonwealth to be aware of particular educational needs. Sometimes it was suggested that the conditions imposed by the Commonwealth reflected too much the requirements of administrative efficiency. This raises questions about Programs intended to meet a perceived national need which are administered through a variety of agencies. The extent to which policy varies, in spite of general guidelines, would appear to reflect differences in the context in which those authorities operated. The issue also raises the question of school authority. Priorities for educational spending within a school may not be congruent with those which are deemed part of a Program to meet a national need.

Criticism was also directed at the effectiveness of the Science Facilities Program. It was argued that concentrating upon capital resources was not the most effective way to improve science education. Some comments about the need for curriculum development and increased recruitment of qualified teachers[2] were made in Chapter One. These were matters of public comment as evident in a Parliamentary debate in 1971.

> I have pointed out frequently in this House how the Government introduced grants to schools for science blocks without giving the slightest consideration to ways of providing teachers and supporting laboratory staff for these laboratories. I have said that in many instances science laboratories provided under the legislation are not staffed by competently trained science teachers, nor are they adequately equipped or serviced by trained laboratory staff. (Barnard, CPD, 1971 : 1265)

However it was always hoped by people associated with implementing the Program that improved facilities would attract qualified scientists to teaching and encourage them to remain at a school longer[3]. The extent to which this occurred is a facet of the Program worthy of investigation, particularly in light of the value placed by Gorton (1966) on the primary importance of good teachers.

One other aspect of effectiveness concerned more especially the Program in the government schools of Victoria and New South Wales. Some items of apparatus provided in bulk consignments to schools in those States were considered unnecessary, even useless. The astronomical telescope usually was cited as an example of an unnecessary purchase[4]. Yet it is possible that such items may have proved useful over a longer period of time.

The Impact on School Systems

While the main purpose of this study was to examine the impact of the Program on schools it was important to take cognizance of the context in which schools were provided with additional facilities. Government schools received the benefits of these funds through State Education Departments who also provided other material resources. The distinction between different

---

2 See pages 15 - 20.
3 Interview with Professor R. Selby Smith, 18 May 1976.
4 Sydney Morning Herald, 22 July 1968 : 7.

sources of funds for apparatus provided was often nominal. For these reasons it would seem important to include a consideration of the impact of the scheme on the administration of science teaching in school systems.

The additional financial resources which this Program placed at the disposal of administrators in State Education Departments was bound to have wide repercussions. Such administrative matters as the system by which schools were supplied with apparatus could have been affected by the additional financial resources available. Moreover State Education Departments could use the resources to stimulate the development of new subjects and new curricula. Even policy decisions concerning the commitment of State resources, as for example in the employment of laboratory assistants, could have been influenced by the presence of Commonwealth funds. Such changes as these at a systemic level would also affect the work of schools. These effects would not be revealed by considering differences between schools as most schools in a system would have been affected similarly.

In order that these system-wide effects are not neglected a study of the impact of the Program on school systems has been made. An additional aspect of such a study was that it could examine any policy differences in Education Departments which were operating under the same policy guidelines.

A Review of the Framework

From the statements of intention, alleged outcomes, and criticisms of the Science Facilities Program a number of questions about its impact were devised. They are summarized in Appendix A. These questions have been written as they arise and no attempt has been made at this stage to consider the inter-action between the issues involved. It was not possible to report on all of these issues in this report. Some, particularly those concerned with students' achievements and attitude, will be the subject of subsequent reports. This Report concentrates upon those questions concerned with the way science is studied and taught in schools. It is in that area that one might expect to observe the more immediate changes wrought by the improvement of facilities.

Studies Related to the Provision of Science Facilities : A Review

Englehardt (1966) considered that the term 'facility' was often wrongly used. Facility was too often used as a synonym for teaching space. He argued that a teaching space only became a facility when it was equipped with apparatus and occupied by teachers. Usage of the term facility during the period of the Science Facilities Program has suggested that it would be more appropriate if facilities were taken to include the material resources for teaching science. In addition the provision of ancillary staff has been considered as an aspect related to science facilities.

Published articles about science facilities form two groups : descriptive and analytic. Descriptive studies include those which assess or recommend standards for school science facilities. Frequently they have been limited to the provision and design of rooms. Their purpose was immediate and practical : to influence the type of science rooms provided in schools. Some of these articles were also interpretative. Proposed designs were based on an assessment of an existing or desired curriculum or teaching method. Connections between facilities and the teaching process were assumed but not investigated.

In the second group are the analytic studies. These studies attempted to examine systematically the possible effects of varying standards and types of provision of science facilities. Various aspects of science facilities were treated as independent variables. The outcomes investigated were diverse, ranging from facets of teaching style, through achievement, to aspects of attitudes and interest. This second group of studies is small in number suggesting a rather neglected area of work.

The Provision and Design of Science Rooms

In Britain the Industrial Fund for the Advancement of Scientific Education in Schools stimulated reconsideration of what constituted appropriate science facilities. Because of its financial contribution to the building of science facilities its standards were widely accepted. The brochures it published proved a source of guidance for those planning science facilities (Industrial Fund, 1957a, 1957b). The standards it adopted for its own buildings reflected an awareness of the central role of the laboratory in modern science teaching. The design of science facilities in Britain has gained more recent stimulation from the Oxford Project (Department of Education and Science, 1967). In Australia the Commonwealth Standards Committee was strongly influenced by these standards. The Industrial Fund had addressed itself to the number of rooms, size of rooms, specialization of rooms, ancillary services and design. (Savage, 1958). Of particular importance was the principle that a science room ought to have a number of 'fallow periods', being vacant for between one third and one quarter of the teaching time. The suggestion became the policy of the Science Teachers' Associations (The Four Associations, 1960.)

This development in Britain paralleled principles enunciated in the United States. Johnson (1956 : 14) recommended that science rooms in United States schools should not be used more than 70 percent of the available teaching time. The National Science Teachers' Association (1970) adopted the principle of fallow periods but with a maximum usage rate of 80 percent. When the Commonwealth Standards Committee urged a standard 75 percent utilization it was within the mainstream of overseas patterns.

A number of publications from the United States made general recommendations about the type of science facilities which would suit the new curricula introduced during the sixties (Arkansas Department of Education, 1966; California Department of Education, 1964; Martin, 1960; Mississipi Department of Education, 1966; Schlessinger, 1963). The common theme was the central role of experimental work in the new curricula and the need for flexible classroom-laboratories for teaching. This intention was consistent with the orientation of the Commonwealth Standards Committee toward dual purpose science rooms. A review of science facilities (Baas, 1973) considered this trend to flexible multi-functional science rooms to be a feature of developments in science room design. It was, in his view, evidence of

> a primary concern for individual student's involvement in the methodologies and results of the scientific process.
> (Baas, 1973 : 3)

Baas' view received support from a study by Novak (1972). In that study of exemplary facilities an evolving pattern was detected. The chain of evolution was from separate lecture and laboratory space with massive fixed furniture, through integrated classroom laboratories to flexible open space provisions. As the author concedes the result could perhaps have been partly influenced by the tacit assumptions made when selecting exemplary schools (Novak, 1972 : 22). However his general assessment of trends in this area does match those of other observers such as Baas (1973). In addition to elucidating an evolving pattern in the nature of science facilities Novak (1972) made an attempt to link this pattern with concomitant developments in curricula, educational technology and teaching roles. The nature of the study precluded the empirical testing of these hypothesized links.

Articles concerned with science facilities in other countries follow a similar approach. The Ontario Department of Education (1968) in a publication on the design of science facilities argued for maximum flexibility.

The purpose, it said, was to permit various methods of operation in rooms which could be adjusted to the personal preferences of teachers and changing requirements in organization, curricula and methods. Laboratories, it said, should also be multifunctional in that they should allow effective teaching in different sciences. One issue of the Australian Science Teachers Journal (1974) was devoted to changes in science facilities. In that issue contributors from New South Wales (Turner, 1974), Victoria (Hall, 1974), Queensland (Robins, 1974), Western Australia (Betjeman, 1974) and Tasmania (Fish, 1974) described the most recent developments in science room design in the Australian States. A common emphasis was on the more flexible designs which had been developed to suit modern science curricula. Articles by Fish (1974) and Betjeman (1974) explicitly related the design changes which had occurred in response to the perceived needs of modern science curricula. Prosser and Woolley (1974) discussed the architectural ramifications of science facilities intended for an open plan school. The booklets published by the Commonwealth Standards Committee (1964, 1973) also show a trend to more flexible designs. The most flexible designs appeared in a supplement published near the end of their period of work (Commonwealth Standards committee, 1975). It is interesting to note that when one member of that Committee reviewed its work attention was concentrated on the development of flexible designs (Field, 1974).

A difficulty with the commonly recurring theme of greater flexibility is that different meanings were attached to it. In some places just one of the possible interpretations was intended while in others it seemed to include several simultaneously.

1 It could refer to a room in which the basic furniture can be quickly and easily rearranged for a given lesson or during a lesson. In this sense the term versatility would seem appropriate.
2 Sometimes the term flexibility was applied to rooms where accommodation arrangements can be altered to suit the preference of teachers or course requirements. Since most buildings last longer than the courses for which they were intended this is an important attribute. Rooms with the capacity for such substantial alteration could be considered adaptable.
3 Rooms which were designed for the teaching of more than one science subdiscipline were sometimes called flexible. More appropriately they should be called multifunctional.
4 Rooms designed for particular requirements of science courses which emphasize group discussion and/or individual progression were called flexible. Often this was a misuse of the term for they were unsuited to any other course.

While flexibility was often mentioned its usefulness as a concept, either in description or specification, is limited by the fact that it encompassed such a variety of meanings.

The Effects of Science Facilities on the Teaching Process

It has been noted that the potential relationship between the provision of science facilities and the teaching of science was usually expressed in terms of providing suitable facilities for a new curriculum. Englehardt (1966) explored the possible influences which the nature of science rooms could have upon teaching practices. Two means of influence were distinguished. Firstly, the provision of suitable science rooms could remove a barrier to certain activities. In this sense rooms were a potentially limiting factor. Secondly, the presence of suitable rooms may suggest the possibility of new activities. Hence the notion of 'suggestive space' was advanced. It was conceded that in practice it may be hard to isolate each means of influence. Yet the argument served the valuable purpose of visualizing facilities as exerting more than a limiting influence.

Several articles considered facilities as possible limitations on certain sorts of practical work (Dark and Squires, 1975; Robertson, 1962). Kerr (1964 : 73) produced evidence that, in English schools, insufficient laboratory facilities, over-use of laboratories, a shortage of qualified teachers, lack of assistance and large classes impaired the effectiveness of laboratory work. Kelly and Monger (1974a, 1974b) reported an evaluation of Nuffield 0-Level Biology course materials. They (Kelly and Monger, 1974b : 715) drew attention to apparent inconsistencies between the objectives and content of the course, teachers' understanding of those objectives and content, and the actual conduct of the course. Among reasons for these inconsistencies, they postulated that lack of facilities may have influenced the way the course was conducted. In an evaluation of the Nuffield A level Biological Science Project lack of facilities was cited as a factor which could have influenced the decision to adopt the course (Kelly and Nicodemus, 1973) but not the achievement of students (Kelly, 1972). Brown (1977) reported that teachers in schools with poor science facilities viewed the Scottish Integrated Science Scheme less favourably than those with good facilities.

In an exploratory paper Englehardt (1966) had argued that the type of room provided could have a suggestive influence, as well as a limiting influence, upon the teaching of science. In addition, he developed a procedural planning model which related goals, methods and facilities. This model incorporated a number of basic determinants of educational specifications: the pattern of science teaching in the school, the number of students in each space, the services required and the location in relation to the school. In the empirical study which followed, Englehardt (1968) investigated a number of aspects of the relationships between characteristics of science rooms and science teaching methods. Nearly 500 teachers in 59 schools in the New England States of the USA were interviewed. Their responses to questions about teaching practices were related to Englehardt's observations of characteristics of the rooms in which they taught. His results were illuminating for some characteristics of the architectural space were found to be significantly associated with teaching practices. It was found that classroom laboratories were significantly associated with the use of 'enquiry methods' in science laboratory work especially when the teachers had adequate preparation time, easy access to the laboratory area and taught mainly in one room each. Other significant associations were reported between suitable sinks and the frequency of laboratory work in Biology and Earth Sciences, the provision of individual laboratory space and the frequency of individual projects, and the proximity of the library and the use of library assignments. It needs to be remembered that information about the practices which teachers followed was derived from interviews with the teachers, with the possibility that the answers may have been biased. Other features also suggest that the findings should be treated with caution. Some of the spatial variables may have been associated with other attributes of the school which were not specified. Moreover the possibility exists that teachers were attracted to schools which had the facilities they sought. Englehardt assumed that teachers were influenced by the facilities which were at the school. However, despite these cautions, the proposition that facilities do influence teaching methods was an assumption of the Program under review and will need examination.

Assuming that Englehardt's (1968) results were not just the results of the operation of some unmeasured personality variables there are two possible explanations of his positive results. Firstly, his examination of spatial influences included consideration of the presence of necessary features. It was not restricted to design differences. Secondly, by conducting the investigation within a specific context, science, it was possible to choose dependent variables which were most likely to be influenced by the presence or arrangement of facilities. However it should be noted that Englehardt's (1968) study suggested an association between facilities and certain teacher practices rather than causation. Alternatives to the postulate that facilities influence teaching practices exist. Dawson (1964) suggested that new curricula such as BSCS Biology influenced the science facilities in schools. In addition it is possible that good teachers might exert great efforts to secure good facilities in their schools.

Teaching Methods in Areas other than Science

Outside the specific context of teaching science there have been studies of the effects of facilities on teaching. Many of the examinations of open education have not been able to separate 'open education philosophies' from 'open space design' because the schools were built for that purpose (Lovegrove, 1974, 1975). In the Australian Open Area Schools Project an attempt was made to look specifically at the effect of architecture on teaching. Fitzpatrick and Angus (1974) described some of the beliefs of teachers in open plan schools. In general those teachers felt uncertain of what changes in behaviour were expected of them. An observation study (Angus, Evans, and Parkin, 1975) suggested that school design was not a factor which could explain many differences in the nature and frequency of interaction between pupils and teachers. Architectural features did not seem to be a decisive influence on styles of teaching. This conclusion was consistent with those similar studies reviewed by Angus et al (1975). An interpretive comment was made that the differences in the conditions experienced by students in open plan and conventional schools were less pronounced than might be imagined. Improvised modifications in many open plan schools resulted in teachers working in effectively self contained areas.

Drew (1971) reviewed a number of studies of the psychological and behavioural effects of the physical environment. Several of these studies in diverse contexts suggested effects other than the imposition of physical restraint. However there were also a number of studies in which results were inconclusive. Drew (1971) concluded that despite a general awareness that manipulation of the physical environment might produce changes in behaviour patterns, the mechanisms of these changes had not been elucidated. These comments have not yet been extended by studies of open plan primary schools.

The Effect of Science Facilities on Achievement

One expectation of the provision of science facilities was that students would better understand the science they studied. This understanding should be reflected in various measures of achievement. Studies of the effect of science facilities on the achievement of students form a subset of studies of school effects in general. In a review of school effects on educational achievement Guthrie (1970) grouped school factors related to performance in the categories; school facilities, teacher characteristics, instructional materials and student environment. There are disparities between studies in the extent to which they suggest schools contribute to the educational achievement of students. These differences arise because different aspects of achievement are used, different populations are studied, different methods are used to collect data, and different methods of analysis are employed. Since the publication of a study by Coleman (1966) the view has been widely accepted that schools do not greatly influence the educational achievement of their pupils. Part of the reason for this may be that measures of school resources, and learning conditions have been school variables. Within a school there is often much variation between classes in access to resources and in the learning conditions they experience as well as in initial ability (Ross, 1976 : 41). Were studies of school effects to use the class as the unit of analysis rather than the school the effects might be found to be stronger.

In general, studies using a measure of educational achievement involving a large component of verbal or literary skill attribute less influence to school factors than do these studies of achievement in Science or Mathematics. The widely quoted study by Coleman (1966), for example, used a test of reading as a criterion measure and suggested schools had little impact on educational achievement. Some studies reviewed by Guthrie (1970) which used tests of verbal ability, and made allowance for home background, have suggested some features of schools related to achievement in this area. Among the features mentioned were expenditure per pupil, teachers experience, classroom atmosphere, teachers verbal ability, science laboratory facilities, building age, temporary classrooms, library volumes and classrooms per 1000 students. At least some of these features were school facilities though the possibility cannot be dismissed that they were manifestations of unmeasured dimensions. Peaker (1967) studied English Primary school children and suggested that two thirds of the variation in reading comprehension could be accounted for by three factors. In order of importance these were; parental attitudes, home circumstances, and attributes of schools or teachers. Guthrie (1970) makes the useful point that

> Presumably, schools are established to instruct students in moderately well defined subject matter areas, not to increase some quality as amorphous as verbal ability.
>
> (Guthrie, 1970 : 38)

In studies of science achievement it seems that school effects are more strongly correlated to outcomes than is the case in other disciplines (Dyer, 1968). This is shown in the results of the IEA studies of Educational Achievement (Purves and Levine, 1975 : 23-30), in particular in the results of some of the multiple regression analyses in that study. Learning conditions made some contribution to the variance in science achievement in most countries. The contribution was greater when there was less variation in home background, as in Sweden, or when learning conditions did not parallel home background as in England. Keeves (1972 : 220), in a study of students in the first year of secondary school, reported that the number of science periods in a laboratory was associated with higher science achievement. Shaycoft (1967) in a longitudinal study of students from grade 9 to grade 12 showed gains in scores in most subject areas as well as variations in those gains between schools. She concluded that school programs did contribute to educational performance on these achievement tests. However, no measures of such factors as staff quality, resource availability or facility adequacy were included.

Two most interesting studies extended the IEA Science Achievement analysis. Owen (1975) and Wilson (1975) made use of the Population IV (Year 12) and Population II (14 year-old) data respectively for Victoria. Both studies were designed to identify school factors which affected the performance of students in science. Using Dyer's (1969) model a predicted school science score, based on 'home background' and 'sex bias' of the school, was calculated and compared with the actual score obtained by averaging the scores of each student in the sample. Two groups of schools were then identified; one group which performed better than expected and the other which had not performed as well as would have been predicted. A comparison of the two groups of schools was made so that some factors affecting performance might be identified. Wilson found greater differences in facilities between above and below expectation schools among the 14 year-old sample than did Owen among the Year 12 sample.

> The accommodation and facilities available for science, also appeared to be related to the level of achievement of the students in a school. In those schools where students achieved less well than was predicted from their sex and home background, the accommodation for science was inadequate. Many of these schools reported that there were not enough classrooms and that makeshift arrangements were necessary to accommodate some lessons, that many science classes were held out of laboratories, that non-science lessons were held in laboratories and that the laboratories were rarely vacant during the day to enable adequate preparation of the rooms for science lessons.
>
> (Wilson, 1975 : 39)

Owen (1975) did not find such differences between the standard of facilities in 'above' and 'below expectation' schools in the Year 12 sample. It seems as if the different results of these two studies could reflect the different age groups studied. Two possible explanations could be postulated for this difference. One is that good science facilities are more important to the achievement of younger students than those in the final year of secondary school. The alternative is that the results reflect the greater variation in facilities available to younger students. The report of the study of schools in the 14 year-old sample also commented on the effect of facilities upon some teaching practices.

> Few clear relationships have emerged in this study concerning practical work. Teachers in the 'above expectation' and 'below expectation' schools did not display marked differences in opinion concerning the importance of such work. However, the facilities found in the 'below expectation' schools suggested that, at the junior levels in particular, the type of practical exercise possible was very limited and in these schools students were unable to do effective work. Because of the recent trend in Victoria away from teacher oriented science lessons to those based on the individual student's practical experience, it is important that the effects of such methods are known. A study which carefully documents the amount and type of practical work done with different kinds of facilities and the relationship between the type of facilities provided and achievement in junior science, is greatly needed.
>
> (Wilson, 1975 : 43)

Science Facilities and Interest in Science

Many of the early statements about the Science Facilities Project implied that with better school facilities more students would become interested in science and would be encouraged to follow scientific careers. Most publications about science enrolments have been concerned to document trends and interpret them in terms of broad societal changes (Dainton, 1968; Fensham, 1970; Lee Dow, 1971; Stranks, 1969). Broad societal changes are sometimes seen in the status accorded science within schools (Fensham, 1970). It is rare for enrolment patterns to be considered in relation to school attributes as specific as the level of facilities. Taylor, Christie and Platts (1973) made one study of factors relating to the choice of science among able fourth year secondary school pupils in England. They reported that boys other than those who were most able, who were taught in schools with good facilities in early secondary school were more likely to opt for science. Understandably personal characteristics, school policy and teaching style contributed to the choice of discipline for further study. It is interesting that facilities were able to explain some four percent of the total variance or ten percent of the explained variance. The small sample and the imprecise measure of the standard of facilities, which was based on impressions from inspectors, limited the degree to which the results could be generalized. In addition it is possible that better teachers tended to be in schools with better facilities. The measure of teaching style which was used did not assess the quality of teaching. Notwithstanding this, the suggestion that school factors including facilities may influence subject choice is at least interesting.

In a review of pupils attitudes to science Ormerod and Duckworth (1975) do not mention any studies, other than that of Taylor *et al* (1973), of the influence of facilities upon attitudes or interests. They do indicate that the age range over which pupils interests in science seems to be aroused coincides with the late primary and early secondary school years. This is a conclusion which has significant implications for the allocation of resources within schools.

A Plan for the Evaluation

General Considerations

The relatively recent emphasis on the evaluation of wide-ranging social and educational programs has had repercussions on techniques of evaluation. In general the techniques which are applied are now broader. Some of this has resulted from evaluators considering that, previously, too much attention had been paid to measurable changes in student behaviour but too little to educational processes and problems identified by schools. One development was to make greater use of observational data within the framework of flexible research designs, and thus allow unanticipated events to be taken into account (Stenhouse, 1975 : 115). Nevertheless there are highly experienced evaluators who argue for rather tighter design and more rigorous data collection (Cooley and Lohnes, 1976). Conflicting approaches to evaluation are now common.

One attempt at resolving these conflicts was that proposed by Sheldrake and Berry (1975). They were concerned with the illuminative approach espoused by Parlett and Hamilton (1973) as well as more traditional methods of testing. They argued that both approaches had value for the higher education project in which they were engaged.

> ...while recognizing the need to be reflective
> and interpretive we have also supported our
> views with empirical evidence where possible.
> (Sheldrake and Berry, 1975:3)

There was a recognition that crucial information was missed by a detached observer while the involved observer developed views and interpretations that were partly a result of his own participation. In short the two approaches were needed to give a balanced evaluation. Sheldrake and Berry (1975) place the two approaches on a two dimensional grid of research style. One dimension was concerned with whether the research was analytic or descriptive while the other categorized the research method as involved or detached. In fact, these classifications are probably too simple. Evaluation methods are probably multifaceted.

Maling-Keepes (1977) has reviewed some of the features of recent evaluation studies with the intention of defining key characteristics through which they could be compared and examined. She argued that the growing diversity in approach was partly attributable to two factors: the varied background of the evaluators and the diverse nature of the programs being evaluated. Concerning the nature of the programs she observed that few were short-term well-defined programs with specific goals. Most were long-term programs for which goals were loosely specified, and sometimes implicit; and where the program varied over time. Maling-Keepes (1977) observes that while the variety and volume of evaluations have multiplied, methods have received little systematic attention. The key features proposed by Maling-Keepes will help to systematize discussion of evaluative methods. An important aspect of the development of them was the fact that the methods of evaluation were always considered in the context of the program being evaluated. Different methods suit different programs or, more precisely, different methods are likely to be appropriate to different questions about any given program.

Specific Considerations

The Science Facilities Program was an example of a program which extended over a considerable time and which had global rather than specific objectives. It had been administered not centrally but federally through several agencies. Given these features it was similar to some of the programs Maling-Keepes (1977) regarded as having given rise to a diverse range of evaluation methods. However, two constraints precluded certain approaches to its evaluation. Firstly, there were no systematic data which described the provision of science facilities at the time the Program commenced. Hence its impact on existing facilities was difficult to assess. As an alternative it was decided to assess the contribution of the Program to facilities being used and to determine whether the provision of facilities in schools at the end of the Program were satisfactory : satisfactory being determined according to the Program's own standards.

The second factor which precluded certain approaches to evaluating the Program was the time that the evaluation commenced. When the evaluation began the Program had finished. Hence the opportunity to study the effect upon a school of gaining new facilities under this Program did not exist. The absence of before and after data on individual schools meant that use had to be made of existing variations in school facilities. Schools which had different standards of science facilities could be chosen, aspects of their science teaching studied and the relationships between the two investigated. In this way it was hoped to explore possible effects of the standard of facilities on science teaching. However, the very effectiveness of the Science Facilities Program in removing cases of extreme shortage did limit the range of the independent variable.

A third consideration was that rather than embark upon a thorough achievement and attitude testing program the results of the IEA[5] study would be available. That extensive and thorough program was conducted in 1970 at which time the Science Facilities Program was not complete. If

---

5   International Association for the Evaluation of Educational Achievement; (Comber & Keeves, 1973).

the Program was effective greater variations in the standard of facilities would have existed between schools than in 1975. Some additional data about students in those samples were also available[6]. However in order to use the data additional information was required about the science facilities in those schools in 1970.

Four Phases of the Evaluation

As a result of these considerations the evaluation of the Science Facilities Program was planned to include four phases. These were chosen to relate to the three levels of impact on schools and the fourth level of indirect impact, through system-wide effects, on schools.

1   The first phase was a study of the facilities for teaching science in schools and the contribution of the Science Facilities Program to those facilities. It was planned to include such features as the availability and quality of rooms, the availability of apparatus and the provision of ancillary services.

2   The second phase was planned to be a study of the effects of facilities on the teaching learning process. The main part of it was intended to be a series of visits to schools in which teachers would be interviewed, students would complete a questionnaire and general observations made. In addition some survey data about teacher retention and some IEA data about teacher attitudes was to be used.

3   The third phase was planned as a study of some outcomes of science education : achievement in, interest in, and attitudes to science. Data obtained in 1975 would be used for enrolment patterns but IEA data were to be reanalyzed in conjunction with information about facilities for the bulk of this phase.

4   Finally, a study of the administration of the Program and its wider impact on educational systems was planned. To this end it was intended to examine official records and to interview a number of people involved with implementing the Program.

Time and space has prevented much of the work undertaken in the third phase being reported in this volume. This study of the influence of facilities on student achievement in and attitudes to science will appear in a subsequent report.

---

6   This additional data included;
       (a) for the Year 12 sample, the Higher School Certificate results for 1970, and the Commonwealth Secondary Scholarship result two years earlier,
       (b) for the sample of 14 year-olds the results on a Science test administered two years later.

CHAPTER THREE

CONDUCTING THE EVALUATION

This chapter describes the way the plan, which was discussed in Chapter Two, was applied to this evaluation. For this plan to be implemented it was necessary to define some concepts more closely, to construct appropriate indices, to devise sampling procedures and to develop questionnaire and interview schedules. These procedures as they applied to both the survey and the school visit phases are described. In addition the procedures followed in the survey, the school visits, and the visits to education departments are also described.

The Survey of School Facilities

The School Questionnaire

As indicated in Chapter Two, the first level at which the Science Facilities Program was to have an impact was upon the science facilities in schools. Information about facilities was not uniformly available from records for the schools of every system. Nor was it possible to visit the number of schools needed to give an accurate assessment of the provision of facilities. In order that an impression of the present facilities could be obtained a questionnaire, to be completed by the teacher in charge of science, was developed.

The questionnaire was intended to provide information to:
1. assess the adequacy of the present provision of science facilities in Australian schools including an estimation of the contribution of the Science Facilities Program to those facilities,

2. test some hypothesized relations between the standard of science facilities and such outcomes as teacher mobility, student enrolment patterns and teaching practices, and

3. generate data to be used in the selection of schools for case studies in which the impact of facilities on the teaching process could be examined further.

That part of the questionnaire which was concerned with present facilities was so structured that information was obtained about four facets of science facilities. The aspects considered were:

1. the availability of science rooms in relation to the schools science teaching program and in relation to the school enrolment,
2. the quality or functional adequacy of science rooms in the school,
3. the adequacy of the supply of apparatus to the school,
4. the number of support staff for science in relation to the school size.

The responses to questions about rooms were obtained in such a way that it was possible to associate the data with the age and source of finance for the room. Information about the use to which each room was put was also sought in addition to details of the non-science rooms used for science. As certain items of apparatus had proved controversial when supplied to the government schools in two States, schools were asked about the usefulness of those items in comparison to other items generally felt to be useful.

A copy of the School Questionnaire is included in Appendix B. In developing the trial form three government schools in Victoria were visited so that discussions could be held with senior science staff. A first trial form was administered to eight government schools in that State while the second and third trial forms were used in a total of 29 schools. Of these 29 schools, 18 were Victorian Government schools, three were Victorian Catholic schools, five were Victorian Independent schools, and the remaining three were Government schools from other States. Science co-ordinators involved in these trials were invited to comment upon and criticize the questionnaire whilst completing it. In addition copies of the questionnaire were sent to a number of people concerned with science education in each State. As a result of this process a number of questions were modified and some were eliminated. In particular the checklist for the functional adequacy of science rooms was modified. The trial versions enabled some initial analyses to be performed to obtain an indication of the range of values on, and the discriminant power of, several indices.

Science Room Indices

The development of appropriate indices of the provision of science rooms was crucial to the assessment of the adequacy of provisions. Indices of room availability and room quality were developed.

The most important indices of room availability were those derived from the Commonwealth Standards Committee. When assessing the number of science rooms required by a school the main criterion adopted was that there should be a science room available for every science lesson held. Moreover the committee incorporated the notion of fallow time in specifying that each room should be used for only 75 percent of the total teaching time.

On this basis the number of science rooms required in a school is given by

$$N = \frac{\Sigma P}{0.75 \times T}$$

where ΣP = the total number of science periods in a week

T = the number of teaching periods on which the timetable is based

Hence the adequacy of the number of science rooms (Q1), or the science room availability, could be calculated as a percentage excess, or deficit if negative.

$$Q_1 = \frac{(R-N) \times 100}{N}$$

where R = the actual number of 'equipped science rooms'.

This index includes all available science rooms, whether they were demonstration theatres or laboratories. However, the thrust of the Commonwealth Standards Committee was to encourage the building of dual-purpose classroom laboratories. In addition Englehardt (1968) certainly suggested that it was the availability of dual-purpose rooms which was influential in shaping the science teaching priorities in the school. Hence, an index based only on rooms which were equipped for students to do experiments was developed (Q2). Thus:

$$Q_2 = \frac{(S-N) \times 100}{N}$$

where S = the number of rooms equipped for student experiments

The Western Australian Education Department adopted a similar approach to this but specified an 85 percent usage rate for rooms. Hence on that criterion:

$$N_a = \frac{\Sigma P}{0.85 \times T}$$

and $Q_3 = \dfrac{(R-N_a) \times 100}{N_a}$

In the indices Q_1 and Q_2, room availability was based on the actual science teaching program of the school. They therefore allow that different schools may have different science orientations and, though of similar enrolment, have different needs. However, these indices suffer the disadvantage of not taking account of the fact that schools may have reduced their science program as a result of having a shortage of facilities. An alternative approach is to base the assessment of the science rooms required upon the school's enrolment. Thus, every school of similar size is treated as having a similar potential commitment to science teaching. This approach was in general that followed by most of the State education systems. Two basic variants existed within this approach depending on whether junior (up to Year 10) enrolments were treated differently from senior (Years 11 and 12) enrolments in assessing school needs.

Thus, in the New South Wales State education system, assessments of need were based on seven science rooms for a school of one thousand pupils (CDE, File 68/2764).

Hence, $N_b = \dfrac{7 \times E}{1000}$ where E = total school enrolment

and, $Q_4 = \dfrac{(R-N_b) \times 100}{N_b}$ where R = total science rooms

In the Victorian State education system assessments were based on:

(i) the estimated average amount of science taken up to Year ten;
(ii) the average retention of students to Years 11 and 12;
(iii) the average proportions of students in Years 11 and 12 taking science subjects and the time commitment involved. (CDE, File 71/5752)

This gave an indication of the number of science rooms needed.

$N_c = \dfrac{(E + 2 \times (Y + Z))}{200}$ where E = total enrolment
Y = enrolment in Year 11
Z = enrolment in Year 12

Hence, $Q_5 = \dfrac{(R-N_c) \times 100}{N_c}$

The South Australian Education Department based its estimates of science accommodation needs on two premises. One was that science rooms should be used for only 25 of a possible 35 teaching periods each week. The other was that laboratories should be able to accommodate 30 to 35 students (CDE, File 68/2764). The practical planning which followed from these premises specified three science rooms (including one demonstration room) for schools of 300 students, and six science rooms for schools containing 600 students. Schools enrolling 1000 students were entitled to two additional science rooms, while those with 1300 students could claim four additional science rooms (CDE, File 68/2764). On this basis it was possible to calculate the number of science rooms required by schools (Nd) and the adequacy of the actual provision.

$$Q_6 = \frac{(R - N_d) \times 100}{N_d}$$

In Queensland the basis for planning science accommodation was not as clear. Until the mid-sixties planning was based on the provision of one Physics and one Chemistry laboratory for every 600 students (CDE, File 68/2764). From the mid-sixties onward a senior science block incorporating three laboratories was planned for schools with Year 11 and 12 students. In addition a school's requirement for laboratories for junior classes was based on the enrolments in Years eight, nine and ten. Up to 350 students entitled a school to two laboratories, schools with 350 to 500 students were to have three laboratories, while those schools with between 500 and 900 students were planned to have four junior laboratories. Very large schools were to be provided with proportionately more junior science rooms (CDE, File 68/2764). From these complex criteria it was possible to estimate schools' requirements for science rooms (Ne) and hence the adequacy relative to those requirements.

$$Q_7 = \frac{(R - N_e) \times 100}{N_e}$$

In Tasmania the provision of science rooms in different High Schools was compared using the ratio of number of science rooms to the school enrolment. This suggested two simple indices for comparing schools. One was the number of science rooms per 1000 students.

$$L_1 = \frac{R \times 1000}{E}$$

The other was the number of dual purpose rooms per 1000 students.

$$L_2 = \frac{S \times 1000}{E}$$

Of these various indices it was intended to make most use of Q_1, Q_2, L_1, and L_2. They represented the simplest measures of the two basic approaches to school needs : science lessons and school enrolments.

The quality, or functional adequacy, of rooms was measured by means of a list of important features of science rooms. The science co-ordinator was asked to rate each of the science rooms in the school for 14 key features[1] using a four-point scale from 'non existent' to 'adequate'. Thus, the total score for each room ranged, in principle, from 0 to 42 and, in practice, from 10 to 42. The score range described rooms which were cramped with minimal or inaccessible services of gas, electricity and water, and poor working and seating conditions to rooms which were spacious and provided with adequate accessible service points and in which conditions were conducive to easy variations in work patterns. Since the same person within each school rated that school's rooms it was possible to compare rooms from different sources of funds and different ages.

The Sample

It was considered that information obtained from a sample yielding a high response would be more reliable than that from a survey of all schools which could at best expect only a moderate rate of response. Hence, a sample of schools was drawn for the survey. This reduced the extensive use of schools and enabled resources to be directed to achieving a high response rate. While sampling could be random, non-response is usually not random.

The schools were chosen from a sampling frame which listed all secondary schools, other than special schools, in Australia. The frame was stratified by State, system (Government, Catholic and Independent) and location (metropolitan and non-metropolitan). Within each stratum, schools were grouped into various sub-strata. For example in Victoria, government schools were classified as either technical or high schools. In the sample drawn no distinction was made between non-systemic and systemic Catholic schools. Such a distinction was not officially recognized for most of the period over which the Science Facilities Program operated.

---

1 These were derived from the brochure published by the Commonwealth Science Facilities Committee and entitled The Design of Science Rooms (Commonwealth of Australia, 1973).

The selection of schools from the sampling frame was governed by the following criteria.

1. The selection should be random within stratified groups.
2. The sample of schools should reflect the various types of school in the population.
3. In accord with the system of administration of the Science Facilities Program sufficient schools should be chosen from each State.

A simple random sample would not have been the best possible for two reasons. Firstly it would lack precision in the representation of each stratum. Secondly by giving each school an equal probability of selection it would over emphasize small, rural schools in relation to the population which they served.

Accordingly a stratified probability sample was chosen for each State. This stratification does not imply a great departure from randomness since schools were still selected at random, by a random start constant interval method from each stratum. It does, however, reduce the standard error (Moser and Kalton, 1975 : 85) as a consequence of each stratum being correctly represented in the sample. The sampling was performed so that each school had a probability of selection proportional to its size. The index of size which was used was the number of 14 year old students at the school. This information was uniformly available for all schools and has the advantage of being relatively uncontaminated by such things as school retentivity.

The basic probability samples were to contain 50 schools in each of New South Wales, Victoria, Queensland and South Australia, 40 schools in Western Australia and Tasmania, and all 21 schools in the Australian Capital Territory. However, while such a sample would be adequate for government schools it would contain too few non-government schools in some States for any reliable estimate to be made for those schools. Therefore an oversample was taken of the non-government school strata such that in any State there were approximately 15 Catholic and 15 Independent schools. To achieve this the sampling fraction was multiplied by an appropriate integral value for each stratum. This technique enabled the basic probability sample to be retained for analyses where weighting would prove too complex but provided a disproportionate stratified sample for between strata comparisons. A summary of the sampling details is contained in Appendix C.

Table 3.1 Questionnaires Returned from each State and School System

State	Government N	%	Catholic N	%	Independent N	%	Total N	%
ACT	12	92	4	80	2	67	18	86
New South Wales	38	97	15	88	13	93	66	94
Victoria	37	97	15	88	15	94	67	94
Queensland	38	100	14	88	13	93	65	96
South Australia	38	97	13	100	13	100	64	98
Western Australia	31	100	17	100	12	92	60	98
Tasmania	36 [b]	95	11	85	8	89	55	92
Australia	230	97	89	92	76	93	395	95

Notes   a   Total number of questionnaires dispatched = 415
        b   This figure includes 7 matriculation colleges

The seven Matriculation Colleges of Tasmania were unique in enrolling only students in Years 11 and 12 with no other government schools in that State enrolling students in those years. To gain some understanding of the provision of science facilities in those colleges a questionnaire was sent to each of them. This was treated separately as an additional sample.

Administration of the Survey

Permission was sought from the Directors-General of Education in each State, and from the Chief Education Officer of the Australian Capital Territory, to approach schools directly for the survey and subsequent stages of the project. Permission was granted in each case. In each State the Director-General nominated, at our invitation, a liaison officer for contact with schools.

A brief statement about the evaluation was submitted for publication in the Science Teachers Association journals in each State. This statement mentioned in particular the proposed survey as the initial phase of the project. A statement about the project was also included in the ASTA notes of the Australian Science Teachers Journal.

In October a letter was sent to the Principal of every school in the sample inviting the participation of that school and informing him that the project officer would soon be communicating with the science co-ordinator. In fact four letter forms were used depending on whether the school was a government or non-government school and whether the school had recently taken part in another ACER study.

Table 3.2 Number of Questionnaires Returned by State and Date

State	\multicolumn{5}{c	}{Questionnaires Returned Before}	Later Returns	Non-Returns
	Nov 17	Nov 24	Dec 1	Dec 8	Dec 15		
ACT	5	3	3	3	1	3	3
New South Wales	44	6	6	2	3	5	4
Victoria	38	8	7	6	5	3	4
Queensland	38	6	8	10	1	2	3
South Australia	44	7	4	6	1	2	1
Western Australia	41	8	5	3	1	2	1
Tasmania	25	6	4	5	4	11	5
Australia	235	44	37	35	16	28	21
Cumulative %	56	67	76	85	88	95	

The questionnaire was posted to science co-ordinators on 21 October 1975. It was accompanied by a letter explaining the project and requesting a reply by 14 November. A stamped and addressed envelope for reply was included, together with a letter of endorsement from the President of the Australian Science Teachers Association.

If no reply had been received by 19 November a reminder letter was sent to the science co-ordinator. Two weeks before the end of the school year, if no reply had been received a second reminder letter was sent to the school and the Liaison Officer was asked to contact the school. Those schools which had not replied by the last week of the school year were either telephoned or visited by the Project Officer direct. Copies of the letters to schools have been included in Appendix D.

As a result of this follow up procedure 95 percent of all questionnaires posted were returned. This compares favourably with the return rates often reported for mail questionnaires (Oppenheim, 1966 : 34). Moreover the rate of return from each school system in each State was sufficiently high for the returns to be analysed with some confidence. The percentage returned for each school system and State is shown in Table 3.1. The effect of the follow up procedure is shown in Table 3.2. Only 56 percent had replied by the due date, 76 percent by the date requested in the reminder letter and 95 percent by the end of the year. This roughly corresponds to the observation of Moser and Kalton (1975 : 266) that the same proportion of people sent questionnaires respond to each mailing.

Data Management

The returned questionnaires were coded according to a prepared coding manual and the data punched on computer cards. These cards were then used to generate an SPSS[2] computer data file. Some of the variables on the file thus created were primary variables from the questionnaire while others were secondary variables created by computation involving the primary data. An analysis of frequency distributions[3] enabled any discrepant values to be identified and corrected. The file was able to be used readily for subsequent analyses.

The file consisted of 13 sub-files, there being two sub-files for each State and one for the ACT. In each State one sub-file consisted of the basic sample and the other of the schools in the oversample. Two series of weighting variables were calculated and assigned to each school according to the stratum of origin. One was a series of weights to be applied within State analyses. It allowed for oversampling of non-government schools and for the non response of some schools. The second was a series of weights to be applied to national analyses. In addition to the factors contributing to the within State weights it allowed for the different size of each State. Hence by using the appropriate weighting variables in the analyses it was possible to use sample statistics to estimate population parameters. The weighting variables used have been included in Appendix C.

The School Visits

The Purpose of the School Visits

In the second phase of the evaluation a small number of schools were selected for more detailed observation and analyses than was possible in the survey. The purpose was to examine and clarify the effects of good facilities on science teaching. Chapter Two drew attention to the claim that the Science Facilities Program had improved 'the quality of science education'. Two approaches were adopted. The first involved interviews with teachers and observation of the use made of facilities. Little research had been done on the effects of good science facilities, and this loosely structured approach was intended to allow the identification of concomitant[4] effects of good

---

2   Statistical Package for the Social Sciences (Nie et al, 1975).

3   The SPSS programs FREQUENCIES (Nie et al, 1975 : 194) and CROSSTABS (Nie et al, 1975 : 218) were used for this.

4   Maling-Keepes (1978) argues that concomitant effects is a better term than unanticipated outcomes for these effects are not really unexpected. Stake (1967) argues for a fuller countenance of educational evaluation which considers <u>inter alia</u> a wide range of outcomes.

facilities. The other, complementary, approach was to systematically analyse differences in aspects of 'the quality of science education' among schools with different standards of facilities. To do this it was necessary to define more specifically those changes which were expected to result from better facilities.

Selection of Schools

The schools used for case study observations were drawn from the sample already involved in the questionnaire analysis. Again it was important that the schools studied included a wide range of standards of science facilities.

The Science Facilities Program had concluded when the evaluation was conducted, therefore a 'before and after' study was not possible.[5] Schools were chosen for investigation using the differences between types of schools revealed by the survey. The survey data had demonstrated that important variations in the availability of dual-purpose science rooms, existed between schools of different type. A technique of clustering schools[6] according to the extent to which they were provided with science rooms was used. The clusters formed were of schools which were most similar in the provision of science rooms. Then at least one school from each of the clusters or terminal groups was chosen for study. From the larger groups more than one school was chosen. 'High', 'middle', and 'low' schools from each government school system (except Tasmania) as well as from the two clusters of non-government schools were included. Thirty schools, from all States, were visited in the school study phase: twenty-two were government secondary schools, including one Matriculation College. Eight were non-government secondary schools.

A copy of the letter sent to each school requesting permission to visit has been included as Appendix D. Schools were most helpful in assisting to fit the activities for the visits into the time available.

---

[5] Though a few schools which had recently acquired new suites of rooms were visited as a separate venture.

[6] The technique used the Automatic Interaction Detector (Sonquist and Morgan, 1964). Its application to this problem has been discussed elsewhere (Ainley, 1976).

Teacher Interview and School Observation Schedules

The reasons for including some relatively open methods of information gathering in this evaluation have already been discussed. From the information gathered in this way case study descriptions of each school were developed. It was also intended to draw generalizations and identify common features after grouping the case studies. Therefore it was considered necessary that comparable information should be obtained from each school. This implied that common procedures be followed in schools, and that common themes be used in interviews. As a result a core of information which was comparable between schools was obtained, in addition to observation and comment which was unique to each individual school. A sufficiently large number of schools was visited so that each school visit could be considered in a wider context and so that some generalizations could be inferred from the results. In these respects the approach adopted had much in common with that of Goodlad and Klien (1974) in a study of elementary schools. That study made use of visits to 67 schools in the United States. Data was gathered from three sources: interviews with teachers, interviews with principals and observation of activities (Goodlad and Klien, 1974 : 34). The interviews and the observations were structured around 12 rather broad categories[7] so that the information gathered in different schools was comparable. By using this approach the authors were able to suggest broad conclusions which could be applied to elementary schools in the United States.

In each school which was visited the science co-ordinator, every teacher of Year 9 Science, the Principal and the laboratory staff, were interviewed. For the interviews with the science co-ordinator and the science teachers, a tape recorder was used. These interviews lasted about thirty minutes. A guide for these interviews which had been prepared during some trial visits to schools, was used. There were, therefore, common questions but digressions were invited so that the interview was not restricted to the guide. Interviews with the school principal and the laboratory staff were not recorded on tape but each followed a pre-determined pattern between schools. Less formal discussions with other science staff members and informal visits to classes, were also arranged.

---

[7] The categories were; milieu, instructional activities, subject matter, materials and equipment, involvement, interaction, inquiry, independence, curriculum balance, curricular adaptation, expectancy, and staff utilization.

The guide for interviews with the science teachers was constructed around the following general issues:

1. the teachers' opinions of the facilities available,
2. the teachers' opinions of aspects of the facilities or their deployment which affect science teaching,
3. the teachers' purposes in science teaching in relation to experimental work,
4. the adequacy of the facilities available for preparation and study, and
5. the importance of good facilities for satisfaction in teaching science.

The guide for interviews with the science co-ordinators centred upon some extensions of these issues to more general concerns:

1. the suitability of the facilities available for the science department,
2. the degree to which the available facilities could be fully utilized,
3. the priority given to particular areas in using facilities,
4. the science curricula of the school, their organization, type and usage,
5. the organization of the science department and the morale of its members, and
6. extra science activities available for students in the school.

The use of the interview guides did not prevent specific concerns of individuals being discussed. They merely provided a base of common ground between the interviews. In addition these issues provided a guide to the observations made in the school and classrooms. A particularly detailed analysis of the schools actual facilities was made.

The Student Questionnaire

In developing the student questionnaire it was decided to focus attention upon Year 9 science teaching. This decision was based upon a consideration of previous studies by Owen (1975) and Wilson (1975). It was inferred from these studies that facilities had a greater effect on junior science teaching than that in Year 11 and 12. In addition such a choice was likely to achieve maximum variation in the facilities available to science classes. The survey results suggested that in Years 7 to 10 there was greater variation in the quality of facilities used than in Years 11 and 12. Year 7 was not part of the secondary school system in three States and Year 10 students in some States were involved in assessment and moderation procedures. Year 8 had the disadvantage of being the first year of secondary school in three States while Year 9 had the advantage of containing most 14 year-old students about whom other science data existed.

The views of students were considered to be of greatest potential value in providing information about two main possible effects of science facilities:

1. the science classroom environment or classroom conditions as they influence learning; and
2. the nature of the science teaching and learning process or the type of activities receiving greatest emphasis in science classes.

These two dimensions correspond to the two approaches to the assessment of the classroom learning environment which were identified by Randhawa and Fu (1973). One approach was based upon 'student perceptions of their classroom environment' through such instruments as the Learning Environment Inventory (Anderson and Walberg, 1974) while the other concentrated on the activities which characterized the class through a Class Activities Questionnaire (Steele, House and Kerins, 1971). In the present study each of these two dimensions formed separate sections of the questionnaire which was developed.

The Science Classroom Environment

The stated objectives of the Commonwealth Standards Committee concerned both the environment in which science was studied and the activities employed in teaching science. Three concepts seemed to be important for the environment of science rooms : involvement, organization and stimulation through variety.

The concept of involvement occurs many times in documents concerned with the Committee's deliberations. New science curricula which emerged during the sixties were to be accommodated in the new science rooms. Such curricula were seen as emphasizing learning through what might be called guided discovery (Commonwealth of Australia, 1976 : 15) with pupils actively involved in doing experiments, participating in discussions, and contributing to class deliberations. Even when the teacher demonstrated an aspect of science, the environment was to be such as to allow every student to see clearly and be involved (Commonwealth of Australia, 1973 : 11). In comments made about one of the best science rooms designed by the Committee, one member referred to an arrangement which achieved

> a more intimate setting... with the likelihood of better pupil-pupil and pupil-teacher discussion. (Field, 1974 : 36)

Smith (1967 : 5) deplored the lack of pupil practical work in the first two years of secondary school where practical work consisted almost entirely of demonstrations by the teacher with few experiments performed by the pupil. During the sixties the curricula used in science changed so that pupils were more actively involved in science learning. The Standards Committee wished to accommodate and facilitate this development.

Another concern of the Commonwealth Standards Committee was organization. Rooms should be well organized places of work where students could conduct experiments effectively with 'the necessary equipment, services and working benches' available and

> conveniently located so that the teacher [could] exercise effective supervision over the activities of the class. (Smith, 1975 : 1)

The design brochure (Commonwealth of Australia, 1973) produced by the Standards Committee gave considerable attention to the space requirements of a room for orderly working, the storage and distribution arrangement, and the conditions which would be helpful to good management.

The third concern of the Committee was that science lessons should be stimulating through the variety of methods used. Stimulation was seen as coming through both provision for varied and flexible instruction and provision of a wide variety of stimulating materials in the room. In its final report the Committee stated that a science room should be suitable for all kinds of activity including <u>inter alia</u>, demonstrations, pupil experiments, group discussions, films, or a mixture of activities at the one time (Commonwealth of Australia, 1976 : 16). Individual members of the committee stressed the same point. One member argued for the need to provide variety in teaching through

> a laboratory ... designed to allow complete flexibility in the type of activity to be followed at any given time in the one lesson. (Smith, 1967 : 6)

Another member of the Committee (Field, 1974 : 35) in commenting on two of the best examples of laboratories built to its plans specifically drew attention to the different possible arrangements of furniture to suit the teaching method. Stimulation through a wide variety of teaching materials was also important. One of the Committee expressed as his view of the richness of the materials to be available in a science room.

> It should be an exciting place where interesting models, charts and books, rocks and minerals, plant and animal specimens and science apparatus are displayed on the walls or in display cabinets. (Smith, 1967 : 6)

Figure 3.1   A Science Room Built under the Science Facilities Program.

Figure 3.2   An Activity-Based Science Lesson.

As further evidence of its desire to provide for varied teaching the Commonwealth Standards Committee had agreed on the need for such ancillary facilities as 'project rooms' and 'growing rooms'.[8] (Commonwealth of Australia, 1976 : 13)

While a number of instruments have been developed to assess students' views of their classroom environment, most were considered inappropriate for this study. Such instruments as the Learning Environment Inventory (Walberg, 1969, 1975), the Classroom Climate Questionnaire (Walberg and Anderson, 1968) and the Science Classroom Inventory (Northfield, 1976) were more orientated to the social than the physical environment. These inventories were based on a theoretical model of the class as a social system enunciated by Getzels and Thelen (1960). Consequently scales measuring student views of their science room environment were developed.

Concepts similar to those mentioned previously existed in studies of teacher characteristics, teacher behaviour and environmental press. In a study of some six thousand teachers Ryans (1960) identified three patterns of teacher behaviour.

Pattern X - warm, understanding, friendly versus aloof, egocentric, restricted behavior.

Pattern Y - responsible, businesslike, systematic, versus evasive, unplanned, slipshod, teacher behavior.

Pattern Z - stimulating, imaginative, surgent, versus dull, routine, teacher behavior.
(Ryans, 1960 : 382)

Pattern Y and Pattern Z seemed to be analogous to two of the concepts discerned in the work of the Science Facilities Committee. In a review investigating teaching behaviour and student achievement Rosenshine (1971) saw Ryans' Pattern Y as overlapping with both goal directed behaviour and organized behaviour. There was moderate and consistent association of these variables with higher student achievement (Rosenshine, 1971 : 100). Keeves (1971 : 254) identified a process variable, which was called 'The Emphasis on Work Habits and Order' and which was similar to Pattern Y.

Pattern Z was very similar to the classroom process variable[9] which Anthony (1967) called Stimulation. Anthony's measure of stimulation included assessing variety in materials, techniques, and feedback to students.

---

8 At the direction of the Minister funds were not made available for these ancillary facilities.

9 This was defined as 'a process or force in the classroom which is considered essential for optimum educational achievement' (Anthony,1967:167).

Rosenshine (1971) included these two variables in the category of studies using flexible or varied behaviour. Keeves (1971) also used a variable called 'stimulation for learning' which incorporated measures of the variety of methods used by teachers in classrooms.

Ryans' (1960) Pattern X did not quite correspond to the notion of involvement which was being sought. A much closer analogue was the second process variable which Anthony (1967) related to achievement: Self Involvement Opportunities. Keeves (1971) included two process variables similar to this: Affiliation with Class and Interaction with Students. While they have something in common with both Anthony's (1967) Self Involvement Opportunity and Ryans (1960) Pattern X they do not correspond directly to the notion of involvement being studied.

Hence, the three concepts discerned in the stated and implied intentions of the Commonwealth Standards Committee when designing rooms were also found in studies of teacher behaviour and classroom processes. The science room environment section of the questionnaire was structured around the following three major concepts.

I   Involvement : An analogue of Anthony's (1967) self involvement opportunities, as found in a classroom process study.

O   Organization : An environmental analogue of Ryans' (1960) Pattern Y (businesslike behaviour) which was intended as a measure of the orderliness and convenience of the workplace in having space to work and being able to obtain the necessary apparatus and services when required.

V   Stimulation through Variety : An environmental analogue of Ryans' (1960) Pattern Z but refined in the manner suggested by Anthony (1967) and Keeves (1971) to mean variety in materials and techniques of teaching.

Activities in Learning Science

The principal justification for building laboratories in schools must surely be that students are thereby able to conduct experiments. It was therefore considered desirable to ascertain whether students enjoying better facilities than their peers in other schools would report different emphases in the science teaching which they experienced. During the sixties and seventies, increased importance was attached to providing students with first hand experience of the phenomena studied in science, and to using activities which incorporated elements of original investigation. There is little doubt that first hand experience and original experience have become crucial elements in modern science curricula (Lee Dow, 1971; Ramsay and Howe, 1969; Ramsay, 1972).

Science rooms built under the aegis of the Australian Science Facilities Program were intended to accommodate and foster these teaching methods. This was evident in articles by Fish (1974) and Betjeman (1974) who were involved in science room design in State systems of education. The intentions of the Commonwealth Standards Committee were also clear. Standards were set so that schools would have sufficient science rooms of suitable design to allow student experimental work, as appropriate, in any science lesson.

> In many of the syllabuses being introduced in different Australian states, the laboratory is assuming a new role. The teaching approach in the past has tended to be dogmatic, with the laboratory being used merely to reinforce work done in the classroom and to develop experimental techniques. Often it has not been used at all for the junior classes. The laboratory has now become a primary place of learning where the students make observations and perform experiments for which the results are not known in advance, and thus experience adventure in the discoveries of science.
> (Commonwealth of Australia, 1973 : 4)

It was stated by at least one member of the Committee that shortages of science rooms, apparatus and laboratory staff were principal impediments to the development of laboratory and activity-based science teaching (Smith, 1967). Through the Science Facilities Program it was intended that at least the first two of these barriers would be reduced.

The development of instruments through which students can report upon the emphases in the science teaching they experience has proved teasingly difficult. The IEA 'Description of Science Teaching' scales (Comber and Keeves, 1973) and further modifications of them by Coxhead (1974) and by Kelly (1976) were considered for possible use in this study.

One of the two IEA scales was concerned with the emphasis upon 'laboratory work' as opposed to 'textbook learning'. The second attempted to assess the type of laboratory work: structured as opposed to unstructured. In the IEA study the use of responses to the scales had been distorted by a printing error in the instructions given to students. As a result the reliabilities were low (Peaker, 1975 : 195).

Coxhead and Whitfield (1975) challenged the theoretical content of these scales and argued that the assumption that more practical work meant less textbook use and the belief that more unstructured experimental work implied less structured experimental work were unsound. From these considerations Coxhead (1974) developed and used a modified form of the IEA questionnaire.

Another approach to modifying the IEA scales was that used by Kelly (1976). In this study the data collected in 1970 was used. A new factor analysis was conducted and the face validity of each item examined. As a result two scales were proposed. One was described as 'learning science through exploration' while the other was called 'science teaching by appeal to authority'.

The results of a trial questionnaire in Victorian schools prior to the main study suggested that the most promising approach was to use the items which had been used in the initial IEA study. Two changes were made to the format. A five point, rather than a three point, response key was used. In addition to this, the instructions were modified so that a more specific meaning was given to each of the five categories. There was insufficient time to try this form prior to the main study. It was hoped that the pattern which Kelly (1976) had found in 1970 data would still be valid.

The three factors which emerged from the analysis of the main study were of direct relevance to the Science Facilities Project. They resembled the concepts of laboratory work, enquiry learning, and textbook learning around which the original IEA scales were formed but did not assume the same bipolarity. Scales which were able to be formed from these three factors had sufficiently good reliabilities to be used as measures of class activity in science. The interpretation of the factors and hence the attributes assumed to be measured by the scales are listed as follows:

- E - Encouragement to Activity and Exploration : the extent to which students are given encouragement to participate in active science learning in and outside school.
- T - Textual : the degree to which science teaching is based upon textbooks.
- P - Practical : the emphasis upon practical work in science classes.

Characteristics of the Student Questionnaire

In its final form, the student questionnaire was administered to almost 3000 Year 9 students in 29 Australian schools. A copy of the questionnaire is included as Appendix E. The selection of schools has been previously discussed. Within each school three or four Year 9 science classes were chosen at random so that a total of about 100 students from each school were included. Choosing classes seemed important because many of the attributes being studied were possibly more characteristic of classes than of schools. This choice made it possible to use the class as the unit of analysis.

Table 3.3   Factor Analysis of Student Questionnaire Views of Science Classrooms (Section A)

Item	Factor Loadings			Item Allocation[c]			
	1	2	3	I	O	V	Rejected
1	41						
2			40			o	
3		32			o		
4		37			o		
5	31			o			
6			36			o	
7							o
8	36			o			
9	52			o			
10			49			o	
11	35			o			
12	32			o			
13			33			o	
14		38			o		
15		49			o		
16	42	36			o		
17		74			o		
18		62			o		
19			43			o	
20	38			o			
21	44	30					o
22			(29)			o	
23							o
24			(23)			o	
25							o
Percent Variance	19.0	6.4	5.1				

Notes: a Only loadings greater than 0.30 are recorded and decimal points have been dropped.

b Where items with a loading less than 0.30 were included in a scale the loading has been shown in parentheses.

c I = Involvement
O = Organization
V = Stimulation through Variety

Before examining the results obtained through the questionnaire its structure was analysed. A factor analysis of Section A, dealing with the classroom environment, confirmed the basic structure found in the trials. A three-factor solution extracted factors consistent with the original interpretation: Involvement (I), Organization (O), and Stimulation through Variety (V). Four items were rejected but it was possible to form a seven-item scale to measure each of the hypothesized aspects of the science room environment.

The results of the factor analysis are shown in Table 3.3

Table 3.4 Factor Analysis of Student Questionnaire
Views of Science Classrooms (Section B)

Item	Factor Loadings			Item Allocation[b]			
	1	2	3	E	T	P	Rejected
26			56			o	
27		54			o		
28	44			o			
29		50			o		
30	35			o			
31			42			o	
32		58			o		
33	45			o			
34	40		36	o		o	
35		40			o		
36			59			o	
37	42			o			
38		46	55		o	o	
39	39			o			
40	43			o			
41	39			o			
42	34			o			
43							o
44			44			o	
45		48		o			
Percent Variance	15.0	10.9	9.7				

Notes: a Only loadings greater than 0.30 are recorded and decimal points have been dropped.

b E = Encouragement to Explore
T = Textual
P = Practical

A factor analysis of responses to Section B dealing with activities in learning science revealed the presence of three factors: Encouragement to Explore (E), Textual (T), and Practical (P). The results of the factor analysis are shown in Table 3.4. The scales formed were not completely independent of each other. Two items, numbers 34 and 38, loaded on more than one factor. Since the nature of the items suggested that this was a logical outcome the scales were constructed with each of these items included in two scales.

Table 3.5 Scale Statistics for the Student Questionnaire Views of Science Classrooms

Scale	I	O	V	E	T	P
Number of Items	7	7	7	9	6	6
Between Students (N = 2991)						
Reliability (Coefficient α)	0.59	0.75	0.55	0.64	0.66	0.66
Mean	19.6	23.8	19.0	24.1	17.7	18.8
Standard Deviation	4.7	5.7	4.6	5.3	4.8	4.4
Between Classes (N = 105)						
Reliability (Coefficient α)	0.82	0.89	0.68	0.73	0.84	0.85
Mean	19.5	23.6	18.9	24.3	17.7	19.0
Standard Deviation	2.3	3.3	2.6	2.6	3.3	3.1

Notes : I = Involvement
O = Organization
V = Stimulation through Variety
E = Encouragement to Explore
T = Textual
P = Practical

Reliabilities[10] were calculated for each scale in two ways. Firstly, the values using the student responses were calculated. Secondly, class means for each item were computed for each of the 104 classes and the reliability of each scale using class means was calculated. Reliabilities and other important statistics are presented in Table 3.5. The reliabilities were quite satisfactory for research purposes,[11] especially since classes rather than students were the units of analysis. A listing of the items forming each scale is presented in Appendix F.

Data Management

The student questionnaire was administered to intact classes. An SPSS file of student responses to the questionnaire was built and an examination made of the frequency distributions[12] for each item. The student responses were

---

10 The SPSS program RELIABILITY was used (Nie et al, 1975).
11 Nunally (1967 : 226) suggests that for basic research reliabilities of 0.6 to 0.8 are adequate.
12 Using the program FREQUENCIES (Nie et al, 1975 : 194)

then aggregated[13] to give a file of class mean responses to which was added to the facility variables from the original survey data and facility variables from observations during the school visits.[14] The facility variables were both school variables and class variables. Appendix G contains a list of the variables related to facilities which were added to the file.

Systemic Effects and Administration

One of the purposes of the project as outlined in Chapter Two was to detect system wide effects of the Science Facilities Project and to study some features of its administration. To this end examinations of official records, a series of interviews, and the analysis of some other data were used.

The files of the Commonwealth Department of Education were made available for this project. In addition to providing information about policy development these records contain detailed records of the administration of the Program. In each State Education Department access to records relating to the administration of the Science Facilities Program was obtained. A number of interviews was held with people who could provide details about the functioning of the Program at both State and Commonwealth level. Some additional data gathered during the Program by Cohen[15] were also used. These data resulted from an unpublished survey conducted for the Science Teachers Association of Victoria (STAV). This survey was of teachers' reactions to the Science Facilities Program in that State, and to the items of apparatus which had been supplied. Survey data collected by the Commonwealth Department of Education was also used. These data were collected from all non-government schools in 1964, 1967 and 1970. It included detailed information about the science facilities available in schools. The 1970 survey also included the opinions of school Principals about the effects of the Science Facilities Program

---

13 Using the program AGGREGATE (Nie et al, 1975 : 203)

14 Using the program ADD VARIABLES (Nie et al, 1975 : 151)

15 D. Cohen conducted a survey for STAV in 1967. Science teachers were asked about their reactions to aspects of the Science Facilities Program. Data from the survey were made available to the Schools Commission for this Project.

CHAPTER FOUR

SYSTEMIC FEATURES OF THE SCIENCE FACILITIES PROGRAM

General Organization

Legislative Provision

The legislation which enabled assistance to be provided for school science facilities was encompassed in five Acts of the Commonwealth Parliament. While there existed a common intention in each there were some variations which reflected the way in which the Program was developing. All were devoid of detail concerning how assistance was to be applied.

The initial Act[1] covered the financial year from 1 July 1964. Contained within the one Bill was provision for assistance to science facilities and technical training. On subsequent occasions provision for assistance to science facilities was made in separate legislation from that for technical training. Smart's (1975) interpretation of this feature of the 1964 Act was that it allowed the government to mollify critics of the aid given to non-government schools. Of the combined sum the proportion given to such schools could be made to appear small. In subsequent years, even when the Acts were separate, the proportion of total Commonwealth funds given to non-government schools was quoted. Of the purpose and means of application the Act specified little; it merely stated the total amount of money to be allocated to each State without any division between school systems, and briefly stated the purpose for which the money was to be applied.

> (3) Payment of an amount to a State under this section is subject to the condition that the amount will be applied by the State, as approved by the Minister, for purposes in connection with laboratories and equipment for use in the teaching of science in schools at the secondary level of education.
> (Commonwealth of Australia, PP,1964)

---

[1] The States Grants (Science Laboratories and Technical Training) Act 1964, Act No. 50 of 1964.

Subsequent Acts in 1965[2] and 1968[3] were similarly brief. In two respects they differed from the initial legislation. Firstly, they were specifically science laboratories Acts and did not encompass the field of technical training. Secondly, they covered triennia rather than a single year. The latter development was important in that it enabled schools and State Education Departments to plan more effectively. It is interesting to note that Commonwealth Standards Committee recommended to the Minister in 1965 that a continuing three year program be implemented (CDE, File 64/8924). This would have been an advantage to schools and systems in that they would have been able to plan three years ahead. The Act of 1967[4] altered the schedule limiting payments to States for the remainder of the 1965-68 triennium enabling payments to non-government schools to be doubled. Subsequently the 1968 and 1971 Acts incorporated the double rate to non-government schools. Because the quadrennium from 1 July 1971 was to conclude the Program, the Act[5] which was passed by Parliament in 1971 differed from previous legislation. Rather more detail[6] about the way funds were to be allocated was provided. The limit to be provided for Government, Catholic and Independent schools in each State was specified in the schedule. This was because allocations among the total available for non-government schools were determined according to needs known to the Commonwealth government at that time. Previously the allocations were determined by the Federal Minister on the basis of demographic statistics. The Act even provided that the amounts specified for Catholic and Independent schools could be varied by regulation, provided that the total non-government allocation was unaltered, and the total sum for all schools remained the same.

The Allocation of Funds

Even though the legislation covering the period from 1964 to 1971 presented the allocations to each State, the primary division of funds was always between government and non-government schools. The basis for allocating funds

---

2   The States Grants (Science Laboratories) Act 1965, Act No.40 of 1965.
3   The States Grants (Science Laboratories) Act 1968, Act No.12 of 1968.
4   The States Grants (Science Laboratories) Act 1967, Act No. 9 of 1967.
5   The States Grants (Science Laboratories) Act 1971, Act No.65 of 1971.
6   Smart (1975 : 182) suggests that such detail was omitted from the early legislation to avoid a possible constitutional challenge.

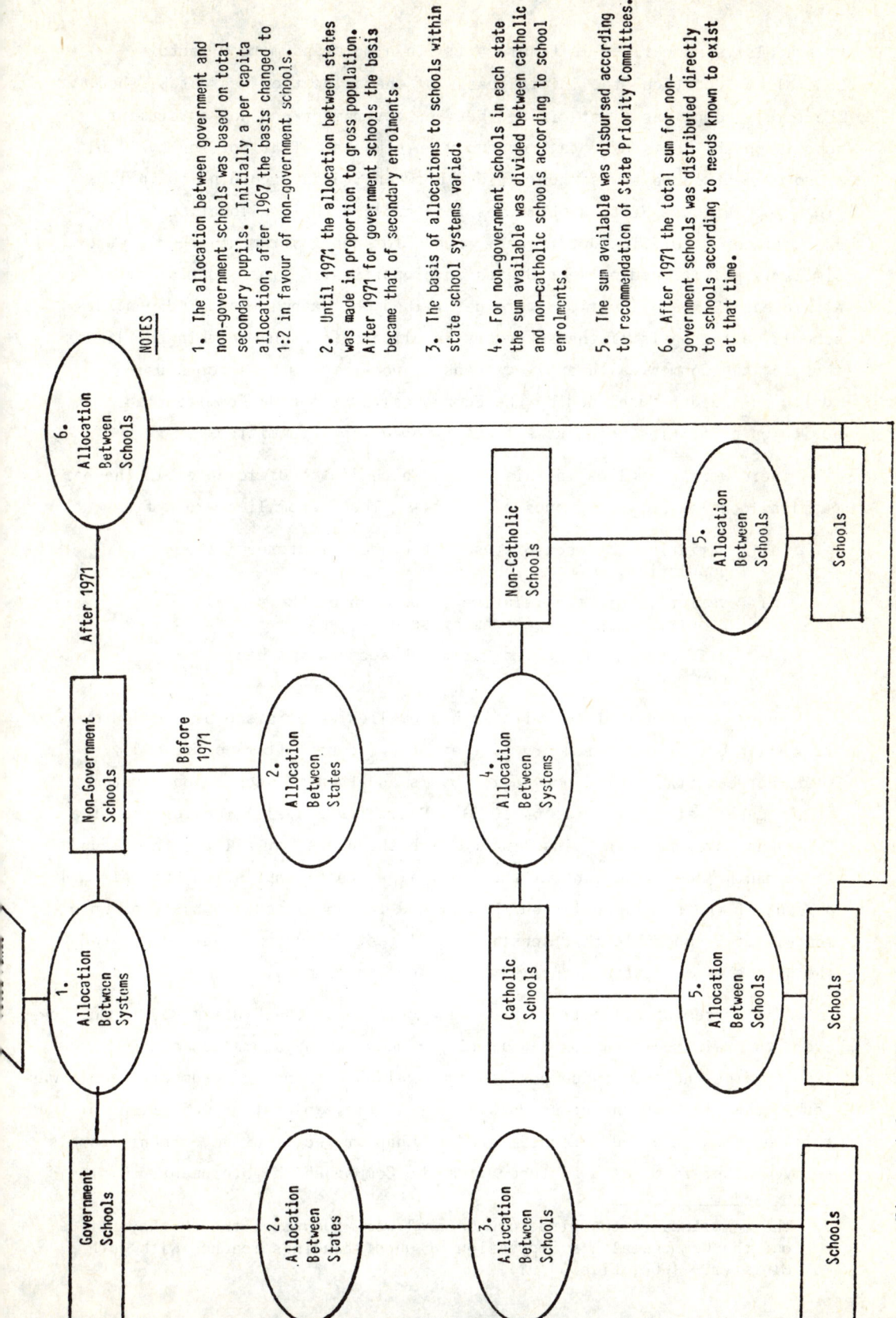

NOTES

1. The allocation between government and non-government schools was based on total secondary pupils. Initially a per capita allocation, after 1967 the basis changed to 1:2 in favour of non-government schools.

2. Until 1971 the allocation between states was made in proportion to gross population. After 1971 for government schools the basis became that of secondary enrolments.

3. The basis of allocations to schools within state school systems varied.

4. For non-government schools in each state the sum available was divided between catholic and non-catholic schools according to school enrolments.

5. The sum available was disbursed according to recommendation of State Priority Committees.

6. After 1971 the total sum for non-government schools was distributed directly to schools according to needs known to exist at that time.

Figure 4.1 Allocation of Funds under the Science Facilities Program.

to schools is summarized in Figure 4.1. In a memorandum to Directors-General of Education[7] the initial basis of the allocation was established. The total amount was first divided between government and non-government schools on the basis of total secondary enrolments. That portion available to government schools was then divided between States according to their gross population. State authorities then applied their allocation to schools as their own priorities determined. Funds for non-government schools were similarly partitioned between States in proportion to gross population. Within each State allocations were determined for Catholic and Independent schools on the basis of the secondary enrolments in each. Within the limits thus set the Commonwealth applied funds to non-government schools using advice on 'needs' furnished by the Commonwealth Standards Committee and advice on priorities which came from State Advisory Committees.

There were anomalies in this system which led to differences in the per pupil allocation between groups of schools. These anomalies arose from :

(a) variations between States in the age structure of the population,

(b) variations in the relative proportion of the school population in non-government schools, and

(c) differences in the Year at which secondary school commenced.

The problems associated with such anomalies were raised by the South Australian Government which argued that it would be better to first divide funds between States on a population basis and then between school systems within each State (CDE, File 64/1083). Smart (1975 : 211) records that the Tasmanian Government was dissatisfied with the basis for allocation of funds. As Tasmania had 3.7 percent of the Australian school population but only 3.4 percent of the total population they argued for an allocation based on enrolments. It is possible that constitutional restrictions may have prevented the basing of allocations entirely on school enrolments.

The system of allocating funds was modified as the Program developed. However, the main modification had little to do with the anomalies above. From 1967 onwards the assistance per student available to non-government schools was double that for government schools. Very little explanation was given for this decision save the defence, cited in Chapter Two, that government schools enjoyed other forms of assistance from the Commonwealth government. Smart

---

7   The memoranda to the Directors-General were identical though they set out the Commonwealth's impression of understandings reached with each Minister. (CDE, File 64/917)

(1975) proposed the plausible interpretation that the decision was a result of an earlier government commitment. The government had undertaken to meet eventually the full reasonable cost of those laboratories which had been partly assisted under the Science Facilities Program. In some groups of schools the policy followed had resulted in providing some assistance to as many projects as possible. Consequently, the Commonwealth was committed to meet the residual cost of many ventures. In a letter to non-government schools, in January, 1965, the Minister had made clear the government's intention.

> I should also reiterate that although a State Advisory Committee may perhaps recommend the payment of part only of the cost of a particular project in any one year, it is proposed ultimately that the whole cost will be met provided that the amount appears reasonable in the light of current building costs. Exactly when a school will receive payment will depend upon the priorities set up by the State Committee.
> (Gorton, 1965 : 2)

At the end of 1965 a minute from the Minister was tabled at a Commonwealth Standards Committee meeting. It contained an explicit indication that the government was concerned to know its degree of commitment.

> The next urgent step required in the implementation of the present scheme is to assess the liability of the Commonwealth in respect of the laboratories so far built so that we know where we stand with more precision.
> (CDE, File 65/10157)

To clear this commitment it was necessary to increase the rate of assistance. In addition the Commonwealth had suggested that, provided money was available and the Program continued, it would meet the cost of some previously unfunded projects (Smart, 1975 : 259). To qualify for such assistance the rooms had to have been built to approved standards, and within the assessed needs of the school. The existence of such unfunded projects may have provided a further incentive to double the assistance to non-government schools.

An unfortunate effect of this decision was that it resulted in an exacerbation of the differences between government and non-government schools. No similar increase in the rate of funding was made to government schools.

The undertaking to meet the full reasonable cost of a facility had two important benefits for non-government schools. It enabled them to plan the development of their science facilities within their assessed needs. A long term program could be planned in the knowledge that funds probably would be available eventually. It is likely that this obviated the need for piecemeal additions to many schools. Secondly, it undoubtedly stimulated schools to use their own resources to provide science facilities immediately at a time when the Commonwealth could not finance these. However, even among non-government schools the concomitant result was that the situation could be more rapidly exploited by those non-government schools which had the capacity to borrow and build.[8] Such an advantage would have been short term had the Program met all the needs of non-government schools by the time it concluded.

In 1971 two modifications were made to the system of allocating funds. One applied to non-government schools while the other concerned government schools. It had been intended to base funding to school systems for the final quadrennium on the 'needs' which were known to exist.

> It is our intention in the extension of the scheme
> to revise the basis of allocation of grants among
> States and among groups of Government schools,
> Roman Catholic Independent schools and Independent
> schools other than Roman Catholic, so that the
> grants available will be in relation to outstanding
> needs, which we expect to vary considerably at that
> time. In addition to completing the present program
> we will also seek to continue to make grants towards
> new needs that will arise from time to time.
> (Fraser, CPD, 1969 : 2509)

Needs, in this Program, referred to the absence of a necessary facility rather than the absence of, or the inability to obtain, funds with which to provide the facility (CDE, File 68/2764(1)). For non-government schools the Commonwealth was well placed to plan on the basis of needs. Visits to schools by members of the Commonwealth Standards Committee, and data from questionnaires, had furnished the government with detailed information about school needs. The Minister was obliged to provide Parliament with details of the assistance given to each non-government school.

---

8 Smart (1975 : 266) interprets this as queue jumping. However, it did enable the rate of building to exceed the rate of supply of funds.

Very little information was known by the Commonwealth about the needs of government schools. The Minister had only to provide Parliament with the total amount spent in each State and with the names of schools receiving some assistance.[9] Autonomy of the States to spend money on education had meant that no cumulative records of facilities in government schools existed in the Commonwealth files. State authorities also adopted different criteria for using the money allotted to them and, more importantly, they used different standards for assessing the adequacy of science facilities. At the request of the Minister the Commonwealth Department of Education attempted to determine the information needed from State governments for planning on the basis of needs.(CDE, File 68/2764). In October 1968 the Commonwealth Minister wrote to all State Ministers informing them that officers of the department would be seeking information about the States' needs for science facilities beyond 1971 (CDE, File 68/2764). The eventual request was for rather less information than had been first proposed as there was some evidence of a reluctance among State authorities to provide more information than was strictly necessary. The letter seeking information was sent in December 1969 for reply by February 1970.[10] Unfortunately the data provided were not sufficient for planning on a needs basis. Estimates varied considerably as a result of different criteria of satisfactory facilities being applied, disparate building costs and varied initial conditions.[11] In any case there was potential for injustice in the proposed procedure. The disparity between the States depended partly on the extent to which State funds had been used to supplement Commonwealth funds. If future funding was on the basis of existing needs then those States which had done least to supplement the Science Facilities Program would obtain a greater share. Any departure from a per capita allocation would have attracted criticism not only in Federal Parliament but from the States which received less assistance under such a procedure.[12] As a result

---

9 This was a totally useless piece of information as it normally included every school in the state.

10 It is possibly indicative of tensions between State and Commonwealth authorities that two replies were not received until after April.

11 A note on the file indicates that the information was in some cases reluctantly given and that its reliability varied. (CDE, File 68/2764(3)).

12 For example, Reynolds (1971 : 2827) criticized the allocation on the basis of per pupil difference. While a valid comparison between all government and non-government schools it should not have been applied to comparisons between non-government schools in each State because in that case the allocations were based on assessed needs.

of these considerations the decision was taken to allocate only the non-government schools portion of the funds according to known needs. The total amount to be spent on non-government schools was determined from an assessment made of all needs known to exist at that time.

The total to be divided among government schools was calculated after that for non-government schools was determined. It was decided to maintain the existing proportionate distribution between government and non-government schools under which the former received half the per pupil allocation of the latter. There is evidence that the Minister raised the possibility of changing this policy so that the per pupil allocations became equal (CDE, File 68/2764(4)). It was argued that this ought to be achieved by increasing the total rather than by reducing the amount for non-government schools whose needs had been accurately assessed. The estimate of needs provided by State Departments suggested that nearly $29 million was required but, assuming that the States continued to contribute 30 percent, the Commonwealth needed to provide only $20 million.[13] The proposed formula guaranteed the government schools some $26 million. Hence there was no strong claim for changing the arrangement (CDE, File 68/2764(4)). In retrospect it appears that some States underestimated their needs and that the criteria on which they assessed their needs were generally not so severe as those applied to non-government schools. An additional complication was the rapid escalation of building costs in the seventies. The continuation of the 70:30 ratio of Commonwealth to State funds also seems inappropriate. That ratio which emerged between 1964 and 1971 had included building in new schools but the needs for the final quadriennium were only actual needs in existing schools. It would appear that a strongly argued case from more than one State government based on criteria equivalent to those applied in non-government schools could have resulted in a modification of the policy for distributing funds. It was an opportunity lost for want of such information.

The amount of Money Allocated

The amount of money made available for the entire Program was considerable : over $123 million. Previously described procedures for apportioning the funds resulted in the allocations to various school systems in each State which are shown in Table 4.1. Appendix H contains allocations over various periods of time.

---

[13] The ratio of 30 percent was the actual figure for the period 1964-71. Total costs were estimated on the basis of $29,000 per laboratory which was the non-government school cost at the time.

Table 4.1   Total Funds Made Available under the Science Facilities Program from 1964 to 1975 (Money in $)

State	Government	Non-Government Catholic	Non-Government Independent	Total
New South Wales	28,441,780	12,429,630	3,898,710	44,770,120
Victoria	22,353,020	8,372,765	5,358,415	36,083,200
Queensland	10,411,580	4,829,320	2,744,100	17,985,000
South Australia	7,374,925	1,735,127	1,667,398	10,777,450
Western Australia	5,489,035	2,458,314	1,411,391	9,358,740
Tasmania	2,683,260	979,147	670,683	4,333,090
	76,752,600	30,804,303	15,750,697	123,307,600
Grand Total	76,752,600	46,555,000		123,307,00

Source: Commonwealth Department of Education   File 72/1547.

Some of the problems involved in the method used to divide funds amongst school systems and States have been mentioned. A clearer indication of the anomalies which resulted can be obtained from the calculated per pupil annual grants in Table 4.2. From 1 July 1964 to 31 June 1967 the per pupil grants should have been equal but as can be seen from the 1964-65 figures there were disparities between systems. From 1967 to 1971 per pupil grants should have been equal within government and non-government systems even though nationally the per pupil grants for the latter were double those for the former. In fact similar discrepancies existed for this period as in 1964-65. The year from 1 July 1968 to 30 June 1969 provides a fair indication of these discrepancies as this was the year in which allocations were revised on the basis of more recent statistics. For the four years from 1971 to 1975 per pupil grants have less meaning. The allocation system was changed so that in government schools per pupil grants should have been equal. In non-government schools grants were based on need so that it was not intended that they should be equal.

The result of neglecting differences in population age structure, school retentivity, and whether secondary school commenced at Year 7 or 8 is apparent in the total per pupil sum in each State. A State such as Victoria where secondary school commenced at Year 7 and which had a high retentivity

Table 4.2   Per Pupil Allocations of the Science Facilities Program
(Dollars per pupil per annum)

State	1964 - 65 Govt	1964 - 65 Non-Govt	1964 - 65 Total	1968 - 69 Govt	1968 - 69 Non-Govt	1968 - 69 Total
New South Wales	14.3	14.2	14.3	11.3	24.5	14.7
Victoria	12.1	11.6	11.9	10.1	20.2	12.8
Queensland	15.7	14.0	15.3	13.5	24.3	16.6
South Australia	12.7	19.2	14.0	10.4	37.5	15.0
Western Australia	13.9	15.0	14.2	11.5	25.3	14.9
Tasmania	11.0	15.3	11.9	9.5	27.7	13.2
Range	4.7	7.6	3.4	4.0	17.3	6.8

Notes: a   Enrolment Statistics derived from Schools Bulletins of the Bureau of Statistics refer to the beginning of August.
b   Money allocations derived from Ministerial statements to Parliament.

had a lower per pupil grant than Queensland where Year 8 was the first year of secondary school and retentivity of pupils was low. This can be seen most clearly in the 1964-5 figures which are unaffected by different rates to non-government school systems. These factors combined with differences in the proportion of students in government and non-government schools, to give wide discrepancies between States within government and non-government systems. Among government schools Tasmania received notably less assistance per pupil than Queensland while for non-government schools South Australia was rather more generously assisted than Victoria.

The period from 1964 to 1971 was one in which the method of allocating funds resulted in anomalies. The final quadrennium probably compensated for this in non-government schools, but not in government schools.

The Non-Government School Program

General Organization

That portion of the Science Facilities Program which was directed to non-government schools was administered by Commonwealth authorities.[14] Payments

---

14   At first this was the Education Division of the Prime Ministers Department. After December 1966 the Commonwealth Department of Education and Science was formed and was responsible for the program. From December 1972 onwards the Department of Education was created as a separate entity.

to schools required the co-operation of State governments. The Commonwealth government allocated money for non-government as well as government schools to State Treasuries. Upon notification from Commonwealth authorities the necessary amounts were paid by the State Treasuries to schools.[15] For each Act under which assistance was given it was necessary for the Commonwealth Minister for Education to seek the agreement of his counterparts in the States to continue to transmit grants to nominated non-government schools.

The administration of science grants to non-government schools was characterized by central executive action, devolution of authority for standards and priorities, and considerable school autonomy in spending the money allocated. There were two State Advisory Committees in each State covering Catholic and Independent schools respectively.[16] These committees were provided with information about the needs[17] of individual schools for science facilities. Information about needs was first obtained from questionnaires and checked through visits to schools by members of the Commonwealth Standards Committee. The State Advisory Committees then advised the Minister of the priorities to be given to various projects for buildings and apparatus. On this advice the Minister made offers to schools. An important feature of the procedure was the separate determination of standards by the Commonwealth Standards Committee, and the objective assessment of needs related to those standards. Once a grant was offered to a school it could appoint an architect, consult a member of the Standards Committee, and let building contracts after approval of the necessary drawings had been given by the Minister. This procedure is summarized in Figure 4.2.

After the school received an offer of a grant it submitted sketch plans and other drawings prepared by its architect to the Commonwealth. A member of the Commonwealth Standards Committee was involved in consultation with the school and the architect at this stage. In fact it was on

---

[15] This was necessary because of the provisions of section 96 of the Constitution under which grants can be made to States. There was no way in which grants could be made direct to schools.

[16] The composition of the State Advisory Committees is discussed by Smart (1975). They were relatively informal bodies. The non-Catholic SACs were set up by the Anglican Archbishop in each capital city.

[17] The specific meaning of the term needs in this Program has been noted on page 72. (CDE, File 64/8961).

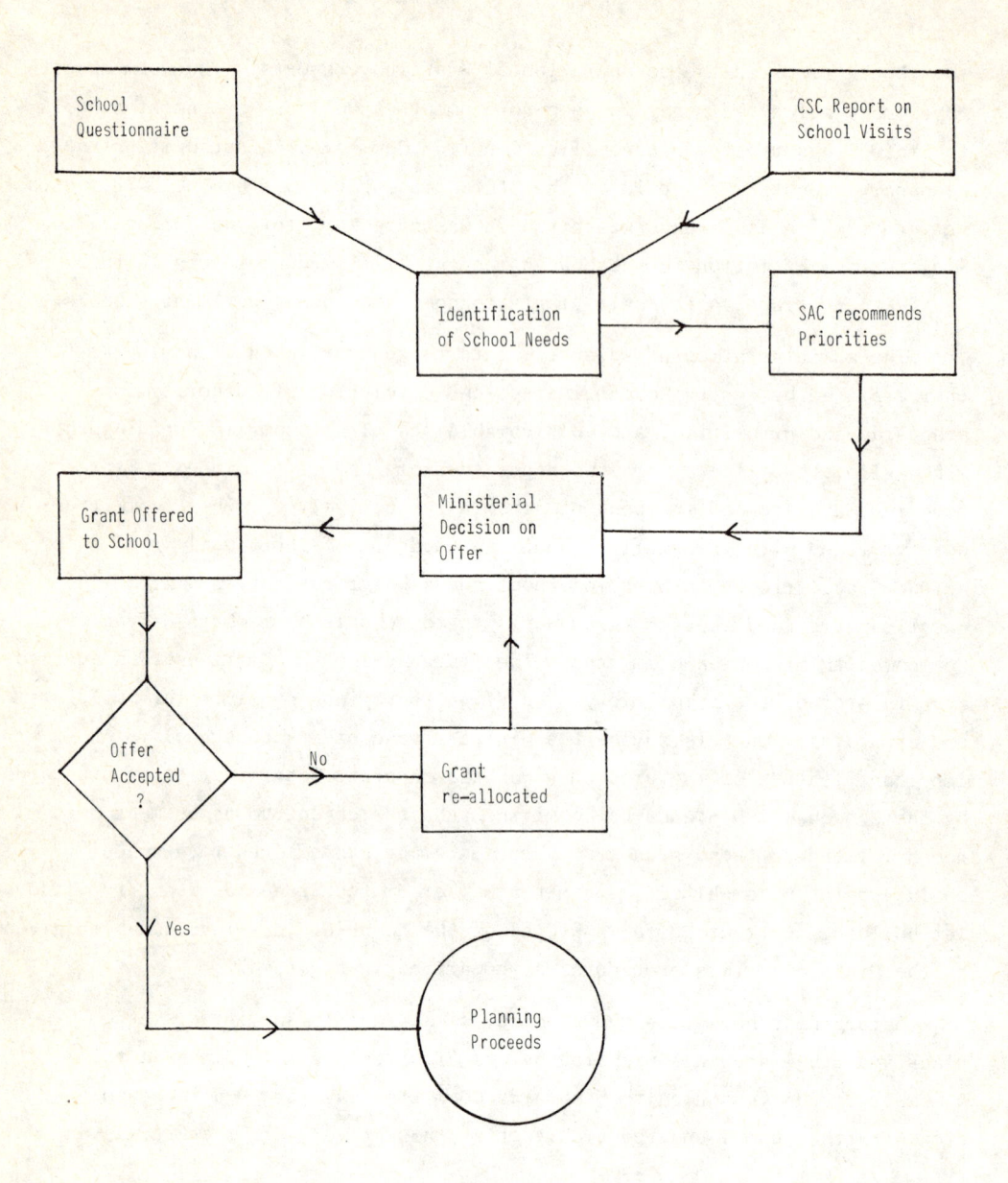

Figure 4.2   Procedure Leading to an Offer of Assistance.

the recommendation of a Committee member, acting for the Committee, that the Minister gave approval for the plan and authorized the commencement of building. Some grant money was paid to the school after it had advised the Commonwealth that construction had commenced. An inspection was made during construction by the Committee member in addition to a final inspection when the building was complete.

Determining Priorities

It is worth extending the comments about the role of State Advisory Committees in the determination of priorities. The priorities which these committees advised upon included which schools should first receive assistance, what proportion of the cost of a facility should be provided, and whether to assist buildings, apparatus, or both. It was hoped that the local knowledge possessed by these committees would ensure that the money was distributed fairly and spent effectively.

At the time that the Program commenced it was decided that only building projects which had begun after 1 December 1963[18] would be eligible for assistance. It was also apparent that insufficient funds existed to assist all eligible schools immediately (Gorton, CPD 1964 : 1325). In the first year of the Program's operation at the request of the Minister (CDE, File 64/8961), the Education Division of the Prime Minister's Department drew up schedules of schools in two categories : those considered to be in immediate need and those whose need for assistance was not so immediate. The priority given to schools in these schedules was outside the terms of reference of the Commonwealth Standards Committee. One heavily weighted criterion for allocation to the category of first consideration was the readiness of the school to commence building (CDE, File 64/8961). When these schedules were prepared they were provided to the State Advisory Committees to decide on priorities and the amounts to be granted. The Roman Catholic State Advisory Committee in Victoria declined to recommend the amounts to be granted. While they were prepared to allot priorities they considered that the Commonwealth Standards Committee was better placed to recommend amounts to be given (CDE, File 64/8946). Certainly there were early variations in the amount of assistance given to projects. Some State Advisory Committees made smaller grants to a large number of schools while others concentrated more substantial assistance on fewer schools. Noting that in Queensland Catholic schools had been granted an average 40 percent of total cost the Standards Committee recommended that grants should be a substantial proportion of the cost[19] (CDE, File 64/8930).

---

18 It is hard to decide when the Program began. An announcement was made in November 1963; projects begun after 1 December 1963 were eligible, the Act passed Parliament and received Royal Assent in May 1964, and finance was available from 1 July 1964.

19 A figure of approximately 80 percent was suggested.

Table 4.3   Percentage of Science Facilities Program Funds Spent on Apparatus - Non Government Schools

State	Catholic	Independent
New South Wales	8	11
Victoria	10	9
Queensland	7	10
South Australia	8	10
Western Australia	9	11
Tasmania	11	11
Australia	8	10

This procedure was followed only in the initial stages of the Program. The Commonwealth Standards Committee set an early goal of visiting applicant schools as soon as possible so that State Advisory Committees could be provided with detailed information about needs[20] (CDE, File 64/8946). The commitment given to meet the full reasonable cost of approved projects relieved some of the pressure on State Advisory Committees and also had other ramifications for their work. In presenting the States Grants (Science Laboratories) Bill 1968 the Minister indicated that not all of the money would be allocated on the recommendation of State Advisory Committees (Fraser, CPD, 1968 : 516).[21] Hence from 1968 some money was allocated by Commonwealth authorities to projects which had been completed within a school's assessed needs, but which had been either not previously assisted, or only partly assisted, by the Program.

---

20   These visits were important because it was found that a school's science facilities were often not well represented on paper. Many listed science rooms were found to be of an unsatisfactory standard (Commonwealth of Australia, 1976 : 6).

21   The statement read as follows:
In relation to Independent schools it has been decided that part of the total amount available will be used, in the first place, to meet the balance of the reasonable cost of science buildings already assisted and then to make grants to schools which have built science laboratories to plans approved by the Minister on the advice of the Standards Committee but for which they have not received any assistance. The other part will be available for allocation on the recommendations of State Advisory Committees for completely new projects at independent secondary schools.

At the beginning of the Program it was intended that the initial emphasis would be laboratories (CDE, File 64/8961). In terms of money spent that emphasis continued so that 90 percent of the money available was spent on buildings. The data which are shown in Table 4.3 reflect the fairly uniform proportion of funds spent on apparatus across Australia. New South Wales and Western Australian Independent schools spent the largest proportion of funds on apparatus while Queensland Catholic schools spent the least. A rather greater variation existed in the detail of spending patterns over time. Victorian Independent schools did not receive substantial apparatus grants until late in the final quadriennium (Commonwealth of Australia, 1976 : 18). By contrast Western Australian Independent schools began the Program by spending money on apparatus (Smart, 1975 : 234).[22]

The Commonwealth Standards Committee[23]

The Commonwealth Standards Committee was an important element in the non-government school section of the Science Facilities Program. Its role included establishing standards for science facilities, providing advice to individual schools in building, providing general advice on laboratory design in schools, and even tendering advice on policy to the Minister. The terms of reference within which it operated emphasized three elements of the advice it would provide.

> To report generally as required by the Minister-in-Charge of Commonwealth Activities in Education and Research upon matters in relation to science buildings and equipment for independent schools, and in particular:
>
> (a) to advise on the standards to be recognised by the Commonwealth in assisting in the construction and equipping of such buildings;
>
> (b) upon reference from the Minister, to advise upon requests for assistance received from individual schools;
>
> (c) to serve as an expert body to which schools developing proposals for improving their science teaching could look for advice as to the best means of meeting their particular needs.
> (Commonwealth of Australia, 1976 : 5)

---

22   Smart also notes that the allocation to girls schools in Western Australia was given early priority because they had been shown to be less well provided.

23   The full title of this committee was the Commonwealth Advisory Committee on Standards for Science Facilities in Independent Secondary Schools.

The work of the Committee in terms of general advice on design and establishment of standards and its specific consultation with schools was of great benefit in the implementation of the Program. The costs incurred in visiting schools and in meetings were not a charge against the Science Facilities Program. Nor, indeed, was the cost of staffing and operating the Science Facilities Section of the Facilities Branch[24] in the Commonwealth Department of Education, debited to the Science Facilities Program. The money allocated for science facilities was entirely expended on the provision of facilities. The administrative and advisory infra-structure was budgeted separately and was an additional benefit to non-government schools.

The standards developed by the Committee included the number of rooms required and the quality of those rooms. Its requirement for sufficient rooms to accommodate all science lessons within a 75 percent usage rate has been mentioned previously.[25] While this was not rigidly applied where the number of rooms calculated was not an integral number, nor where either the school or senior classes were small,[26] it was an important guideline. As a standard it was generally more generous to schools than that which applied in government schools.[27] Likely growth in a school and the potential for reducing class

---

[24] According to the Annual Report of the Department of Education and Science (1971) in 1971 there were 15 established positions in the Science Library Facilities Branch. It can be assumed that about 7 were in the Science Program.

[25] See page 45 for more detail. The statement elaborating this was the following:
> In view of the need to assemble and to remove apparatus and material, a science room should not be occupied by classes for more than three-quarters of the week's teaching time.
> (Commonwealth of Australia, 1973 : 4)

[26] For small senior classes a specially designed preparation room was often provided (Commonwealth of Australia, 1976 : 12). For small schools, which were defined as having less than 28 periods per week, special provision was made.
> Category A   A school that has a total secondary enrolment of about 20 students.
> Such schools should be provided with facilities in an existing room, e.g. wall benches, movable tables, services, storage cupboards, apparatus, etc.
> Category B   A school that has several secondary classes and which needs to provide for science classes of about 18 to 24 students.
> Such schools should be provided with a laboratory of 600 - 750 sq. ft., but do not need a separate preparation/store room.
> Category C   A school that has several secondary classes and which needs to provide for science classes of more than 24 students.
> Such schools should be provided with a laboratory of 960 sq.ft., but do not need a separate preparation/store room.

[27] See page 46.

size were also considered in determining the number of rooms required
(Commonwealth of Australia, 1976 ; 12). Assessing the viability of schools
was a difficult problem as money could be wasted in providing laboratories
in schools which may have closed shortly afterwards.[28]

Concerning the quality of rooms a principle was always adhered to that
basic services such as water, gas and electricity should be easily accessible
to the working area of each pair of students (Commonwealth of Australia,
1976 : 17). A series of working rules was established which was based on
decisions concerning area (92 to 104 m^2 per room), student places (32 for
junior classes), storage preparation area (23 m^2 per room) and specific
matters such as bench and seat heights.[29] [30] In discussions and operations
the Committee expressed a preference for multi-purpose and multi-functional
rooms.[31]

These standards and guidelines were implemented in a number of ways.
The most influential was in discussion with individual schools. Schools were
obliged to have their plans approved by the Commonwealth Standards Committee
to ensure that standards were satisfied. They were also advised that the
Standards Committee should be consulted when developments were first considered (Gorton, 1965). Discussions with schools' staffs often broadened
from the planning of facilities to encompass teaching methods, curricula, and
laboratory organization. An even wider influence was achieved through the
five editions of a design brochure (Commonwealth of Australia, 1964, 1966, 1968,
1971, 1973) and its 'open planning' supplement (Commonwealth of Australia, 1975).
The brochure contained clear specification of requirements for plans to be
approved, general guidance in planning and a number of sample plans. The plans
added in later editions reflected the development of more adaptable, versatile
designs which suited new curricula in Biology and Science. Plans were developed to suit the BSCS Biology course. The group developing ASEP materials was

---

28 This problem was discussed at a meeting of the Committee in January 1970.
    It was difficult to assess the viability of small Roman Catholic schools
    because of structural changes in those systems. In addition the viabil-
    ity of some schools depended on gaining a Commonwealth grant.

29 The decisions taken by the Committee on such matters were accumulated
    from the very first meeting and summarized in a digest of decisions
    prepared by the Chairman (E.D. Gardiner) (CDE, File 72/1296).

30 One member of the Committee at the second meeting recorded dissent from
    the attempt to specify guidelines which he considered too rigid. (CDE,
    File 64/8946).

31 Single science rooms were approved only in large schools.

consulted about laboratories which would best suit its approach (CDE, File 70/6081).[32] In the later years of the Program consideration was given to ways of reducing costs while maintaining essential features of design (CDE, File 71/2233). It would be valuable if these conclusions were documented and made public for future consideration.[33]

Lists of recommended quantities and types of apparatus were prepared for schools in each State. These lists were for guidance only since schools could purchase apparatus of their own choosing subject only to the condition that it be 'non-consumable'. Such lists were most useful for relatively isolated non-metropolitan schools. The apparatus grants for equipping laboratories were made on the basis of $2000 per science room. That this amount was too small was first discussed by the Committee in 1966 (CDE, File 65/10157) and an increase to $3000 and $4000 per room for junior and senior rooms respectively was recommended in June 1967 (CDE, File 67/4951). The Committee was notified that the Minister had approved the increased grants (CDE, File 67/1571) but these were never implemented despite the matter having been raised again in 1970 (CDE, File 70/1390) and 1974 (CDE, File 74/1547(39)).

Through its visits to, and consultation with schools, the Committee built up considerable expertise. It is regrettable that a similar body, or a combined body, was not available to help government schools in a similar way. For government schools it fell to existing staff to administer the Science Facilities Program.

---

32 There was some discussion within the Committee at its 15th meeting in February 1971 as to whether plan 8 (fifth edn) was suitable for other than BSCS Biology. In a letter the ASEP Assistant Director indicated that plan 4 or plan 8 would suit the ASEP material. The Committee discussion appears to have centred on 'flexibility' versus 'specific purpose' considerations.

33 Among the means agreed were runnels rather than sinks, use of standard furniture, timber floors, no drawers in fixed benches, reduced numbers of taps in junior science rooms, restricting fume cupboards to chemistry rooms only etc. It was recommended, however, that architects should always be employed.

As a result of the fund of knowledge it acquired the Standards Committee was an influential source of policy advice for the Minister and the Department of Education. While it was unsuccessful in achieving increased apparatus grants and in having approved provision for much ancillary space (Commonwealth of Australia, 1976 : 13), its advice was accepted in other areas. Particularly when the Department was planning for the final quadrennium of the Program on the basis of needs the Commonwealth Standards Committee's knowledge was essential.[34]

The Government School Program

Commonwealth Constraints on State Policy

The Commonwealth government administered the Science Facilities Program in non-government schools, but State authorities were responsible for spending the sums allotted to government schools. In spending money under the Science Facilities Program State governments were obliged to comply with a number of conditions. Through these conditions the Commonwealth was able to scrutinize the policy of each State. Hence State governments were not completely free to determine their own priorities : they operated within uniform constraints.

The conditions which applied to this Program were specified in a memorandum of discussions between Commonwealth and State Ministers and officials held during February 1964.

(i) The grant must be spent on science buildings and for equipment associated directly with the teaching of science at secondary level.

(ii) The things on which it is spent, and the source should be clearly identified in the State Budget.

(iii) The Commonwealth expects that the State will treat the grant as supplementary and additional to the amount which the State would normally make available for education purposes from its own budget.
(Western Australia, File 64/1207)

Other conditions were also applied. Following discussions between Commonwealth and State officials in May 1964 it was agreed that only non-

---

34 For the final quadrennium finance was estimated on the basis of $31,000 per new laboratory and $16,000 per conversion (Commonwealth of Australia, 1976 : 9).

consumable apparatus[35] would be purchased, lists of apparatus would be approved by the Commonwealth,[36] and normal State spending on science buildings and apparatus would continue. The agreement also allowed some continuation of spending beyond a financial year and attempted to define subjects not eligible for assistance.[37] At the beginning of each triennium or quadrennium the respective States indicated the general program of spending proposed. (CDE, File 72/1547). The Commonwealth Minister would then indicate whether the program was approved. From 1965[38] onward State authorities submitted in advance of each quarter a synopsis of past spending and an indication of anticipated expenditure for that quarter. Advances were then made available to State Treasuries (CDE, File 67/1855). As the Program developed specific scrutiny of spending on apparatus diminished.

Commonwealth authorities were also concerned with the cost of buildings provided in government schools. Early versions of science blocks provided in Queensland schools were noted to be extravagant and wasteful of space (CDE, File 67/1857). Subsequent buildings avoided the separate laboratory and teaching areas which drew Commonwealth comment. Similarly the cost of one science block to be provided by the Tasmanian government was thought to be too great. Indeed further details were sought before approval was given. Only after detailed supporting argument in terms of the proposed use of space and site difficulties, with the inclusion of plans, was the project approved (Tasmania, File 8547).

---

35 Originally defined as apparatus costing more than $20, (CDE, File 64/1081), it was amended to be constrained to a lower limit of $10 in November 1964 (CDE, File 64/1081). Subsequently in July 1965 non-consumable was defined as those articles which may be used repeatedly for a considerable period of time (Tasmania, File 8547). This appears to have been a tacit recognition of the impossibility of closely specifying a term such as non-consumable.

36 The Commonwealth Files indicate that this detailed approval was not so stringently enforced after the first few years of the Program.

37 Domestic Science was not eligible. It was suggested that Geography and Mathematics might be considered in some circumstances.

38 Before 1965 one quarter of the annual sum was paid to State Treasuries at the beginning of each quarter.

The condition which possibly caused most disharmony was that requiring the maintenance of normal State spending. Smart (1975 : 214) notes the difference between the February and May conditions on this matter. The former referred to general educational spending, the latter to spending on science buildings and equipment specifically. While the 1965 Premiers' conference resolved that the reference should be to general spending on education, evidence presented by Smart (1975) suggests that the Commonwealth Minister attempted to maintain State spending on science education. The conflict was greatest between the Tasmanian government and the Commonwealth. In late 1964 the Commonwealth Minister asked the Tasmanian Minister for Education for an assurance that State expenditure on secondary education[39] had not declined, before the grant would be paid (Tasmania, File 8547). Tasmania had spent a considerable sum on science education just prior to the Science Facilities Program. As Smart (1975) suggests, it was difficult to argue that the level of those years should be maintained. In other States there was less conflict over this provision though there is evidence that expenditure from State funds on science education did decline in some instances (Smart, 1975 : 252).

The conditions explicitly stated together with implicit aspects of Commonwealth policy set the boundaries within which State authorities could use the Science Facilities Program. Within those limits policies could and did vary in each State. In many ways the differences between States suggest that rather than being one program of assistance the Science Facilities Program was a conglomerate of seven interlocking schemes.

The Commonwealth Contribution to State Programs

The replies from State Education Departments to the Commonwealth authorities in 1970 provide information about the extent to which the Science Facilities Program contributed to the provision of science facilities in government schools up to 30 June 1971.[40] In the period from 1964 to 1971 it appears that 70 percent of the science rooms built in, and 50 percent of apparatus supplied to, government schools was part of the Science Facilities Program. The 30 percent contribution from State resources to building laboratories suggests that the government schools building program was slower than in

---

39 The assurance sought referred to total expenditure on secondary education but concern was expressed about a decline in science education expenditure.

40 Because some doubt has been expressed by the Commonwealth Department of Education about the reliability of this data it has been checked against State records where possible.

Table 4.4　　　　　Science Building and Equipment Programs

Government Schools 1964-1971

	No. of Science Rooms			Apparatus Expenditure[a]		
	SFP	State	%SFP	SFP	Total	%SFP
New South Wales	652	281	69	2757	5646	49
Victoria	300	130	69	3600	5200	69
Queensland	193	82	70	569	1110	51
South Australia[b]	172	64	73	783	1540	51
Western Australia[c]	97	67	59	371	849	44
Tasmania[d]	54	47	53	339	885	38
Australia	1468	671	69	8420	15228	55

Notes:　　a　Units are thousands of dollars

b　Only includes laboratories and demonstration rooms. The table on Commonwealth Department of Education Files includes preparation storage rooms in addition.

c　Taken from State Education Department files.

d　Includes ten major conversions from the Science Facilities Program and eight from state funds.

Source:　Commonwealth Department of Education, File Number 68/2764(2), Science Facilities Scheme - Proposals for Extension.

---

non-government schools. Since the per capita grant to the latter was double that to government schools a 50 percent contribution from State resources would have been needed to compensate if the rate of building in government schools was to be kept up to that in non-government schools. As shown in Table 4.4 only in Western Australia and Tasmania did this occur.

In the case of Western Australia it was possible to examine the science building program beyond 1971. For the total period from 1964 to 1975 the Science Facilities Program contributed some 146 new rooms and provided for the improvement or conversion of 25 additional rooms. Over the same period State resources were used to provide 137 new science rooms. Hence the contribution of the Science Facilities Program to science room construction was between 52 and 55 percent depending on the weighting given to conversions. Unfortunately this analysis cannot be replicated for other States but it is reasonable to assume that the contribution of the Science Facilities Program, to the provision of science facilities, continued to be substantial.

State Education Departments indicated to the Commonwealth that most of the new laboratories were to meet the increased enrolments attributable to the growing retentivity of school systems (CDE, File 68/2764(2)). It can be inferred from this that additional funds could have been usefully employed to replace existing science rooms of poor quality.

The Cost of Science Rooms

While it is difficult to estimate accurately the cost of building science rooms, there is evidence of considerable variation between State systems. One set of estimates was compiled by the Commonwealth Department of Education (CDE, File 68/337(16)). Estimates of laboratory costs were also among the information provided by state education departments in 1970 (CDE, File 68/2764(2)). A third approach adopted in this project was to estimate an average cost between 1964 and 1971 by combining total Science Facilities Program building expenditure with the number of laboratories provided. While this was a crude approximation it was considered an indicator of relative costs. These cost estimates are recorded in Table 4.5.

Notwithstanding the reservations about the methods used to reach these estimates the correlations between them are fairly high. The variations between States are consistent in each set of data. No simple explanation for the variations is obvious. It does seem that States provided rooms and preparation rooms of different floor area. The 1968 data showed that Victorian rooms were serviced by a larger preparation area than those in other States while Commonwealth science rooms in Queensland schools had a larger teaching area (CDE, File 68/337). The calculated average could have been distorted by funds being used for small building alterations. The Science Newsletter of the Victorian Education Department in May 1972 observed:

> Hundreds of small bills are written against Commonwealth science moneys every quarter, for maintenance, for grounds, for small adjustments, for fittings. These consume tens of thousands of dollars annually. (Victoria, 1972 : 2)

Another source of variation in cost was in the services provided in rooms. For example, rooms in Victorian schools were more extensively provided with water, gas and electricity outlets than similar rooms in New South Wales

Table 4.5   Estimated Building Costs ($ per laboratory)

State	Estimate[a] 1968	Estimate[b] 1970	Average[c] 1964 - 71
New South Wales	23664	27395	24747
Victoria	31666	37500	35679
Queensland	30000	33000	35172
South Australia	26000	-	23227 [d]
Western Australia	27333	32000 [e]	33894
Tasmania	24286	27000 [f] (34000)	27809

Notes
a Taken from Commonwealth Department of Education file number 68/337.
b Provided by State Education Departments in 1970 to the Commonwealth (CDE, File 68/2764).
c Estimated using the method described above.
d South Australia provided some timber prefabricated units as well as solid brick units. The former were more economical than the latter.
e Costs had risen up to $40,000 but new plans were expected to reduce this to $32,000. Rooms built in 1971 in fact cost an an average $30,000.
f Rooms in high schools cost $27,000. In Matriculation Colleges the cost was $34,000.

schools. In New South Wales the existence of a Schools' Building Research and Development Group may have helped to restrain costs. This body was formed in 1965, before similar groups were established in other States. By restraining exuberant architects it ensured that schools received science laboratories at a lower cost. Experience accumulated in New South Wales through developing a wide variety of school buildings since 1945 was valuable in applying the science assistance money as effectively as possible. As a result of cost differences the number of science rooms able to be provided from the Science Facilities Program was not in proportion to the money available.

It also appears that the cost of providing science rooms in government schools was generally greater than in non-government schools. Table 4.6 contains estimates of the cost of science rooms in government and non-government schools. Results are reported for both systems for the period

Table 4.6   Laboratory Costs in Government and Non-Government Schools

	Non-Government		Government
	1964-71	1964-75	1964-71
Minimum estimate	20265	23356	27561
Best estimate	22095	25180	28563
Maximum estimate	24095	26204	28975

from 1964 to 1971 and for non-government schools from 1964 to 1975. The minimum estimate assumed that modified and converted rooms and research laboratories were equal in cost to new science rooms. The maximum estimate excluded these rooms entirely. Finally the best estimate set the cost of such rooms at 30 percent of the cost of a new room. An estimate of costs for non-government schools for the whole Program from 1964 to 1975 was made to ensure that any temporary indebtedness to a completed project in 1971 was not distorting the calculation. The results suggest that it cost about 10 to 25 percent less to provide science rooms in non-government schools than in government schools.

In keeping costs low non-government schools enjoyed some advantages. It was possible for them to only let building contracts at the most propitious time. Some schools, which employed astute managers and bursars, indicated that they let building contracts when there was a minor trough in the building industry. Such tactics were not possible for the large State Education systems. The second advantage was the administrative structure which enabled the school and its advisers, supported by the Commonwealth Department of Education, to closely supervise the planning, construction, and completion of projects. The role played by the Commonwealth Standards Committee was important in helping schools reduce costs and demand what they required from architects in buildings. For government schools no such administrative structure was provided. The supervision of the Program was an additional task for an already heavily committed system. New structures within State systems evolved with the Program but they did not exist in the crucial early stages. In addition the building of laboratories was not so directly supervised by Education personnel. Relationships between the Education Departments and the various Works Departments

Table 4.7 Percentage of Science Facilities Program Used for the Provision of Apparatus in Government Schools.

State	Time Period				
	1964-65	1965-68	1968-71	1971-75	1964-75
New South Wales	6	17	17	18	16
Victoria	75	27	17	10	19
Queensland	0	10	4	5	7
South Australia	39	19	11	6[a]	11
Western Australia	4	11	8	4	8
Tasmania	7	18	29	7	13
Australia					14

Source: Annual Statements of Auditors-General, Commonwealth Department of Education.

Note: [a] Estimated as statement included State expenditure.

varied between States.[41] In some States officers of the Education Department were able to exercise little supervision once general plans had been submitted to the Works Department. Superimposed on these considerations is the general observation of such features as foyers and tiered lecture theatres in government school science blocks which were absent from those in non-government schools. It is worth remembering that cost differences need not automatically be interpreted as being indicative of inefficiency.

State Priorities : Building and Apparatus

In general State Education Departments used a larger proportion of the funds available under the Science Facilities Program for the provision of apparatus than did the non-government school authorities. Among the States there was variation in this policy. The data in Table 4.7 reflect this variation and the variation in policy over time. Victoria and New South Wales spent notably more on apparatus while Western Australia and Queensland used a smaller proportion of funds for that purpose. A possible explanation for this may lie in the perception of New South Wales and Victoria about the standard of science accommodation in their schools. Perhaps science rooms were not seen to be so much of a need as was the case in other States. Accordingly more funds could

---

41 In some States (e.g. Western Australia) private architects were often employed for some tasks but a need to manifest fairness resulted in work being shared amongst firms.

be devoted to apparatus. Interviews with officers of the Western Australian Education Department revealed that in that State it was part of a long term plan to use Commonwealth funds mainly for buildings. State funds were seen as adequate for the provision of apparatus.

Table 4.7 also shows changes in spending patterns with time. Victoria and South Australia began by spending a large proportion of funds on apparatus. In part this was attributable to the difficulties in starting a large scale building program at short notice. Some States apparently elected to spend the money on apparatus in case a surplus was not permitted to be carried into the next year. Other States were prepared for a larger building program and chose to establish buildings as a priority from the beginning.[42] Evidence suggests that State authorities were unprepared for the Science Facilities Program. Many non-government schools had the experience of the Industrial Fund to guide them. In fact it has already been noted that the Commonwealth government took cognizance of a schools readiness to commence building in classifying schools in the category of first consideration for State Advisory Committees. This ensured that in that section of the Program money was expended within the year. For government schools the task was more difficult as Menzies stated in 1965.

> The States have not, for their own good reasons, been able to spend in this year, all the money made available to them.
> (Menzies, CPD 1965 : 1587)

The observation drew a comment from the Opposition.

> There can be only one reason why this has happened. There was no prior consultation with the States as to their real needs, the Commonwealth proposal was not in any way based on a study of the needs of the States, and no attempt was made to dovetail the administration of this scheme with the administrative processes of the States.(Calwell,CPD 1965 : 1773)

This comment was supported by the interviews held with numbers of officials in State Education Departments. In the first years there appear to have been uncertainties about the purpose of the Program, the restrictions on the use of money, and even the administrative procedures which would be followed. Table 4.8 shows the small proportion of available funds expended by the end of the first financial year. These data are testimony to the difficulties of quickly mounting this Program in State Education systems,

---

42   Tasmania decided on this policy and indicated this to the other States. (Tasmania, File 8547).

Table 4.8   Percentage of Available Funds Expended 1964-65
                        (Government Schools)

State	Funds Available ($)	Funds Spent ($)	% Expended
New South Wales	2710000	1975622	72
Victoria	2045200	566562	28
Queensland	1048400	60454	6
South Australia	675400	284146	42
Western Australia	517000	198044	38
Tasmania	284100	129658	52
Australia	7244100	3214486	44

Source: Commonwealth Department of Education, File 69/3376.

especially as it was the first Commonwealth program in secondary education.

The variations in the proportion of available funds spent in the first financial year are also interesting. New South Wales used a high proportion of its funds in that year. It had already embarked on a program of improving facilities and changing curricula. In the late fifties new Physics and Chemistry syllabuses had been introduced and apparatus was being supplied for these courses. As a result the officials in that State were prepared with specifications for apparatus (e.g. oscilloscopes, Quick-fit apparatus) to be purchased with the money which became available. A building program and room designs were also at hand so that the newly acquired financial resources could be used to accelerate existing activities. Tasmania, which also expended more than half the available money within one year, had recently been engaged in a program to improve science facilities. It was fortuitous that these two States were placed in a good position to spend the money made available to them. Other State Education Departments had little time in which to initiate the new programs.

Summary

The administration of the Science Facilities Program was through seven educational systems. As a consequence it is better considered as seven interlocking sub-schemes rather than a single uniform program. Differences existed between the seven sub-schemes in levels of funding and in policy formation. In general non-government schools enjoyed a higher level of funding, while State Education Departments were unable to supplement Commonwealth funding to match this. Non-government schools also had the benefit of an administrative and advisory infra-structure specifically established for this program.

CHAPTER FIVE

CONCOMITANT DEVELOPMENTS IN EDUCATIONAL SYSTEMS

Funds from the Science Facilities Program for government schools were directed to schools through State Education Departments. As a result it was possible for the Program to influence developments in science education at the school system level in addition to affecting science teaching in particular schools. While that Program appears to have assisted systemic changes it could not be argued to have been a major determinant of those changes. These developments in school systems were not explicitly stated expectations though it was hoped that some general developments of this type would result from the Program. For this reason the term concomitant developments has been used. Following the suggestion of Maling-Keepes (1978) this term was considered more appropriate than unexpected outcomes. Such developments were not entirely unexpected. They represent changes sought but often gained in forms which were not anticipated.

Laboratory Assistants

Over the period during which the Science Facilities Program operated more ancillary staff were employed. At the beginning of the Program there were very few laboratory assistants in schools.[1] In 1975 the position had noticeably improved in all except Catholic schools.[2] Such a development does not imply causality. Not only have there been more ancillary staff employed in areas other than science, but some evidence indicates that the demands of new courses created a need for these staff. Consider the comment made in the Science Reports of the Education Department of Western Australia.

> The introduction of the Web of Life programme and the implementation of the recommendation for Achievement Certificate Science will increase even further the need for laboratory assistants in schools.   (Western Australia, 1969:11)

However, there is also evidence that the new facilities influenced decisions to employ laboratory assistants. In the Victorian Education Department a Science Newsletter (Victoria, 1967:67/1248) asked for teacher reaction to a new design for chemistry rooms. The authors commented in the introduction

---

1 See page 14

2 See page 150

that it made a laboratory assistant indispensable. Several officials of Education Departments claimed that the need to maintain and utilize sophisticated equipment, and to manage many consumable items was a persuasive point in arguing for laboratory staff.

In Western Australia it was argued, in 1965, that maximum efficiency was not being obtained from high standard science rooms and equipment because teachers did not have time or the necessary assistance to prepare experiments and demonstrations (Western Australia, File:1277/65). At first the appointment of laboratory assistants was recommended and made only to those Senior High Schools which gained new Commonwealth science blocks. This provided a precedent, as the value of such appointments could then be demonstrated. In 1966, it was recommended that laboratory assistants be appointed to other schools, including some without new science blocks. It was argued that these latter schools were disadvantaged both by lack of facilities and lack of laboratory assistants. Following recommendations made in 1967, country Senior High Schools gained laboratory staff in 1969 (Western Australia, 1969:10). By 1970, 80 percent of Senior High Schools and 25 percent of High Schools had laboratory staff (Western Australia, 1970:4). Beyond that time the employment of part-time and full-time staff grew so that by 1975 all Senior High Schools and many High Schools employed laboratory staff. In addition, 1969 saw the appointment of technicians at some Senior High Schools who gave assistance in dispensing and maintaining special provisions and making equipment for some courses. A Technical Officer for the Education Department was appointed in 1974 (Western Australia, 1974). This completed a coherent system of laboratory assistance which began with the Commonwealth Science Program in 1965.

While this development would have been desirable in any circumstances it is worth noting that it began in Western Australia, as a response to the Science Facilities Program. Western Australia has been mentioned in detail because the development of policy regarding the employment of laboratory staff is better documented in that State. Interviews with officials in some other States confirmed that similar developments had occurred elsewhere.

Curriculum Development

During the period over which the Science Facilities Program operated a number of new curricula were introduced to Australian schools. Some of these were intended for senior students while others were more concerned to provide material for teaching junior science. Courses such as BSCS Biology and PSSC Physics were adopted in most States. Other courses of more local application to particular States were also introduced. The new chemistry courses in South Australia and

Victoria and the revised science courses in New South Wales were examples of this. In none of these courses was development funded directly by the Science Facilities Program. However, in many instances money from that Program was used to assist in the trial and implementation of such new courses.

PSSC Physics and BSCS Biology were first introduced in Victorian schools to Year 11 in 1965 and 1967 respectively. In both cases special equipment was provided to assist schools which were introducing the new programs. This equipment was provided under the Science Facilities Program (Victoria, 1966: A66/147). Well equipped classrooms were found to be important in the trials of BSCS materials. The Director of the BSCS adaptation held the view that poor quality rooms and lack of equipment would have imposed restraints on implementing the course in its full spirit.[3] While the innovation would have proceeded in the face of such adversity it would have been truncated in some specific areas and possibly in its general success. The Director sought and obtained from the Education Department of Victoria assistance with apparatus and material for state school commencing the BSCS course.[4] Those schools received special packs of apparatus according to their size and Biology enrolments (Victoria, 1966:A66/147). The funds for this venture came from the Science Facilities Program.[5] A similar procedure had been followed when PSSC Physics had been introduced.

In Western Australia specific assistance was given to schools introducing Biology in 1969. Funds were made available as a basic grant of $250 plus a pro-rata amount based on upper school science enrolments (Western Australia, File:1968/73). A little more than $16,000 was spent on this purpose and was followed in 1970 by the investment of a further $25,500 to help the introduction of BSCS Biology[6] through the provision of apparatus and films. In both cases the money came from the Science Facilities Program Grants (Western Australia, File:1968/73). A substantial amount of money was also made available for films related to the Chemistry Study course which was introduced to all departmental schools in 1969.

---

3 Interview, D.G. Morgan : 27 July 1976.

4 Private correspondence, D.G. Morgan.

5 Minutes of Commonwealth Science Grant Equipment Committee, Education Department of Victoria : Held by I.M. Hall.

6 Web of Life, or BSCS, Biology had been tried in schools in 1968 and in 1969. It was introduced in all schools in 1970. The money came from the 1969-70 Science Grant.

In New South Wales the trial of new senior science courses began in 1971 as an alternative to the then existing multi-level, multi-strand courses.[7] The Board of Senior School Studies was responsible for these trials in both government and non-government schools. As the trials progressed more schools became involved so that by 1975 nearly half the schools in that State were using trial materials in Year 12. The new courses were used for Year 11 by all schools in 1975 and for Year 12 by all schools in 1976.[8] At an early planning meeting it was considered desirable that schools participating in the trials should be assisted in obtaining apparatus and other material. That assistance was obtained from the Science Facilities Program funds. The new courses used many of the concepts and ideas of BSCS Biology, Chem. Study Chemistry, and Harvard Project Physics. Some $80,000 was made available for each of the first two years of the trials in 1971 and 1972. In fact the cost in 1972 was a little more than this. Half of the money provided went towards providing text books and manuals for the schools participating in the trials, and a further one-fifth was spent on films to support the courses. As the Board of Senior School Studies had no funds of its own to support the trial of the new courses, the material made available under the Science Facilities Program was important to the success of the venture (New South Wales, 180:70/4471

In South Australia some similar developments were reported. A new approach to Chemistry which employed small scale experiments and apparatus was introduced in the mid sixties.[9] While this approach improved safety, especially with respect to the production of noxious gases, reduced the cost of apparatus and the consumption of large amounts of chemicals, it was expensive to commence. New small scale apparatus had to be devised and manufactured to suit the rather inventive experiments which had been developed. Such a venture was helped by the availability of sufficient money to contract the manufacture of this apparatus.[10] Without such support the imaginative work of those developing the

---

[7] The trial science courses mainly involved Physics based on Harvard Project Physics, Biology based on the BSCS program and Chemistry developed from the Chem. Study materials. There were also new Earth Science materials and a few other courses in various subdisciplines tried in the early seventies. All the new courses increased the role of laboratory work in senior science.

[8] The system of various combinations of units of 'single strand' and multi-strand' studies, in principle, provides students in New South Wales with a wide choice of scientific studies.

[9] S. Eberhard, V. Eyers and B. Hannaford were the main developers of small scale chemistry.

[10] Interview with D.J. Anders: 23 April 1976.

new course would have had its impact blunted. Similar support assisted the
introduction of Biology in South Australian government schools. BSCS Biology,
beginning in 1967 was especially assisted by the increased capacity to purchase
new apparatus to service an increasingly popular subject.

These examples of specific assistance for the implementation of new
curricula do not constitute an exhaustive list of such effects of the Science
Facilities Program. Other cases undoubtedly exist where such specific records
were not available. Moreover the implementation of new curricula was also
affected by the existence of better science rooms in schools. The general
existence of better science rooms and more abundant basic apparatus changed
the parameters within which curriculum development could occur. Thus ASEP
could be developed on the assumption that reasonable access to good science
rooms would be possible and that basic apparatus would be available in
schools. The Teachers Guide indicated that the successful use of ASEP
required good science rooms and the availability of certain core equipment
(ASEP, 1974:41). One former Assistant Director of ASEP has explained that
ASEP did not need to produce packages of equipment because most of the
equipment which was required was already available in schools from the
Commonwealth Science Grants (Ramsey, 1974). In Western Australia a new
set of activity centred curriculum materials for Lower School Science was
introduced with the Achievement Certificate in 1971. Prior to this a
survey of the availability of science rooms in schools was conducted. It
was considered important that classes using these materials should have
good access to science rooms. The materials were developed on the assumption
that this was the case.

In two ways the Science Facilities Program became a factor in curriculum
development and implementation. The most obvious was the direct provision of
apparatus to schools implementing new courses. Less obvious were the changes
in the limiting conditions within which those planning and developing curricula
material could operate. While not crucial to the success of the new ventures
the Science Facilities Program did remove some important barriers. However,
the very fact that small proportions of the funds available to the States
were diverted to help schools adopt new curricula indicates that limiting
the Program to the provision of science facilities was not in accord with the
needs of science teaching. The implementation of the Science Facilities
Program shared several assumptions with the new curriculum projects. Not least
of these was a belief in active participation by students in learning through
first-hand experience of scientific phenomena. Since it was a shared goal,
more co-ordination between facilities provision and curriculum development
may have been beneficial.

The Supply of Apparatus

The General Context

A general development in the system through which government schools obtained apparatus was that of granting schools more autonomy to order apparatus which suited their conditions and purposes. In part this development corresponded to the devolution of authority for planning curricula. As school science curricula diversified it was necessary to modify the central control of apparatus supply. The motivation to shift responsibility for the purchase and inventory of science apparatus to schools was also a result of the growth of school systems. Many became too large for such minutae to be centrally administered. There is also evidence that the Science Facilities Program contributed to the changes which occurred.

When the Science Facilities Program began most States controlled the supply of apparatus to schools through an annual requisition system. Schools requested apparatus and indicated existing stock each year. The requisitions were assessed by Science Inspectors, modified, and the material requested sent to schools through a stores branch. The Science Facilities Program altered this by making available additional funds. The requisition system which possibly suited the supply of bare essentials was not so appropriate when it became possible to provide schools with more sophisticated, or special, apparatus. By providing funds which removed pressure on the supply system, the Program enabled consideration of alternative means of providing schools with material.

In the early stages of the Program problems arose which served as salutary lessons for later developments. Because such a largesse had to be spent promptly, bulk issues of equipment were made to all schools, with but minor variation to account for school size. This procedure became the subject of much public criticism.[11] The supply of astronomical telescopes was particularly controversial. It was claimed that those instruments were unwanted and inappropriate in schools. The furore which was generated probably influenced the later decision to allow schools to decide on the apparatus which they needed.

---

11 See for example the Sydney Morning Herald, 22 and 23 July 1968. The article claims science teachers regarded the Science Facilities money as mis-spent and would have preferred to be allocated a budget.

Table 5.1 The Usefulness of Certain Items of Equipment Supplied to Schools - 1967

Ten Most Useful		Ten Least Useful	
Item	Mean Rating [a]	Item	Mean Rating [a]
Motion Projector	3.9	Glass Workers Burner	2.3
Microscopes	3.9	Ultra Violet Lamp	2.5
Refrigerator [b]	3.8	Wind Meter	2.7
Dissecting Microscope [b]	3.7	Centrifuge	2.7
Power Packs	3.7	Oscilloscope	2.8
Electric Balance	3.6	Cloud Chamber	2.8
Overhead Projector	3.5	Thermograph	2.9
Rock Specimen Sets	3.5	Barograph	2.9
Molecular Models	3.5	Telescope	3.0
Incubator[2]	3.5	Vacuum Pump	3.0

Notes:
a   Ratings were on a four point scale : 4 = Very useful, 3 = Some use, 2 = Limited use, 1 = No use.
b   Items supplied to only 50 to 60 percent of schools.

Reactions of Teachers

In 1967 a survey of the reaction of teachers in one State to the Science Grants was conducted by the Science Teachers Association of Victoria.[12] Teachers were asked to indicate the usefulness and quality of 36 items supplied as part of the consignments to schools. There was only one consistent pattern in the indications of quality : most respondents considered most items of satisfactory quality. Interesting differences in the items considered to be useful were revealed. A listing of the most and least useful items is in Table 5.1. A surprisingly large number of the ten most useful items were audiovisual or display materials. The remainder were items used by students. Among the least useful ten items was a preponderance of items which would normally be used by teachers for demonstrations. However, the mean values recorded indicate that not many

---

12 The survey was conducted for STAV by D. Cohen but results have not been published. The raw data was supplied to the Schools Commission for this Project. 222 replies were received representing a response rate of 50 percent.

Table 5.2   Usefulness of Certain Items of Apparatus - 1975

Item	New South Wales Mean Rating [a]	New South Wales Percent Schools [b]	Victoria Mean Rating [a]	Victoria Percent Schools [b]
Electric Balance	3.9	90	3.7	84
Model Skeleton	3.8	100	3.4	90
Aquarium Tank	3.7	92	3.5	90
Oscilloscope	3.5	95	3.2	92
Linear Air Track	3.4	97	3.2	65
Vacuum Pump	2.9	84	2.6	80
Telescope	2.3	82	2.2	95

Notes:

[a] Items were rated on a four point scale : 4 = Often used, 3 = Occasionally used, 2 = Rarely used, 1 = Never used.

[b] The percentage of schools reporting possession of one or more of the items has been recorded.

teachers considered any items without use. Even the telescope was considered to be of 'some' use. Some others (eg. the wind meter) may have found further application in Geography.

When the Science Facilities Project was conducted in 1975 science co-ordinators indicated the usefulness of a number of items about which comment had been made. Table 5.2 records the mean ratings to each of 7 items of apparatus. Results have been reported only for New South Wales and Victorian government schools because only there were these common items made available in the early consignments to schools. It is interesting that teachers in these States hold such similar views in spite of teaching different curricula. The astronomical telescope is considered only 'rarely' used. Of course one might not reasonably expect otherwise. It is perhaps more salient to indicate that only 10 to 12 percent of the schools in each State indicated that the telescope was never used. While such pieces of apparatus could well have been accorded lower priority they are clearly used, albeit rarely, and are not wasted.

A similar result was also reported in the Science Newsletter of the Victorian Education Department (1969:A69/1015). Some 90 percent of schools forwarded priority lists of apparatus to the Department in 1969. High preference was shown to items for pupil use (eg. light ray boxes, rock sets) as opposed to items for teacher use (eg. Van der Graaf generators, gas syringes).

Table 5.3   Preferred Method of Allocating Apparatus to Schools - Teachers' Comments in 1967

	N	Percent
Present Method (Direct Consignment)	65	31
Science Teachers Select from List	56	26
Direct Money Grant to Schools	90	43
	211	100

This confirms the pattern of preferences discerned in both the STAV survey and the Science Facilities Project survey.

Teachers responding to the STAV survey also answered several other questions. In response to being asked to indicate a preferred method of allocation, two-thirds sought a method which placed more responsibility with schools. The details are contained in Table 5.3. It is in that direction that policy has shifted.

At the time that the STAV survey was conducted most schools had only experienced the benefits of the Science Facilities Program by receiving apparatus. When asked about factors limiting effective use of apparatus or other methods of improving science education, other facets of facilities were the most frequently mentioned. It is surprising that preparation time and in-service education opportunities were not more frequently mentioned. Table 5.4 contains a list of the most frequently mentioned issues. While the Science Facilities Program has been said to have overemphasized the importance of physical resources it should be observed that many science teachers shared the view that facilities were important to them.

Table 5.4   Issues Related to the Use of Apparatus - Teachers' Comments in 1967

Limiting Factors		Other Methods of Assisting	
Comment	Percent Mentioning	Comment	Percent Mentioning
Storage space	16	Books and Libraries	21
Inadequate Science Rooms	14	Improved Buildings	19
Lack of Blackout Facilities	14	Audiovisual aids	16
No Instructions for Use	13	In-Service Training	12
Insufficient time	13	More Preparation Time	10

N = 224

Changes in Supply Systems in Each State

Two responses to the problems posed by the availability of funds for scientific equipment could be observed in several State school systems. One involved the establishment of forms of wider consultation on policy, the other involved changes in administrative procedures so that there was greater devolution of authority.

Victoria

The advent of Commonwealth funds for equipment in Victoria resulted in the establishment of an <u>ad hoc</u> committee to help formulate policy in the distribution of apparatus. Membership of this body known as the Commonwealth Science Grant Equipment Committee varied over time but it contained Departmental officials, Inspectors, Science Teachers and Teachers College Lecturers.[13] Initially it decided from teachers submissions what could be considered desirable items of apparatus in a science department, bulk purchases were arranged and were followed by distribution to schools according to a priority list devised by the inspectorate.[14] Several other developments modified this arrangement. The need to supply apparatus for BSCS and PSSC courses reduced the finance available for general major apparatus. Increases in school enrolments and greater emphasis on practical work meant that more Commonwealth funds were diverted to stores branch for the purchase and supply of basic apparatus. When it was observed that the items supplied in bulk were not always the same as those which schools desired, a shopping list system was introduced. Under this arrangement schools could select, from a list, apparatus they required up to an amount determined by the school enrolment. This was used for the Commonwealth funds from 1970 onwards and was later applied to the general equipment supply. Two problems of the shopping list were apparent. Firstly, small schools were often unable to afford an expensive item. Secondly, the movement of teachers could sometimes result in a new science co-ordinator being saddled with apparatus which suited the idiosyncratic interest of a predecessor. To solve the first problem an allocation to establish parity between schools with respect to some basic items was attempted but was quickly limited by dwindling funds. The second problem was tackled by initiating procedures through which

---

[13] The Budget meeting of 10 December 1969 was held at an inner city high school. In attendance were 6 Inspectors of Secondary Schools, 2 Inspectors of Technical Schools, 8 Science Teachers, 4 Teachers College Lecturers, an Assistant Director of Secondary Education, a member from stores branch and the Principal and Science Co-ordinator of the host school. The sub-disciplines in which they had qualified were Physics (5), Chemistry (6), Biology (3), Other Science (2), Geography (2) and Mathematics (1).

[14] Minutes of meetings of the Committee were held by Mr I.M. Hall.

schools could exchange apparatus.[15] It was an interesting attempt but met with little response from schools. In addition to this annual supply there was a basic kit of apparatus supplied to every new science laboratory.

New South Wales

Developments in New South Wales were similar to those in Victoria. In the first stages the extra Commonwealth money was used to provide standard equipment to all schools.[16] This was in addition to the school science departments' normal requisition from State supplies. As a second stage from 1971 onward a Commonwealth Science Grant list was attached to the school requisition.[17] From that list schools could order up to a budget of about $150 per laboratory. In 1974-1975 schools received a cash grant from the Science Facilities Program for science apparatus. A total of $311,000 was distributed in this way. The amount granted depended on school size with the most common grants for High Schools and Central Schools being $900 and $450 respectively (New South Wales, File 71/25623). Schools had considerable freedom in spending that money.[18] Some items left in stock were allocated to schools in need.[19] When no more Science Facilities Program funds were available all apparatus was ordered through the school requisition. However, the intention for the future was to develop a school based system under which schools could spend some of their entitlement through credit at the Government Stores Department and use the remainder to purchase directly from suppliers.[20]

As in Victoria a Science Equipment Advisory Committee was established in 1965.[21] This Committee determined items to be added to, and deleted from,

---

15 Interview with Mr I.M. Hall : 21 October 1975.

16 As in Victoria this included valuable (eg. oscilloscopes), unwanted (eg. anaemometer) and esoteric (eg. telescopes) apparatus. A direct distribution system from suppliers who had been awarded contracts, to schools was used. Some quality control spot checks were made.

17 From 1971 schools were allocated a budget to be divided among departments. General science apparatus was purchased, through government stores, out of this amount. The Commonwealth Science Grant List contained more specialized items of equipment. Some Principals may have reduced the science share of the general budget. Interview with Mr C. Macdonald, 5 August 1976.

18 The general condition was that the money was to be used for science. Where an item was available from the government stores it was to be purchased there. Other items costing less than $250 could be bought directly while those worth more than that amount could be referred to the Special Projects Unit.

19 Interview with Mr J. Jacobsen : 5 August 1976.

20 Interview with Mr C. Macdonald : 5 August 1976.

21 The Committee was composed of nine Science Co-ordinators in schools, a Teachers College staff member, a Staff Inspector (who was Chairman) and the Senior Technical Officer (who was executive officer). In recent years two curriculum officers have joined the Committee.

lists sent to schools and from August 1970 published a series of Science Notes. Science Notes were mainly a guide for use, maintenance and safety of the equipment supplied to schools but they also provided a means for teachers to comment on equipment.[22] Suppliers who gave best value were recommended by the Equipment Committee to the Stores Branch. While the Science Notes provided a lot of information the Committee also used the network of science advisors to reinforce this aspect of in-service education.[23]

South Australia

South Australia saw developments broadly comparable to those in New South Wales and Victoria. A basic bulk order system, with requisitions for items not on the list was augmented by the Science Facilities Program allocation. At first bulk consignments of goods purchased with the Science Facilities Program money were made to schools.[24] This changed so that schools could select from a Commonwealth Science List to the value of their allocation. Both the bulk order and Commonwealth allocations to each school were determined by a formula which took account of science enrolments and the amount of science taught.[25] There were, in the early seventies, special allocations for new courses, new laboratories and small classes. From 1975/76 a single comprehensive catalogue was used. Schools were allocated a budget, ordered available items from the State Supply Department, and had received a cash balance (in three instalments). This balance was to be used for local purchases, repair and maintenance.[26] Thus responsibility for management of resources was transferred to schools. An interesting side issue was that neighbouring schools were encouraged to group and thus share sophisticated apparatus.

Advice on the supply and purchase of apparatus to schools from science

---

22 For example, Science Notes No. 9 (1972) was concerned with the safety of high voltage discharge tubes and of mercury spillage. It also asked for suggestions regarding in-service training. Science Notes No. 8 (1972) contained information about using a set of two organ pipes to demonstrate beats and also some uses of the pH meters. Science Notes No. 11 (1973) contained suggestions for the use of the Overhead Projector.

23 Science Notes 11 : 32-34 (1973) contained a description of the Committee's role and composition.

24 Interview with D.J. Anders : 23 April 1976.

25 Statement prepared by M. Caust, Education Officer, SA Department of Education.

26 Circular to School Principals, 18 February 1975.

teachers came from the Apparatus sub-committee of the Secondary Science Curriculum Committee.[27] By acting as a liaison body with schools it could investigate and seek to rectify problems of supply. It has also been influential in developing policy for the supply of apparatus to schools and has even been responsible for the cataloguing of items held in the State Supply Department (South Australia, 1976:7). It is interesting that the effective and influential Secondary Science Curriculum Committee has been reported to have had antecedents in the ad hoc groups formed in the mid-sixties to provide advice on the purchase of apparatus and laboratory design.[28]

Queensland and Tasmania

The Queensland Education Department has also modified its method of supplying apparatus to schools.[29] Where previously schools requisitioned items from a list and their order was vetted and approved, now a budget system operates. As in the previously mentioned States, schools can order, up to a budget limit, the apparatus they choose. It is possible to order 'off the list' but delay times in delivery are rather long. There was no formal apparatus advisory group.

Tasmanian schools operated in a similar way to those in Queensland when ordering apparatus. However, while the budget system had previously applied to science (since the earlier years of the Science Facilities Program) now the school is allocated a budget and within the school the priority to each subject area is determined.[30] When schools have determined orders they are collated and purchases made through the Supply and Tender Branch. Science departments are able to order items off the budget list.

Western Australia

Western Australia has continued to use a system of school requisitions which are vetted by the Science Superintendent. The process begins in February with requisition lists sent to schools. Given optimal circumstances goods are delivered in October. An automatic data processing system for keeping inventories

---

27 The Secondary Science Curriculum Committee is a large body of more than 40 people. It works through a series of sub-committees : Agenda, Apparatus, Audio Visual, Book, Curriculum Design, Evaluation, Laboratory Design and Science Centre. It is influential in policy and involves a large number of senior science teachers.

28 Interview with D.J. Anders : 23 April 1976.

29 Interview with G. Robins : 7 June 1976.

30 Interview with G. Fish : 24 May 1976.

of stocks is intended to speed the process considerably. The first supplies of apparatus purchased with Commonwealth funds were sent to all schools on the basis of what was deemed necessary. After two years the system moved towards teacher choice based on purchase from a list within a sum determined by school size. This was in addition to the annual requisition and applied only to Commonwealth funded apparatus. It was considered to be a failure because the purchases reflected too strongly the personal preferences of the science co-ordinators. Those idiosyncratic choices did not always suit their successors. As a result the venture was discontinued. Commonwealth money was used only for equipping new laboratories and assisting the implementation of new courses. Energies were devoted to developing an efficient annual requisition system.

The changes in methods of supplying schools with apparatus for science can be partly attributed to the need to respond to the increased diversity among schools while at the same time retaining an efficient and equitable system. However, it does seem that the advent of the Science Facilities Program provided both the impetus and the opportunity to make supplies more appropriate to each school in the system. Methods tried in the Science Facilities Program were often prototypes for the general systems which were developed. At the very least the Program was a proving ground for new systems.

The Design of Science Rooms

Two developments pertaining to the design of science rooms over the years 1964 to 1975 are worth noting. The first was an increase in the extent to which people involved in science education were consulted about room design. Secondly, there was a trend to emphasize more versatile multi-functional rooms rather than fixed bench single purpose rooms.

Procedures

The Victorian Education Department provides one example of increased consultation with science education personnel. A Laboratory Design Committee was established in 1964. Of its seven members, six were experienced practising teachers while the co-ordinator was a senior science inspector.[31] Its

---

[31] At its August meeting the Assistant Director of Secondary Education and two members of the Public Works Department were present. It received suggestions from two science teachers not on the Committee.

recommendations of general policy shaped the development of science rooms to be provided in Victorian secondary schools.[32] The co-ordinator prepared plans which were considered in detail before being modified for presentation to the Public Works Department. Some differences arose between the Public Works Department and the Committee over the width of rooms. The former favoured a 24 feet width which had been used to that date while the Inspectorate and the Committee preferred a 32 feet width. After lengthy discussion rooms were planned with a width of 28 feet. Similar differences arose over whether rooms should be free standing or added to existing structures. At the very least a precedent of involving teachers in planning groups was established.

In Queensland a similar group was responsible for reviewing the design of science laboratories (Robins, 1974:5). However, it only came into existence in the early seventies and was not permanently established. There was less provision for feedback from teachers than in Victoria. In Queensland the best designs were not followed in all laboratories: a distinction was made between State funded rooms and Commonwealth funded rooms. The new designs only applied to the latter. Prior to the formation of this informal group designs were drawn in sketch form by a science inspector and developed by the Works Department.

Since 1965 science teachers in New South Wales have been involved in planning school science facilities (Turner, 1974:9). The planning was co-ordinated through the Schools Building Research and Development Group which was established in that year. This group was staffed by teachers and inspectors from the Department of Education as well as architects from the Public Works Department. It evaluated school facilities, prepared briefs for school design and undertook research in the construction of buildings.[33] The planning of science facilities is now co-ordinated by a research officer who is assisted by the Science Teachers Building Advisory Panel. This group of about 24 people comprised inspectors and a diverse range of teachers. It is not clear whether this development had any link to the Science Facilities Program though it

---

[32] The principal decision was to support multi-purpose rooms rather than separate classrooms and laboratories. In addition recommendations were made about the number of rooms (4 in an 800 pupil school), the type (one for each of Biology, Physics, Chemistry and Science) and requisite features (2 doors, master switches, type of furniture and services).

[33] See New South Wales Education Department, Public School Architecture in New South Wales.

does appear that the Program did allow greater opportunity to experiment
with room design. A lot of the initial work of the Schools' Building
Research and Development Group involved science laboratories.

The Laboratory Design Sub-committee is one of the subsidiaries of the
Secondary Science Curriculum Committee in South Australia. Its five members
include four science teachers and one Principal Education Officer. Its projects
include aspects of science room design such as the provision of servicing using
pillars, bollards and overhead trunking. Recommendations often resulted from
information obtained from school staff and were placed before the full Secondary
Science Curriculum Committee. As a result design features were considered in
the context of curriculum development before being forwarded to the appropriate
section of the Education Department. It has been mentioned in relation to the sup
of   apparatus   that there was a practical necessity to obtain advice about
laboratory design and apparatus at the commencement of the Science Facilities
Program. That informal network of advisory groups was the precursor to the
Science Curriculum Committee.

Design briefs for Western Australian schools have always originated with
the Science Superintendents. The sieving of ideas and trends is therefore
based on the judgment of those people : no formal design groups have existed
until recently. Designs of science rooms are now within the framework of a
document which outlines the general design for high school complexes (Betjeman,
1975). Similar documents guide planning in Tasmania for both High Schools
and Matriculation Colleges (Tasmania, 1975a, 1975b). In Tasmania these
documents were the result of work by two broadly representative committees which
worked with a series of subject area sub-committees. Science was one
of the subject area sub-committees (Hudspeth, 1973). However, this
procedure began only in 1971. Prior to that date a very informal liaison
between Science Supervisor, the Buildings Superintendent and the Public
Works Department existed. In the relatively small education systems in
Tasmania and Western Australia such informal communication seems to have presente
less of a problem than elsewhere.

In Victoria it was possible to trace changed procedures in the planning
of science accommodation to the beginning of the Science Facilities Program.
A similar development came later in Queensland but did not have the same lasting
impact. Evidence of a link with the Science Facilities Program in South Australia is largely anecdotal while in New South Wales science room design was but

Table 5.5   Types of Science Rooms in Australian Schools

Primary Classification	Secondary Classification	Tertiary Classification
1. Separate Facilities	1.1 No services	1.1.1 Classroom only
	1.2 Limited Services (front bench only)	1.2.1 Lecture theatre or tiered demonstration room
		1.2.2 Demonstration room
	1.3 No Teaching Provision	1.3.1 Single Purpose Laboratory
2. Fixed Services	2.1 Bar-bench type (with services on each bench)	2.1.1 Long benches across room
		2.1.2 Long benches down room
		2.1.3 Long benches across room but split with centre aisle
	2.2 Island bench type	2.2.1 4 to 6 seat island benches in room - all services
		2.2.2 2 seat island benches
3. Flexible Arrangements	3.1 Peripheral Services (Moveable writing tables in centre of room)	3.1.1 Sinks in benches around perimeter
		3.1.2 Runnel benches around perimeter
		3.1.3 Perimeter services with peninsula work areas separate from writing area
	3.2 Service Pillars (with moveable benches abutting these)	3.2.1 Long runnel 'pillars' with abutting benches
		3.2.2 Fixed pillars
		3.2.3 Mobile 'pillars' with overhead trunking of services

one function of the design group formed in 1965. Design and planning procedures used in Western Australia and Tasmania appear to have developed without the Science Facilities Program having made a big impact.

The Design of Science Rooms

Trends in the design of science rooms in both government and non-government schools have been in a similar direction but there were variations in the time at which new designs were introduced. To consider the development of design it is worth classifying changes in three stages. The first stage saw the use of separate rooms, or areas, for laboratories and teaching. The second stage resulted in dual purpose science rooms which had large fixed work benches. Most recently, in the third stage, science rooms have been developed which are more versatile and multi-functional. Rooms built in this third stage have often been called flexible. Table 5.5 contains a summary of the types of science rooms built.

Stage one science facilities were discouraged in non-government schools by the Commonwealth Standards Committee from the outset of the Science Facilities program. Most State Departments of Education did not proceed with separate single purpose facilities. Lecture theatres were provided in some Western Australian science suites when a team teaching concept was in vogue. Such facilities are now useful as a school resource but not as a science resource. Science blocks built in some Queensland schools in the mid sixties included laboratories of a type unsuited to class teaching. An example is shown in Figure 5.1. While some early South Australian designs were single purpose laboratories they were also suited to class teaching. In general the concept of separate teaching and laboratory areas was losing favour at the time the Science Facilities Program began. Its demise was hastened by that scheme.

The second, or fixed bench stage, of science room design predominated in the early part of the Science Facilities Program. Fixed benches appear to have derived from a concern to provide adequate services in science rooms. Possibly this was a reaction to previous shortage though equally it can be attributed to the need for stable working areas in Physics and Chemistry, the sub-disciplines for which new facilities were then being provided. Variants of this design are evident in rooms which have long benches either across rooms or down rooms, and in those rooms where the long fixed benches are divided to give a centre aisle (Figure 5.2). The island bench design used in New South Wales government schools and shown in Figure 5.3 is another variant of this theme. It was used in a State where senior as well as junior curricula involved multi-strand science and was possibly intended to cater for that circumstance. Science rooms with fixed benches are still being built and are favoured by many science teachers because of the stability of work areas and the easier accessibility of services.

A combination of pressures to reduce the cost of science rooms and to provide facilities for courses such as BSCS and ASEP led to the development of the stage three science rooms. These rooms, which give emphasis to one or other of the meanings of flexibility, were conceived in the late sixties but few examples were built until the seventies. Among the various forms of this concept there

Figure 5.1   A Single Purpose Laboratory Designed for Chemistry Practical Work.

Figure 5.2   A Dual-Purpose Science Room Based on Fixed Benches.

Figure 5.3   An Island-Bench Design Science Room.

Figure 5.4   A Science Room with all the Services at the Perimeter of the Room.

Figure 5.5   A Science Room with Peripheral Services in which the Desks have been Arranged for Discussion Groups.

Figure 5.6   A Science Room with Separate Laboratory Work Areas at the Edge of the Room.

5.7 A Science Area Incorporating Service Pillars and Movable Benches. The Benches have Holders for Trays of Equipment Obtained from the Service Wall of the Preparation Room.

5.8 A Science Room with Elongated Pillars and Movable Tables.

are two groups. In one group the emphasis has been on peripheral services, and work areas, with movable writing tables in the centre of the room. The other approach involved providing services at pillars to which movable benches could abut.

Peripheral services carried the advantage of separating work areas, with their associated mess and temptations for vandalism, from the commonly used writing areas. This approach is evident in the most recent laboratories provided to government schools in New South Wales (Figure 5.4), Victoria (Figure 5.5), Queensland (Figure 5.6) and elsewhere. It can also be seen in some of the designs used by non-government schools.

Service pillars provide better access to services without students having to move from their work place. A good example of this approach to the design of science rooms has been shown in Figure 5.7. Rooms intended for Chemistry in Victorian schools incorporated elongated 'runnel' pillars with abutting benches (Figure 5.8). The boldest attempt at flexible laboratory space incorporated the use of mobile pillars which plugged into service points trunked though the ceiling. This was tried in several South Australian government schools but the practical problems have proved too great and the approach has been discontinued.

Changes in the design of science rooms have occurred over the course of the Science Facilities Program. It is probable that changes would have taken place without the Program. However, the stimulus given to the design of rooms by the large amount of money available possibly hastened the changes. It also lessened financial constraints which would have inhibited the use of some design features.

Summary

A range of developments in science education were influenced by the Science Facilities Program. The provision of laboratory assistants, new curricula, apparatus supply systems which were more sensitive to the needs of individual schools, and more adaptable room designs have all emerged. All have affected science teaching across systems and have been at least partially influenced by the Science Facilities Program.

CHAPTER SIX

ROOMS FOR TEACHING SCIENCE

Looking at Science Facilities

In Chapter Three the development of the school questionnaire was discussed. Part of that questionnaire was concerned with the adequacy of school science facilities. Information was sought about four aspects of science facilities.

1 Whether the school had an adequate number of science rooms.
2 Whether the school had science rooms of good quality.
3 Whether there was sufficient apparatus available in the school.
4 Whether the school employed laboratory assistants in science.

In order to examine the intercorrelations between these aspects of the questionnaire a factor analysis was carried out. Variables of different sorts were included in the analysis.

1 The indices of room availability for science lessons (Q_1 and Q_2).
2 The total number of science rooms and the number of dual purpose science rooms per 1000 students (L_1 and L_2).
3 The functional adequacy, or quality, of the school's science rooms.
4 The number of equivalent full time laboratory assistants per 1000 students and per 10 science teachers.
5 The direct responses of the science co-ordinator to questions about the adequacy of 'expendable', 'minor', and 'major' apparatus.
6 The Science Co-ordinators' ratings of the degree to which various features of the school's science facilities impeded practical work.

The SPSS program FACTOR (Nie et al, 1975: 468) was used. In the analysis reported in Table 6.1, four principal components had eigen values greater than 1. When a varimax rotation of these components was undertaken the four factors extracted had the loadings shown. From these loadings it was possible to identify the four factors:

1 The availability of science rooms.
2 The provision of support staff.
3 The abundance of apparatus in the school.
4 The quality of science rooms in the school.

Thus the structure of the questionnaire was confirmed. It therefore appeared reasonable to consider each of the original four aspects of science facilities

Table 6.1   Factor Analysis of Responses to the Questionnaire: Science Facilities in Australian schools.

Variable	1	2	3	4
Functional adequacy				-60
Basic apparatus impedes experiments			-77	
Laboratory design				61
Preparation time		-51		
Lack of assistance		-68		
Lack of storage space				65
Expendable apparatus			68	
Minor apparatus			71	
Major apparatus			61	
Laboratory assistants/1000 students		84		
Laboratory assistants/10 teachers		83		
Science room availability (Q_1)	76			
Dual purpose room availability (Q_2)	79			
Science rooms per 1000 students	90			
Dual purpose rooms per 1000 students	88			
Proportion of variance	24.0	22.8	12.9	9.0

Note: Only loadings greater than 0.30 have been recorded and decimal points have been omitted.

separately. The next two chapters present analyses of these four aspects of science facilities. This chapter is concerned with science rooms: their abundance and quality. The next chapter considers the supply of apparatus and the presence of laboratory staff as conditions necessary for the effective use of rooms.

Three types of data were used to examine each aspect of school science facilities. Objective information was provided by the various indices of room availability and laboratory assistance developed in Chapter Three. The science co-ordinator in each school provided information about the functional adequacy of rooms and the stock of apparatus. The science co-ordinator also provided an opinion about the degree to which different aspects of the school's science facilities impeded practical work. These three types of data were considered complementary means of obtaining information about school science facilities.

Table 6.2   Science Rooms Built or Renovated Since 1964 in Schools Established Before 1964.

	Government		Catholic		Independent	
	% Schools with <20% New Rooms	Mean % New Rooms	% Schools with <20% New Rooms	Mean % New Rooms	% Schools with <20% New Rooms	Mean % New Rooms
New South Wales	5	60	0	90	8	54
Victoria	8	53	0	85	7	75
Queensland	8	59	10	86	7	83
South Australia	14	47	0	86	0	81
Western Australia	6	57	9	81	0	87
Tasmania	10	74	0	96	0	86
Australia	8	57	2	87	6	73

The Availability of Rooms for Science Lessons

The Contribution from the Science Facilities Program

One measure of the impact of the Australian Science Facilities Program on science accommodation was the number of additional rooms received by schools which already existed in 1964. In some States it was difficult to establish the source of funds provided for each science room. Therefore the total rebuilding program since 1964 was considered rather than only those rooms identified as provided through Commonwealth funds. An additional reason for this decision was the Commonwealth requirement that State governments should continue to provide funds for some rebuilding of science rooms (Smart, 1975: 170). The results in Table 6.2 were obtained from the school questionnaire. These results show that very few of these previously existing schools had less than 20 percent of their present science rooms added since 1964. Most government schools of this vintage had 40 percent or more of their present rooms added during the period when the Science Facilities Program was operating. The mean for government schools was 57 percent. By comparison most non-government schools had more than 80 percent of present rooms built since 1964. Thus while most schools in Australia received additional science rooms, non-government schools gained more new rooms per school than government schools.

In addition to noting the differences between government and non-government schools, two other comments about these data seem warranted. Firstly, the post 1963 building program had its greatest impact on Catholic schools. This probably reflects the poor conditions which existed in those schools before 1964. The Science Facilities Program appears to have rectified that problem. Secondly, the non-Catholic Independent schools in New South Wales appear to have gained less benefit than their counterparts in other States. The explanation for this probably lies in the history of the Industrial Fund. The Fund was most active in New South Wales (Smart, 1972). Hence, for the Independent schools in that State, it pre-empted the Science Facilities Program. Schools which were assisted by the Fund would not have been assessed as needing so many additional rooms from the Science Facilities Program.

Science Rooms for Science Lessons

It has been observed previously that a number of authorities was responsible for administering the Science Facilities Program. These authorities used different criteria to assess the number of science rooms which a school needed. Table 6.3 shows the correlations between the indices of need which were derived from criteria stated in Chapter Three. All were found to be correlated. However, two groups were distinguished. One consisted of those indices which related the number of rooms to the amount of science taught. The second group of indices related the number of rooms to the school enrolment. One index (Q_7), which was based on Queensland criteria, was poorly correlated with the others.

Table 6.3 Correlations Between Various Indices of Need for Science Rooms.

		Q_1	Q_2	Q_3	Q_4	Q_5	Q_6	L_1	L_2	Q_7
Q_1	(Commonwealth)		89	100	61	60	57	60	55	35
Q_2	(Commonwealth)			89	56	55	49	58	62	21
Q_3	(WA)				61	60	57	60	55	35
Q_4	(NSW)					94	90	99	97	42
Q_5	(Vic)						81	92	89	21
Q_6	(SA)							89	86	63
L_1									97	48
L_2										43
Q_7	(Qld)									

Notes a Decimal points have been omitted.
       b Indices are defined on pages 44 to 47.

Table 6.4   Availability of Science Rooms in Secondary Schools (Q_1) in 1975
(Percentages of Schools in Each Category)

	Government	Catholic	Independent	Total
Less than -30	11	8	1	10
-29 to -15	27	19	5	24
-14 to 0	27	16	23	25
1 to 15	14	9	31	14
16 to 30	10	13	27	11
Greater than 30	11	34	13	15
Total	100	100	100	100
Number of Schools	230	89	76	415

Two authorities, the Commonwealth Standards Committee and the Western Australian Education Department, assessed the needs of schools according to the amount of science taught. The influence of the Commonwealth Standards Committee on government policy for funding the final quadrennium of the Science Facilities Program was discussed in Chapter Four. Particular mention was made of the fact that the final quadrennium was intended to meet school needs which were known to exist in 1970. In practice only the needs of non-government schools were known accurately. The amount of money to be allocated to government schools was calculated in proportion to the sum determined for non-government schools. One measure of the effectiveness of the Science Facilities Program could be considered to be the extent to which the availability of science rooms in schools at the end of the Program satisfied the criteria of the Commonwealth Standards Committee. Two indices which have been discussed previously were used. Q_1 related available science rooms to the number of rooms specified by the Committee's formula. Values of Q_1 were the percentage excess of science rooms which a school possessed relative to its assessed needs. Its assessed needs were based on provision of sufficient science rooms for every lesson and an allowance of 25 percent non use. An ideal value for Q_1 would have been zero. Q_2 was similar but considered only those rooms which were equipped for students to do experiments.

Values of Q_1 and Q_2 were calculated from information provided in October 1975, just three months after the Science Facilities Program finished. Therefore, it was possible to use this data to assess whether the Program had met the needs of schools for science accommodation. The results in Table 6.4 show the percentages of Government, Catholic and Independent schools with varying levels of science room provision. Where the value of Q_1 was less than -30 the school was considered seriously deficient in that it had too few science rooms to possibly accommodate all science lessons. Schools for which Q_1 was less than -15 but greater than -30 were classified as 'deficient'. Science lessons could be held in science rooms only at the cost of imposing restraints on the scheduling of other classes. Even so, insufficient time would have been available for the maintenance and servicing of science rooms to allow them to be used to best advantage. A value of Q_1 equal to -15 corresponded to the 85 percent room usage regarded as suitable by the Western Australian Education Department (CDE File 68/2764(147)). Those schools which had a value of Q_1 greater than -15 but less than 0 were regarded as having an adequate, but less than ideal, number of science rooms. It was possible for such schools to accommodate all science lessons in science rooms with only minor inconvenience.

It was clear that at the conclusion of Science Facilities Program the provision of Science rooms in Australian secondary schools was better than in 1963 when two-thirds of science classes were not held in science rooms. Yet from the data in Table 6.4 it was also apparent that about one-tenth of schools had a serious shortage of science rooms for their needs and an additional one quarter had a shortage which would impose constraints upon the teaching they provided. Moreover it was in the government schools that these deficiencies were most marked. Very few Independent schools had a shortage of science rooms.

The same cut-off points were applied to Q_2. This implied that only rooms equipped for students to do experiments were satisfactory science rooms. To assume this is possibly a little harsh but it was the clear preference of the Commonwealth Standards Committee to build dual purpose rooms (Commonwealth of Australia, 1976 : 15-16). The results obtained by applying the same cut-off points to Q_2 as were used for Q_1 are shown in Table 6.5. It can be seen that an even greater difference existed between government and non-government schools when dual purpose rooms alone were used. Nearly one quarter of the government schools were seriously deficient in dual purpose rooms. Restricting science rooms to those equipped for student experiments made little difference to non-government schools : only a few could be considered seriously deficient.

The comparison of government with non-government schools across Australia suggested non-government schools were better provided with science rooms. However, the administrative units responsible for implementing the Science

Table 6.5   Availability of Dual Purpose Science Rooms in Secondary Schools (Q_2) in 1975

	Government	Catholic	Independent	Total
Less than -30	23	8	1	19
-29 to -15	29	19	10	26
-14 to 0	25	18	27	24
1 to 15	9	10	33	11
16 to 30	5	17	19	8
Greater than 30	9	28	10	12
Total	100	100	100	100
Number of Schools	230	89	76	405

Facilities Program included State Education Departments as well as the Commonwealth Department of Education[1]. Therefore it was necessary to compare the availability of science rooms in different States. In order to show the variation between and within the school systems in the States two statistics were computed. The mean values of Q_1 and Q_2 were recorded in Tables 6.6 and 6.7 respectively. In addition, the percentage of schools 'seriously deficient' in science rooms (Q_1 less than -30) or dual purpose science rooms (Q_2 less than -30) was entered in each Table.

Table 6.6   Room Availability (Q_1) for School Systems in Each State in 1975

	Government Mean	Government % <-30	Catholic Mean	Catholic % <-30	Independent Mean	Independent % <-30
ACT	-8	0	25	0	16	0
New South Wales	-8	13	0	13	7	0
Victoria	-4	5	33	7	14	0
Queensland	16	13	48	0	13	0
South Australia	-12	18	18	0	13	8
Western Australia	-8	6	-2	6	6	8
Tasmania	13	10	7	0	28	0
Australia	-3	11	17	8	12	1

1   Refer to Chapter Four for a description of the changes in title of the Commonwealth Departments which were involved.

Table 6.7 Dual Purpose Room Availability (Q_2) for School Systems in Each State in 1975

	Government Mean	Government %<-30	Catholic Mean	Catholic %<-30	Independent Mean	Independent %<-30
ACT	-8	0	25	0	8	0
New South Wales	-14	24	-5	13	0	0
Victoria	-7	8	30	7	8	0
Queensland	-10	27	48	0	6	0
South Australia	-21	40	10	8	7	8
Western Australia	-21	39	-3	6	6	8
Tasmania	7	29	4	10	21	0
Australia	-12	23	14	8	6	1

The data which are recorded in Tables 6.6 and 6.7 provide a more complete description of the availability of science rooms for science lessons. It was apparent that in addition to variations between the mean values for States and school systems there were variations within systems. Moreover there were greater variations within some school systems than others. Roman Catholic schools not only had a higher mean for Q_1 and Q_2 than other non-government schools but they also included a greater proportion of schools seriously deficient in science rooms. That school system contained both well and poorly provided schools. In part this can be explained by the general diversity within the Catholic school system which includes well established colleges as well as small parochial secondary schools. However in addition to this the variation of Q_1 and Q_2 within the Catholic school system increased as a result of changes in its administrative structure (Bourke, 1974). As far as possible the Commonwealth Standards Committee took account of the structural change in Catholic education (Commonwealth of Australia, 1976). Indeed, the Committee occasionally encouraged neighbouring schools to share science facilities. Yet, in spite of this, the process of consolidation and reorganization resulted in some science rooms being built in schools whose secondary enrolment subsequently declined or ceased while other schools grew so rapidly that their science room provision was no longer adequate. In one country town, visited by the Project Officer, a Roman Catholic school had a science room provided through the Science Facilities Program but had since ceased to enrol secondary students. The government school in the same town was sorely pressed for science accommodation.

Variation also existed among government schools in Queensland. The mean value for Q_1 was higher than for other government school systems. Q_2 was lower than Q_1, indicating a high proportion of demonstration rooms, but still reasonably high compared with other government school systems. Yet an unexpectedly large number of schools were seriously deficient in science rooms (13 percent) or dual purpose science rooms (27 percent). This can be explained by an uneven distribution of science rooms. One contributing factor was the disparity between metropolitan and non-metropolitan schools in Queensland. The data in Table 6.8 show the mean values of Q_1 and Q_2 for schools in urban and rural locations. In Queensland the disparity is greatest. Even within the metropolitan region large variations existed. Two schools which were visited had an abundance of science rooms as a result of a decline in student enrolment. Facilities provided when the schools were larger now served a declining number of students.

In Tasmania also there was an apparent discrepancy between the high mean values of Q_1 and Q_2 and the large proportion of schools considered seriously deficient. This discrepancy arose not because of marked differences between metropolitan and non-metropolitan schools but rather because of the difference between High Schools and Matriculation Colleges. Matriculation Colleges are well provided with science rooms ($Q_1 = 72$). Other secondary schools do not have such an abundance of science rooms ($Q_1 = -1$).

Table 6.8 Mean Values of Room Availability (Q_1) and Dual Purpose Room Availability (Q_2) by School Location for Government Schools in 1975

	Q_1 Metro.	Q_1 Non-Metro.	Q_2 Metro.	Q_2 Non-Metro.
ACT	-8	-	-8	-
New South Wales	-8	-9	-14	-13
Victoria	-3	-3	-6	-9
Queensland	33	6	5	-21
South Australia	-15	-6	-27	-8
Western Australia	-13	0	-28	-7
Tasmania	10	15	5	7

Grouping Schools with Similar Provision of Science Rooms

To extend the description of science room availability across all possible categories of schools by State, school system, location, type, and coeducational status would have produced a voluminous set of tables. It was therefore considered useful to cluster schools according to the extent with which they were provided with science rooms using a technique known as the Automatic Interaction Detector, or AID, (Sonquist and Morgan, 1964).

The application of the AID to this problem has been described elsewhere (Ainley, 1976). The criterion used was the availability of dual purpose rooms, Q_2. The predictors entered were those characteristics by which schools are commonly identified: State, school system, location, coeducational status and type. School type referred to the number of years of secondary schooling offered. The splitting was controlled by specifying that the variance should be reduced by at least 0.6 percent as recommended in the OSIRIS manual (Institute for Social Research, 1971) and also that each group should contain at least fifteen cases so that small idiosyncratic groups were not formed.

The sample first split on school type with schools which proceeded only to Year 10, together with Matriculation Colleges, being better provided than other schools. The upper group split further between States as shown in Figure 2 while the lower group was next divided on school system with non-government schools being better provided for than government schools. The full pattern of the splitting is shown in Figure 6.1. The terminal groups of schools which were formed are described in Table 6.9.

The AID, at each successive step, forms groups which 'account for' the maximum possible amount of variance in the criterion. The terminal groups therefore represent the clustering or grouping of schools which 'explains' more of the variation in the criterion than any other possible grouping based on those 'predictor' variables entered. Thus the classification formed is the most economical description of the availability of science rooms.

From the AID analysis it emerged that three variables were most important in distinguishing schools on the basis of dual purpose room availability. These were type, school system, and State.

Schools which only enrolled students up to Year 10 had a greater number of science rooms for the amount of science taught than other schools which offered a complete secondary program. This was because senior students generally placed greater demand on science rooms than students in Year 10 and below. Throughout Australia

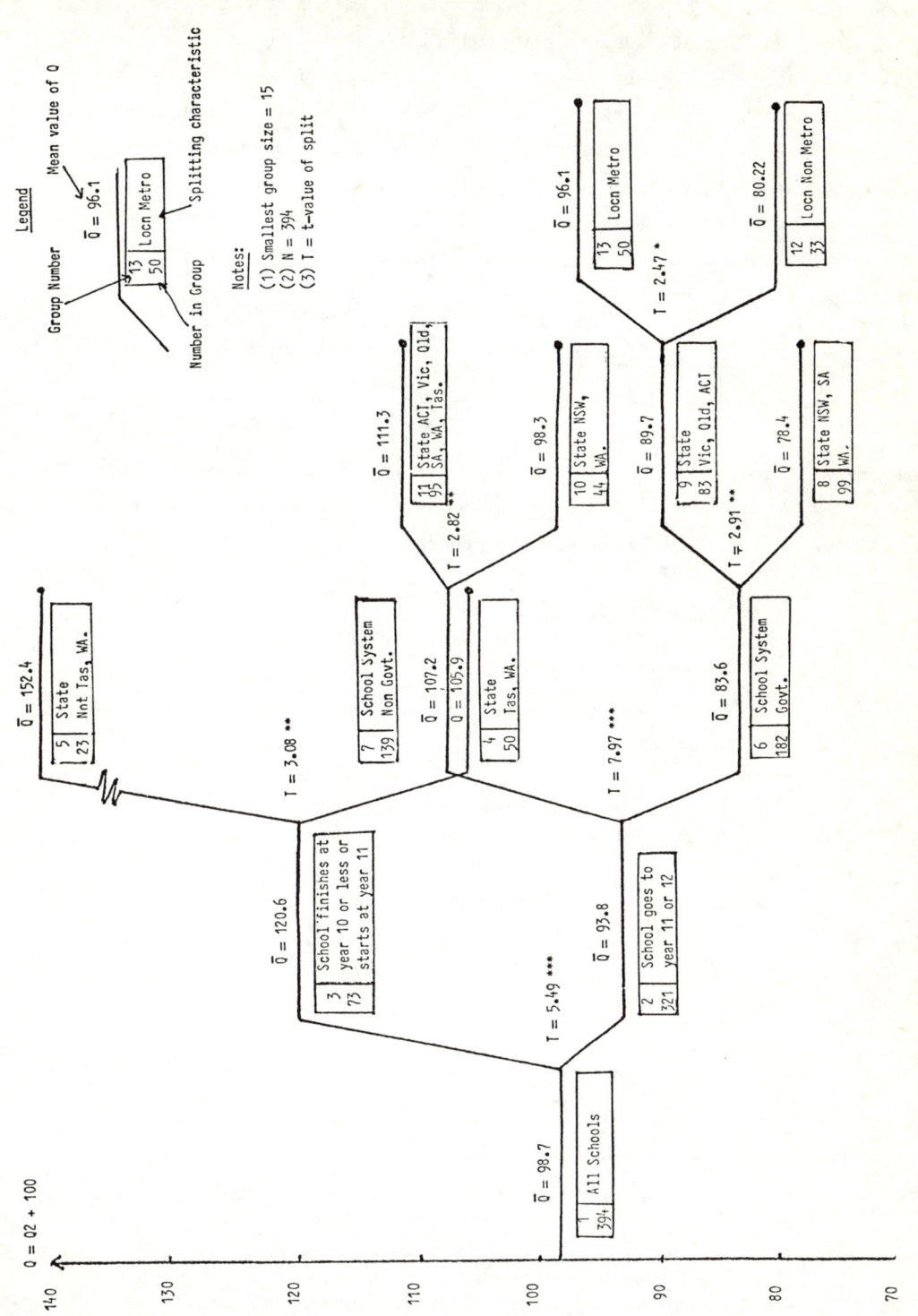

Figure 6.1: AID Analysis to Determine Distribution of Availability of Science Rooms in Australian Secondary Schools

students in Years 11 and 12 study sufficient science to result in an average of more than one science subject per student. This can be seen for Year 12 in Table 6.14. Since these subjects generally occupy as much time as the single junior subject, Science, studies in Years 11 and 12 make greater use of science facilities than Years 7 to 10. In addition to this, schools which proceeded only to Year 10 (except Tasmania) were often non-government schools and were often small. Their small size meant that their one or two science rooms adequately met their modest requirements for science accommodation.

Table 6.9   Clusters of Schools with Similar Provision of Science Rooms

Terminal Group Number	Q_2 [a] Mean	Description of Group	Number of Sample Schools in Group	% [c] 14 yr. olds
8	-21.6	Government schools proceeding to Year 11 or 12 in NSW, SA and WA	99	42
12	-19.8	Government schools proceeding to Year 11 or 12 in non-metropolitan areas of VIC and QLD	33	13
13	-4.9	Government schools proceeding to Year 11 or 12 in metropolitan areas of ACT, VIC and QLD	50	20
10	-2.7	Non-government schools in NSW and WA which proceed to Year 11 or 12	44	9
4	5.9	Government schools in TAS [b] and those schools in WA which proceed to Year 10 only	50	3
11	11.1	Non-government schools in states other than NSW or WA which proceed to Year 11 or 12	95	12
5	52.3	All schools in NSW, VIC, QLD or SA which proceed only to Year 10 or less	23	1

Notes: a   An ideal value of Q_2 would be zero (o). A positive value indicates an excess, while a negative value indicates a deficit.

b   The seven Matriculation Colleges which form part of Group 4 have a higher value of Q than the rest of the group. An AID analysis which specified a smaller group size would separate these from schools which proceed only as far as Year 10.

c   This column shows the percentage of 14-year-olds throughout Australia in the schools described in each group.

Other splits made by the AID reinforced the divisions discussed previously. The results confirmed the importance of the school system by indicating that it accounted for more of the variance between schools than any variable other than school type: and it has been observed that type was partly associated with system. Differences existed between States for government schools and, to a smaller extent, for non-government schools. The latter differences would be expected on two grounds. Firstly, the allocation of money for the Science Facilities Program was divided between States on the basis of school population and took no account of differing emphases on science. Secondly, State Education Departments (for government schools) and State Advisory Committees (for non-government schools) differed in the proportion of their allocation spent on buildings rather than equipment (Smart, 1975). For example, among non-government schools, Western Australian Independent schools placed greater emphasis on equipment. This was also true for New South Wales Independent schools. In 1975 these schools were among those which were less well provided with science rooms than their counterparts elsewhere. By contrast the Western Australian Education Department allocated a large proportion of the money available to them to buildings.

Metropolitan schools were significantly better provided than non-metropolitan schools only in the government school systems of Victoria and Queensland. In no other case was a split made on the basis of location. Nor was there any difference detected between girls, boys and coeducational schools which was not previously removed by the school system to which they belonged. One of the disparities which existed at the beginning of the Science Facilities Program was that girls schools were ill-equipped for science. It seems that that disparity has now been removed.

The Provision of Science Rooms in Schools

So far this chapter has considered the availability of science rooms for the science lessons taught each week. This corresponded to the approach of the Commonwealth Standards Committee. Availability of science rooms was believed to be a potential influence upon the nature of the science teaching which was conducted. However the indices Q_1 and Q_2 tend to underestimate the provision of rooms in schools which teach much science and exaggerate the provisions in those which teach a diminished amount. Hence, variations between States were due not only to differences in the provision of science rooms in schools but to different demands made upon science facilities. Varying demands upon the science facilities provided could have arisen from three sources.

1   Variations existed in the time allocated to Science each
    week for Years 7 to 10.

2   Some students in Years 7 to 10 may have studied no Science
    at all and therefore not used the facilities at all.

3   Schools differed in the extent to which senior students in
    Years 11 and 12 chose to study science subjects.

The Demand placed upon Science Facilities

From the information provided in the responses to the questionnaire it was possible to calculate:

1   the amount of time allocated to science teaching per week for
    students who studied science in Years 7 to 10,

2   the proportion of students at each Year level who did not study
    science at all,

3   the average amount of time spent in science per week for all
    students in a given year (by combining 1 and 2), and

4   the proportion of Year 12 students enrolled in science subjects.
    This fourth calculation used a Science Enrolment Index. The value
    of this Index was calculated for each school by dividing a
    weighted sum of science subject enrolments by the total Year 12
    enrolment. The weighted sum was calculated by scoring students
    enrolled in one science subject as one, those enrolled in two
    subjects as two, etc., and weighting enrolments in each of the
    Wyndham Science courses in NSW (about half of the schools in
    1975) in an appropriate way. This procedure may be stated as
    follows:

$$S = \frac{\Sigma E_i}{T}$$ where E_i = the enrolment in each Science subject
T = total year 12 enrolment.

and for Wyndham Science Schools in NSW

$$S = \frac{\Sigma E_i W_i}{T}$$ where W_i = the weight applied to each level
= 2.0 for level 1
= 1.5 for level 2F
= 1.0 for level 2S and level 3.

The amount of time allocated for the teaching of science differed significantly between the States in each Year level. From the data in Table 6.10 it can be seen that in Victorian schools rather less time is spent in the study of science than in other States. By contrast in Western Australia,

Table 6.10 Mean Number of Hours per Week per Class Allocated to Teaching Science in 1975 (Science Students only)

State	Year 7	Year 8	Year 9	Year 10
ACT	3.4	3.3	3.4	3.7
New South Wales	3.4	3.4	3.4	3.7
Victoria	2.3	2.4	2.6	3.1
Queensland	-	3.3	3.6	3.6
South Australia	-	3.1	3.8	3.9
Western Australia	-	4.0	4.0	3.9
Tasmania	3.2	3.2	3.4	3.5
Australia	2.9	3.1	3.3	3.5

Note: The data in this table have been calculated for those classes which study some science. Non science classes have been excluded.

where science is one of four subjects in the Achievement Certificate 'core', considerably more time is spent in studying science. Only Year 10 students in South Australia study as much science as students in Western Australia. There was no significant difference in the time given to science between Government, Catholic and Independent schools. Neither was there a significant difference between boys, girls and coeducational schools. However, as can be seen from the data in Table 6.11, Year 7 and 8 students in non-metropolitan schools spent more time in science lessons than their city counterparts.

Table 6.11 Mean Number of Hours per Week per Class Allocated to Teaching Science at Year 8 in City and Country Schools in 1975 (Science Students only)

State	Year 7 Metro.	Year 7 Non-Metro.	Year 8 Metro.	Year 8 Non-Metro.
ACT	3.4	-	3.3	-
New South Wales	3.3	3.5	3.3	3.4
Victoria	2.0	2.6	2.3	2.7
Queensland	-	-	3.2	3.4
South Australia	-	-	3.0	3.4
Western Australia	-	-	4.0	4.0
Tasmania	3.2	3.2	3.2	3.2
Australia	-	-	3.0	3.3

Table 6.12   Percentage of Students in Year 10 who did not Study Science in 1975

	Government	Catholic	Independent	Total
ACT	2	0	0	1
New South Wales	0	0	0	0
Victoria	9	3	0	7
Queensland	31	14	4	27
South Australia	6	3	0	6
Western Australia	0	0	1	0
Tasmania	1	3	0	2
Australia	8	3	1	7

Tables 6.10 and 6.11 refer to the amount of time allocated to science for those students studying some science. In practice not all students, even in the lower secondary school, were students of science. While in Years 7 and 8 nearly all students in secondary school took some science, by Years 9 and 10 a number had apparently dropped science completely. In addition there was considerable variation between States in this pattern. In Year 9, nearly one quarter of Queensland secondary students studied no science at all: in other States very few Year 9 students omitted science. Among Year 10 students more than one quarter of Queensland students included no science in their course. Other States had a much smaller proportion of such students. Victoria had the next largest with seven percent. Table 6.12 shows the percentage of Year 10 students in each State and school system who did not include science in their curriculum. The State differences were significant. In addition differences between school systems were also significant. There was a larger proportion of non-science students in Government schools than Catholic or Independent schools.

It is interesting to note that the students who studied no science were mainly girls. In Queensland schools about one half of the girls in Years 9 and 10 studied no science at all, but virtually no boys excluded science. Those girls who did not take science were following a course of commercial studies for which science appears to have been considered inappropriate.

As a consequence of the variations in the percentage of students not doing science it was necessary to calculate the amount of time allocated to science per week for each pupil. Hence those students whose allocation

Table 6.13   Mean Number of Hours per Week Allocated to Teaching Science Per Pupil in 1975 (All Students)

State	Year 7	Year 8	Year 9	Year 10
ACT	3.4	3.3	3.3	3.6
New South Wales	3.4	3.4	3.4	3.7
Victoria	2.3	2.4	2.6	2.8
Queensland	-	3.3	2.7	2.6
South Australia	-	3.1	3.8	3.7
Western Australia	-	4.0	4.0	3.9
Tasmania	3.2	3.2	3.4	3.5
Australia	2.9	3.1	3.2	3.3

Note: The data recorded in this table have been calculated for all classes including those who study no science.

was zero were included in the calculation. The results have been shown in Table 6.13. Since this measure combined the time allocation for science with the proportion of students who studied that subject it provided an indication of the demand made per junior secondary school student on science facilities. In two States that demand was notably low: Victoria and Queensland. In the case of Victoria this was a result of a small time allocation to science while in Queensland it was a consequence of a significant number of girls opting out of science. These data suggest an explanation for some of the differences in the mean values of Q_1 and Q_2 for

Table 6.14   Mean Values of the Science Enrolment Index for School Systems in Each State in 1975 (Year 12)

	Government	Catholic	Independent	Total
ACT	125	107	148	124
New South Wales	116	119	120	116
Victoria	89	104	109	94
Queensland	127	118	138	127
South Australia	131	114	139	131
Western Australia	147	124	167	147
Tasmania	113	105	153	119
Australia	117	111	127	117

the government schools in each State. Queensland and Victoria appeared to be better provided because the demand of their lower secondary school science classes was less.

Schools differed in the science orientation of senior students' courses as well as in the demands of their lower school students. The Science Enrolment Index provided an indication of the propensity of Year 12 students to pursue scientific studies. Mean values of this index, for schools which have Year 12 students, for each State and school system are shown in Table 6.14. Clearly in States such as Western Australia and South Australia senior students placed greater demands on science facilities than in States such as Victoria. Interestingly, the difference between States was significant at the 0.001 level, but the difference between school systems was not significant at even the 0.05 level.

The data in Table 6.14 provided an explanation of one other division which was made by the AID analysis. Schools which enrolled students up to Year 10 were better provided with science rooms than other schools. The results in Table 6.14 show that in most States the mean value of the Science Enrolment Index was greater than 100. It can be inferred from this that senior school students generally placed more demand on science rooms than students in Year 10 and below. Students in the junior secondary school take the equivalent of one science subject each. Those in Years 11 and 12 take an average of more than one subject each.

Number of Science Rooms per 1000 Students

The analysis of demands placed on science facilities revealed that there were considerable differences, at both the lower and upper secondary school levels, between States. It was therefore considered desirable to examine the provision of science rooms in schools with a measure which was independent of the amount of science taught. In the discussion of the various indices of need, it was observed that those based on enrolments were highly correlated with each other but less strongly correlated with indices based on the number of science periods taught. The most direct measures of the number of science rooms for a given school population were L_1 and L_2: the number of science rooms and dual purpose rooms respectively per 1000 students. Hence L_1 and L_2 were considered suitable for making comparisons. For Q_1 and Q_2 a logical basis had been derived from the work of the Commonwealth Standards Committee. The only clear guidance for a similar cut-off point for L_1 and L_2 was the statement by the New South Wales Education Department (CDE File 68/2764(150)) that seven science rooms were needed in a school of 1000 students. The South Australian Education Department considered eight science rooms, including three demonstration rooms, appropriate for a school of that size. (CDE File 68/2764(146)). Hence the indices L_1 and L_2 were used for comparative purposes rather than for assessing standards.

Table 6.15 contains mean values of L_1 and L_2 for the school systems in each State. The differences between government and non-government schools which had existed on Q_1 and Q_2 were also present in L_1 and L_2. However L_1 showed a distinction between Catholic and Independent schools which had not been apparent in Q_1 and Q_2. This was presumably a result of Catholic schools having larger classes so that while they could accommodate science lessons in science rooms, those rooms were rather more crowded than in Independent schools.

Among government schools there were some interesting differences from the pattern of Q_1 and Q_2 values. South Australian and Western Australian government schools were among the best provided in terms of science rooms per 1000 students. Schools in those States made heavy demands on their rooms, hence they had lower values of Q_1 and Q_2. Victoria, which had relatively high values of Q_1 and Q_2, and New South Wales contain the government schools least well provided with science rooms. In Victoria this is compensated by a reduced science teaching program and small senior enrolment in science subjects. One can only speculate why schools of the two largest educational systems were the

Table 6.15 Science Rooms (L_1) and Dual Purpose Science Rooms (L_2) per 1000 Students by State and School System in 1975

	Government L_1	Government L_2	Catholic L_1	Catholic L_2	Independent L_1	Independent L_2	Total L_1	Total L_2
ACT	7.9	7.9	8.3	8.3	9.7	9.0	8.3	8.2
New South Wales	6.2	5.8	6.8	6.5	10.7	10.0	6.5	6.1
Victoria	6.1	5.8	6.9	6.7	10.6	10.0	6.6	6.3
Queensland	9.2	7.5	8.7	8.7	11.6	10.9	9.4	7.9
South Australia	7.9	7.3	7.7	7.4	13.3	12.6	8.3	7.6
Western Australia	8.3	7.3	9.4	9.3	11.1	11.1	8.6	7.8
Tasmania	6.8[a]	6.1[a]	9.2	9.2	17.9	17.1	10.3	9.8
	(9.9)	(9.0)						
Australia	7.2	6.5	7.5	7.2	11.2	10.7	7.5	6.9

Note: a The figure quoted is for High Schools and District Schools. The figures in parentheses include the Matriculation Colleges.

least well provided with science rooms. A possible answer is that these two government school systems spent relatively more on apparatus than building in the early stages of the Science Facilities Program. This was discussed in Chapter Four.

While the differences between girls, boys and coeducational schools were not significant there was an interesting difference between metropolitan and non-metropolitan schools. The data in Table 6.16 show this unexpected result. Non-metropolitan schools had more science rooms per 1000 students than metropolitan schools in the Government, Catholic, and Independent school systems. Yet, in spite of this, it can be recalled that non-metropolitan schools held no advantages in science rooms for science lessons. In fact among the government schools of Victoria and Queensland they were at a disadvantage.

It can be seen that an examination of science room provision using enrolment-based indices yielded some differences from that using indices based on the number of science lessons taught each week. While the overall correlation between the two types of index was moderately high some specific differences between the two approaches exist. Differences arise because of:

1. different emphases on science between States,
2. variations in class size because of the relative abundance of other resources, and
3. different locations which necessitate small senior classes.

As was discussed in Chapter Four, the Science Facilities Program was administered separately in government and non-government schools and separately in each State. The total allocation was divided between government

Table 6.16   Science Rooms (L_1) and Dual Purpose Room (L_2) per 1000 Students by School Location in 1975

	Government	Catholic	Independent	Total
L_1 (Rooms/1000 students)				
Metropolitan	6.6	6.9	10.8	7.0
Non-Metropolitan	8.1	8.6	13.2	8.3
L_2 (Labs/1000 students)				
Metropolitan	5.9	6.7	10.2	6.4
Non-Metropolitan	7.4	8.6	12.9	7.7

and non-government schools on the basis of school population and between States on the basis of gross population[2]. Such a division took account of neither initial conditions nor differing emphases on Science. Within systems school needs and school priorities were determined by using a variety of means, some enrolment-based and some period-based. It is regrettable that a more uniform policy was not followed.

The Quality of Science Rooms

The Functional Adequacy of Rooms

Two types of data provided information about the quality of science rooms in schools and the impact of the Science Facilities Program. One was the response to a checklist of essential features which was developed to assess functional adequacy. Its development was described in Chapter Three.

The science co-ordinator was asked to rate each of the science rooms in the school on each of fourteen items, using a four point scale ranging from 'non existent' to 'adequate'. Thus, the total score for each room ranged in principle from 0 to 42 and in practice from 10 to 42. The score range described rooms which were 'cramped with minimal or inaccessible services of gas, electricity and water, and poor working and seating conditions' to rooms which were 'spacious and provided with adequate accessible service points and in which conditions were conducive to easy variations in work patterns'. A problem with interpreting results from such a scale is that different persons were used to rate rooms in different schools. However, within each school, the same person rated that schools' rooms and comparisons of different types of room (by age or source of funds) are possible. Moreover an analysis of some of the questionnaire returns suggested that this source of unreliability was not very great. The returns from a group of schools in the Melbourne area with similar rooms were considered. These were schools of light timber construction built in the late fifties and early sixties to which two-room Commonwealth Science blocks had been added between 1967 and 1970. The results shown in Table 6.17 suggest that the variation was not great. The internal consistency (Cronbach's α) calculated for the scale using this sample was 0.68.

---

[2] This was varied after 1971 as is described in Chapter Four.

Table 6.17   Different Ratings of Similar Rooms - Melbourne Schools

	Mean	Standard Deviation	N
Science Facilities Program Rooms	37.4	2.05	16
Original LTC Rooms	29.8	3.07	24

It was found that science teachers rated the rooms they identified as coming from the Science Facilities Program as more functional than other rooms in which they taught science. This applied in both government and non-government schools. The mean ratings of rooms provided under the Science Facilities Program and other rooms, according to the scale previously described, are recorded in Table 6.18. Rooms about which there was uncertainty as to the source of funds were included with 'other rooms' so that for some States an estimation of the rating of Science Facilities Program was not possible because there were too few identified cases. The data in Table 6.18 were interpreted as indicating that an improvement in the standards of science rooms resulted from the Science Facilities Program. Such an improvement was an intended outcome of the Program. The activity of the Commonwealth Standards Committee was directed towards this improvement both through its publication, The Design of Science Rooms, (Commonwealth of Australia, 1973) which included suggestions

Table 6.18   Mean Ratings of Science Room Quality by Science Teachers

	Government Schools			Non-Government Schools		
	Science Facilities Program Rooms	Other Rooms	Significance of Difference	Science Facilities Program Rooms	Other Rooms	Significance of Difference
New South Wales	38.5	33.7	**	38.6	30.0	*
Victoria	35.6	30.7	**	37.9	32.8	*
Queensland	36.4	25.2	**	37.2	29.9	*
South Australia	-[a]	30.9	-	36.4	27.8	*
West. Australia	37.2	31.5	**	37.6	(27.5)	*
Tasmania	31.1	30.1	ns	37.3	(35.4)	ns

Note: a   Too few schools in this group were able to identify rooms.
        b   * $p<.05$,   ** $p<.001$

Table 6.19   Percentage of Schools Where Rooms Rated As
              A Significant Impediment to Practical Work

	Laboratory Facilities				Lack of Storage			
	Govt.	Cath.	Indep.	Total	Govt.	Cath.	Indep.	Total
ACT	8	–	–	5	25	0	0	15
New South Wales	13	7	0	11	37	0	33	30
Victoria	19	14	0	17	22	14	14	20
Queensland	40	14	7	33	18	7	14	16
South Australia	13	15	0	12	37	23	0	33
West. Australia	10	6	8	9	7	13	8	8
Tasmania	8	10	0	8	36	10	0	31
Australia	18	11	3	16	27	8	19	22

about the design of, and possible plans for, science rooms and through its consultations with individual non-government schools. As far as government schools were concerned the additional funds enabled State Education Departments to reconsider and improve existing plans for science rooms. Often this involved the establishment of <u>ad hoc</u> committees[3] of senior science teachers to advise on possible laboratory designs. Such committees considered general questions of policy, developed sketch plans and amended draft plans when these had been prepared.

Aspects of Rooms which Impede Practical Work

Schools from all systems considered the new rooms provided under the Science Facilities Program to be more functionally adequate than the older rooms. Hence the overall adequacy of the science facilities in a school often reflected the proportion of new rooms provided under the Program. In general during 1975 government schools were using more old rooms which were considered less suitable for teaching science.

A similar pattern was apparent when teachers were asked whether laboratory facilities were an impediment to practical work. As seen in the data in Table 6.19 about one government school in five considered laboratory facilities a 'significant' problem. This applied to one in ten Catholic schools and only

---

[3] The role of these committees was discussed in Chapters Four and Five.

three percent of Independent schools. A surprising 40 percent of Queensland government schools replied in these categories. It seemed that while some Queensland schools had sufficient rooms the quality of the older science rooms was not good.

The replies as to whether lack of storage space was seen as an impediment to practical work gave a less clear picture. The results are also shown in Table 6.19. It can be seen that lack of storage space was regarded as a 'significant' problem in a number of government and non-government schools. Of course lack of storage space would be a problem which depended upon the amount of apparatus to be stored. In the next chapter it will be seen that Catholic schools were not so well provided with apparatus as government or other non-government schools. Hence storage space was not a problem to them.

Access to Science Rooms

Classes Not held in Science Rooms

The proportion of science lessons which are not held in science rooms is sometimes taken as a measure of the availability of science rooms. However the association between these two measures is not direct. In the limiting case insufficient science rooms (say Q_1 less than -.25) would necessitate science lessons to be held in non-science rooms. Where there were sufficient rooms available the scheduling of science lessons for science rooms depended on the skill of the timetable co-ordinator, the degree to which specialist science accommodation was seen as a priority, the interests of the science teachers, and the nature of the curriculum, as well as upon the availability of rooms. Schools were observed where a bare minimum of rooms was fully utilized. For example, one Catholic school had a minimum of science rooms but all were fully utilized. The timetable was staggered so that Years 7, 8, 9 and 10, and 11 and 12 took lunch and morning and afternoon breaks at different times. Consequently, science rooms were continuously occupied. The result was that nearly all science lessons were accommodated in specialist rooms. By contrast some other schools had a surfeit of science rooms which were often unused. In one particular government school science rooms were left vacant while science classes were held in normal classrooms. This was the result of two factors. The teachers did not appear to view practical experience as relevant to the syllabus they were teaching and a lack of equipment and poor laboratory design limited the attractiveness of the science rooms which were available.

Table 6.20 Percentage of Science Lessons held in Non-Science Rooms in 1975

	Government		Catholic		Independent		Total	
Years -	7-10	11-12	7-10	11-12	7-10	11-12	7-10	11-12
ACT	4	4	4	0	1	0	3	3
New South Wales	8	5	16	2	6	5	9	5
Victoria	7	4	15	0	5	1	8	3
Queensland	22	8	8	0	7	2	18	6
South Australia	24	13	21	3	16	14	23	12
West. Australia	9	8	23	7	5	2	11	8
Tasmania	7	0	10	1	0	0	7	0
Australia	12	6	15	2	6	3	12	5

It should not be assumed that the holding of science lessons out of science rooms only arises out of lack of facilities or difficulties of planning. It can also be part of a planned program which makes use of school resources outside the science room. In some Western Australian government schools it is intended that one science lesson each week for Years 7 to 10 should take place in the library. Thus science lessons are in a non-science room not through a restraint imposed by facilities but as part of the planned use of school resources.

The proportions of science lessons held in non-science rooms in various school systems are shown in Table 6.20. Throughout Australia little more than one lesson in ten for Years 7 to 10 was held in a non-science room. The figure was a little higher (one in seven) for Catholic schools and rather lower (one in 20) for Independent schools. Queensland and South Australian government schools held rather a lot of science lessons in non-science rooms. In Queensland this seemed to be a matter of choice influenced by the nature of the science curricula, the teachers' views of practical work and the unattractiveness of some old science rooms which were available. In South Australia there was considerable demand placed upon the facilities because a lot of time was allocated to science. In addition many of the 'open plan' schools and teaching methods stress moving to facilities as needed rather than being continuously in a specialist room.

At senior level, in Years 11 and 12 only one in 20 science lessons were held in non-science rooms, the proportion being a little larger for government than for non-government schools. In South Australia the figure rose to one in eight for government schools, in part due to the provision of science courses for non-academically oriented students. In general it seems that Years 11 and 12 were well accommodated in available science rooms.

Access to New Rooms

Table 6.21 records the proportion of lessons in various subjects held in rooms provided under the Australian Science Facilities Program. Only schools which identified some rooms as coming from that source have been included in the calculations so that the figures are an indication of the priority given in using these facilities. In non-government schools where the provision has been most abundant the pattern of use seems more uniform across the various subjects and age levels. However, in government schools, where this source of funds had provided a smaller proportion of available science rooms, there was a different pattern of use. In general senior Physics and Chemistry enjoyed most use of these facilities while junior science classes and senior science other than Physics and Chemistry had less opportunity to use the facilities. In Queensland government schools the difference was most marked between Years 11 and 12 science classes and those for Years 7 to 10. Victorian and Western Australian government schools used the Science Facilities Program rooms for senior Physics and Chemistry plus some junior science. Biology and 'other' senior science had less access to the Science Facilities Program rooms in those States.

Table 6.21   The Use of Rooms Provided under the Science Facilities Program

| | \multicolumn{5}{c|}{Government} | \multicolumn{5}{c}{Non-Government} |
| | \multicolumn{4}{c}{Years 11 and 12} | Yrs 7-10 | \multicolumn{4}{c}{Years 11 and 12} | Yrs 7-10 |
	Chem.	Phys.	Biol.	Other	Sci.	Chem.	Phys.	Biol.	Other	Sci.
New South Wales [a]	55	79	60	59	50	73	78	92	75	73
Victoria	88	91	40	33	48	67	78	91	75	74
Queensland	91	86	79	54	18	88	79	75	80	74
South Australia [b]	-	-	-	-	-	76	72	85	63	77
West. Australia	87	87	31	25	40	85	86	83	78	71
Tasmania [c]	-	-	-	-	-	63	65	83	76	82

Notes: a The distinction between these disciplines may be less clear in schools which were operating under the Wyndham scheme science courses.
b Too few schools identified rooms from the Science Facilities Program to enable calculations to be made.
c Because of the separation of High Schools and Matriculation Colleges calculations were not made for Tasmanian government schools

The pattern in government schools throughout Australia suggests that junior science only benefited from the new rooms to the extent that they were able to occupy those rooms which the senior students vacated. There appear to be many reasons why this occurred, including the fact that concern with laboratory work in junior science is a more recent development than concern with practical work and experimentation in senior science subjects. In addition it was sometimes tacitly assumed that the Program was to be directed towards senior rather than junior science, reflecting the predominant concern at the time the Program began. These factors tended to reinforce the desire of science co-ordinators to maintain new facilities in good condition, if necessary by excluding less manageable classes in Years 7 to 10. This concern should not be lightly dismissed. In many schools damage to facilities was a problem which had to be considered by the science co-ordinator when planning the use to which they would be put.

However it can be argued that a suitable science laboratory is even more important for junior than senior students. In keeping with theories of cognitive development junior science curricula emphasize rather more the concrete experience of practical work and integrating practical with theory. If this is accepted it is unfortunate that junior science in government schools should have benefited least directly from the provision of science rooms under the Science Facilities Program.

Summary

The Australian Science Facilities Program contributed substantially to the rebuilding and renovating of science rooms between 1963 and 1975. A large proportion of rooms now used for teaching science was built during this period. The money made available under this Program enabled rooms which were considered to be of better quality to be provided. Non-government schools had more of their rooms replaced or renewed than did government schools, and within government schools senior Physics and Chemistry classes had greatest access to the better rooms.

In terms of the criteria stated by the Commonwealth Standards Committee only about one school in ten was 'seriously deficient' in science rooms when the Program concluded. However if only rooms which were equipped for student experimentation were considered, one in five schools were 'seriously deficient'. Most of these schools were government schools. As a consequence of these deficiencies one in seven schools regarded its laboratory facilities as an impediment to practical work. One in ten science lessons in Years 7 to 10, and 1 in 20 senior science classes were held in non-science rooms. It should be remembered that this was sometimes the result of choice, or was due to timetabling problems, rather than the lack of available rooms.

It seems that the impact of the Science Facilities Program was to provide rooms of better quality and to substantially improve the availability of science rooms. However it should be noted that the needs of schools as they would have been assessed by the Commonwealth Standards Committee have not been completely satisfied. Junior science classes in government schools are rather too often held in non-science rooms or poor quality science rooms.

CHAPTER SEVEN

MAKING USE OF SCIENCE ROOMS

Facilitating Effective Use of Rooms

In Chapter Six the availability and quality of rooms provided for science teaching were considered. For those rooms to be used effectively they would need to be well equipped with apparatus and serviced so that teachers might easily exploit their potential. The factor analyses suggested that the abundance of apparatus and the provision of assistance in the laboratory were separate considerations from room availability and room quality. This chapter will consider the abundance of apparatus and the presence of laboratory assistants in Australian schools.

Funds from the Science Facilities Program were used to provide apparatus as well as rooms. The money used for apparatus was rather less than for buildings, and policy was less uniform. Aspects of policy concerned with spending on apparatus were discussed in Chapter Four. In general, whenever a new laboratory was built either money for apparatus, or apparatus itself, was provided to equip the laboratory. In government schools other apparatus was provided while in some non-government school systems funds for apparatus were made available to schools to equip existing laboratories. The policy regarding the provision of apparatus was rather more varied than that regarding the provision of buildings. In the opinion of some members[1] of the Commonwealth Standards Committee the Science Facilities Program had met most non-government school building needs but had not been quite so effective in supplying apparatus.

Laboratory assistants did not come within the ambit of the Science Facilities Program. Yet it was suggested in Chapter Four that the new facilities were a stimulus to the provision of laboratory staff. In some cases[2] an argument was advanced that effective laboratory staff were an important

---

[1] Interview with Dr J. DeLaeter, West Australian Institute of Technology, July 1976.

[2] See page 97.

Table 7.1 Percentage of Schools with Frequent Deficiencies in Apparatus

	\multicolumn{3}{c}{Expendable}	\multicolumn{3}{c}{Minor}	\multicolumn{3}{c}{Major}
	Govt.	Cath.	Indep.	Govt.	Cath.	Indep.	Govt.	Cath.	Indep.
ACT	8	0	0	0	0	0	16	0	0
New South Wales	11	0	0	13	0	0	32	7	15
Victoria	0	0	0	0	0	0	22	14	0
Queensland	3	7	0	5	7	0	21	43	7
South Australia	0	0	0	0	8	0	13	31	8
Western Australia	3	0	8	3	12	8	3	29	17
Tasmania	0	0	12	3	0	0	8	0	0
Australia	4	2	1	6	2	1	22	17	7
All Schools	\multicolumn{3}{c}{4}	\multicolumn{3}{c}{5}	\multicolumn{3}{c}{20}

adjunct in gaining maximum use from the new buildings. Since schools were not given additional funds with which to employ laboratory assistants there were variations between schools in this matter. The employment of laboratory staff depended upon the financial resources available for recurrent spending and the policy of the school system.

The Supply of Apparatus

School science co-ordinators were asked, when completing the questionnaire, whether the supply of 'expendable', 'minor', and 'major' apparatus was adequate.[3] The response was given on a five-point scale for each of the categories of apparatus. The two lowest ratings referred to 'deficiencies most of the time' and 'general deficiencies in many items frequently'. The percentages of schools from each school system in each State which gave either of these responses are shown in Table 7.1.

Schools throughout Australia apparently regarded the provision of 'expendable' and 'minor' apparatus as satisfactory. Only four percent reported frequent deficiencies in 'expendable,' and only five percent in 'minor' apparatus. The least satisfied were the government schools in New South Wales where one in eight schools reported deficiencies. The supply of 'major apparatus' caused more disquiet. One fifth of schools reported

---

[3] These categories were defined as in the ASTA survey of 1961 and are described on page 14

Table 7.2 Correlations between Various Measures of the Adequacy of
          Apparatus

	Basic	Exp	Min	Maj
Lack of Basic Apparatus Impedes Practical Work (Basic)		-55	-56	-54
Supply of Expendable Apparatus (Exp)			50	42
Supply of Minor Apparatus (Min)				48
Supply of Major Apparatus (Maj)				

Note: Decimal points have been omitted.

frequent and general deficiencies in this area. Government and Catholic schools were less well provided in general than Independent schools. However, the government schools of Western Australia were especially well-stocked, and in South Australia and Tasmania also, relatively few government schools reported deficiencies. By contrast, a large proportion of Catholic Schools in Queensland, South Australia and Western Australia reported difficulties with 'major' apparatus. 'Major' apparatus included very expensive items of which few were required (e.g. cathode ray oscilloscopes) as well as moderately expensive items required in greater numbers (e.g. microscopes). This latter category presented schools with most problems and microscopes were frequently mentioned. These instruments are used a lot in modern science courses in situations which necessitate students having easy access to them. They were often provided under the Science Facilities Program, but apparently, were required in greater numbers.

Another measure related to the supply of apparatus was the indication of whether lack of basic apparatus impeded practical work. Of course answers to a question of this nature would have depended not only on the availability of apparatus but also on its accessibility and the willingness of staff to improvise. Where science teachers were able and willing to improvise a shortage of apparatus would not have seemed such an impediment to practical work. Notwithstanding this caveat an indication that a lack of basic apparatus impeded practical work correlated well with the more direct answers about the supply of apparatus. The correlation coefficients have been shown in Table 7.2. Moreover the uniform pattern of the correlation coefficients suggests that the responses about a lack of basic apparatus as an impediment to practical work were related to the sufficiency of all three categories of apparatus. No one category seemed to predominate.

Across Australia some eight percent of schools regarded a lack of basic apparatus as a significant problem impeding practical work. There were variations between States and school systems in the extent to which

Table 7.3 Lack of Basic Apparatus regarded as a Significant Problem in Practical Work (Percentage of Schools)

State	Govt.	Cath.	Indep.	Total
ACT	8	0	0	5
New South Wales	18	7	0	15
Victoria	3	0	0	2
Queensland	8	7	0	7
South Australia	0	8	0	1
Western Australia	0	24	0	2
Tasmania	6	10	8	7
Australia	9	6	1	8

this problem was reported as significant. The percentages of schools in each State and system, which regarded a lack of apparatus as a problem in practical work, has been shown in Table 7.3. The differences reflect not only differences in actual supply but rather how well the supply matches the demand of the courses which are conducted. New South Wales Government schools and Western Australian Catholic schools more frequently reported a lack of basic apparatus as an impediment to practical work. Most Independent schools did not regard this as a significant problem. Hence, while one fifth of the schools claimed frequent deficiencies in major apparatus only one in twelve regarded their deficiencies as a significant problem in arranging practical work. One can only assume that the difference was made up of schools which had developed improvised means of coping with shortages.

While the results in Table 7.3 suggest a generally satisfactory situation, the schools which reported that lack of apparatus was 'sometimes a problem' should be mentioned. In this category were placed some 35 percent of Government schools, 44 percent of Catholic schools and 22 percent of Independent schools. Thirty-five percent of all schools were in this category. This represents a large proportion of schools for whom shortages of apparatus impeded work on more than rare occasions.

The results of this survey refer to apparatus generally available in science subjects. A more specific study (Lucas, 1975) of Physics apparatus has been reported for New South Wales, Queensland and South Australia. Of sixty items of apparatus studied, a number considered to be 'essential' were in relatively short supply in Queensland. It was argued that this restricted Queensland teachers to the PSSC course for which schools had been equipped. The comparison made by Lucas (1975) of Queensland with South Australia was in general agreement with the present survey. However, it seemed that New South Wales teachers were more critical of the apparatus available to them than would have been expected from Lucas' (1975) study. The most plausible explanation of this discrepancy seemed to be that the present survey was conducted at a time when New South Wales schools were adopting new curricula. A number of new senior science courses were being introduced, and changes had also been made in the junior science courses. These curricula required new apparatus. Stocks of new apparatus may not yet have been built up. In Queensland, schools were able to continue to teach PSSC Physics while in New South Wales all schools were to adopt the new senior courses from 1976 onwards. Lucas (1975) observed that because Queensland schools had been specifically equipped for PSSC Physics courses, deficiencies became most notable when a different approach was attempted. In addition Lucas (1975) claimed that the poorer availability of experimental apparatus lead to a diminished student interest.

Laboratory Assistants in Schools

Funds were not available under the Science Facilities Program for the employment of ancillary staff. Over the period in which money was available for material facilities more laboratory assistants were employed by schools. It was suggested in Chapter Four that the motivation for this in several instances came from a desire to fully exploit and properly maintain the new facilities. The argument that laboratory assistants could assist in fully exploiting material facilities became widely accepted. For this reason an examination of the provision of laboratory assistants in Australian schools was carried out.

Four pieces of information related to the assistance provided to science teachers in schools. The most direct measures were the ratios of laboratory assistants per 1000 students (A_1) and laboratory assistants per 10 science teachers (A_2). Only data related to A_1 has been reported in this chapter. The two other measures were less direct. These were answers to questions of whether 'lack of assistance' or the 'amount of preparation time involved' were seen as impediments in arranging practical work. It was reported in Chapter Six that in a factor analysis all four measures loaded on the same factor. The correlations between these measures are indicated by the coefficients

Table 7.4 Correlations between Measures related to the Provision of Ancillary Staff.

	A_1	A_2	A_3	A_4
Lab. Assts/1000 students (A_1)		88	-30	-47
Lab. Assts/10 teachers (A_2)			28	-51
Lack of Assistance (A_3)				64
Lack of Preparation Time (A_4)				

Note: Decimal points have been omitted.

reported in Table 7.4. It can be seen that while lack of preparation time was negatively correlated with the number of laboratory assistants, the association was not strong. Factors other than lack of laboratory assistants must have been associated with a perceived lack of preparation time. Clearly teaching loads, or a poorly organized store room would be two such possibilities.

The data recorded in Table 7.5 show the provision of laboratory assistants in various schools. The provision of laboratory assistants in schools has improved dramatically since 1961. The results of the ASTA survey (Keeves, 1966) which were reported in Chapter One indicated that very few schools then had laboratory staff. Increased employment of laboratory staff was coincident with the Science Facilities Program. In Chapter Five it was suggested that this may have been an important indirect effect of the Program. South Australian government schools in particular

Table 7.5 Laboratory Assistants per 1000 Students in 1975

State	Govt.	Cath.	Indep.	Total
ACT	2.1	1.4	1.5	1.8
New South Wales	1.5	0.8	1.2	1.3
Victoria	1.0	0.3	2.3	1.0
Queensland	2.3	0.2	1.6	1.9
South Australia	2.7	0.2	1.8	2.5
Western Australia	1.5	0.1	1.5	1.2
Tasmania	1.6	0.3	1.5	1.5
Australia	1.6	0.5	1.8	1.4

Table 7.6 __Percentages of Schools in which Aspects of Assistance rated as a Significant Impediment to Practical Work.__

State	Lack of Assistance			Preparation Time		
	Govt.	Cath.	Indep.	Govt.	Cath.	Indep.
ACT	0	50	0	0	0	0
New South Wales	24	53	31	29	13	31
Victoria	27	57	27	27	29	7
Queensland	8	57	36	8	29	21
South Australia	3	69	46	3	38	31
Western Australia	7	57	0	3	37	0
Tasmania	9	80	50	14	30	37
Australia	18	57	29	19	23	17
All Schools		24			20	

appear to have employed laboratory assistants extensively. Generally both Government schools and Independent schools were well serviced by ancillary staff. Victorian government schools were a little less well staffed than those of other States. This was largely a result of the poorer provision in that States' technical schools. It was Catholic schools which languished most for want of laboratory assistants. The recurrent costs of employing such staff are high so that schools without other financial resources could not always afford such staff. In schools where laboratory staff were not employed it was likely that teaching staff had demanding teaching allotments. Such circumstances would militate against gaining full benefit from the facilities.

Government schools which were relatively well provided with laboratory assistants did not regard 'lack of assistance' or the 'amount of preparation time' as impediments to practical work. Notably few government schools in Queensland, South Australia and Western Australia reported difficulty from these sources. More than half the Catholic schools in each State regarded lack of assistance as a significant problem. Consistent with this, more Catholic schools regarded the amount of preparation time involved as a significant problem. Among the government schools of New South Wales and Victoria, lack of assistance and the amount of preparation time involved were seen to impede practical work in one quarter of the schools. Few government schools in other States considered these aspects to be a problem.

Facilities as an Impediment to Practical Work

It was of interest to know which aspects of science facilities were most commonly regarded as impeding the conduct of practical work. In Table 7.7 the aspects of facilities which were most frequently reported as impeding practical work are recorded. No entry was made for those school systems in which fewer than ten percent of schools considered any aspect of their facilities to be a significant problem. On the basis of the data in Table 7.7 facilities do not appear to be regarded as a significant problem by Western Australia Government or Independent schools, or Independent schools in the Australian Capital Territory.

The most commonly reported problems for Catholic and Independent schools were those deriving from non-material resources: lack of laboratory assistants or the amount of preparation time involved. Any deficiencies in physical provisions were not seen to be serious. Large numbers of Queensland Government schools were critical of their laboratory facilities. Some 40 percent of these schools considered their inappropriate laboratory facilities to be a significant problem in practical work. In other Government schools lack of suitable storage rather than general aspects of laboratory facilities were the most frequently mentioned difficulty. This suggests that attention may need to be given to ancillary science areas, storage, and preparation rooms in those schools.

Two conclusions appeared to emerge from these data. One was that there was a difference between those factors which government and non-government schools considered to be impediments to practical work. Non-government schools were more concerned with support services, but government schools were more frequently critical of their buildings. The evidence presented in Chapter Six suggests that, rather than representing different attitudes, this difference was probably the result of the levels of assistance received from the Science Facilities Program.

The second conclusion concerns those aspects of facilities which were not mentioned as problems. No group of schools mentioned a shortage of apparatus as a significant problem. Indeed laboratory facilities were mentioned directly and frequently only by Queensland government schools, while in other states it was storage space which drew unfavourable comment. It can be inferred from this that schools in general do not regard a lack of physical resources as an impediment to practical work.

Table 7.7 Aspects of Facilities Least and Most Frequently Regarded as Significant Impediments to Practical Work.

Least Frequent Impediments

	Government Aspect	%	Catholic Aspect	%	Independent Aspect	%
ACT	P,A	0	B	0	B	0
New South Wales	L	13	S	0	B,L	0
Victoria	B	3	B	0	B	0
Queensland	P,A	8	B,S	0	B	0
South Australia	B	0	B	8	B,S	0
Western Australia	P	3	L	6	P,A	0
Tasmania	B	6	B	10	L,S	0
Australia	B	9	B	6	B	1

Most Frequent Impediments

	Government Aspect	%	Catholic Aspect	%	Independent Aspect	%
ACT	S	25	A	50	-	-
New South Wales	S	37	A	53	S	33
Victoria	P,A	27	A	57	A	27
Queensland	L	40	A	57	A	36
South Australia	S	37	A	69	A	46
Western Australia	-	-	A	56	-	-
Tasmania	S	36	A	80	A	50
Australia	S	27	A	57	A	29

Notes: Code B = Lack of basic apparatus
L = Inappropriate Laboratory facilities
P = Lack of preparation time
A = Insufficient Laboratory assistance
S = Lack of suitable storage space

The aspect of facilities most frequently cited as a significant problem has been entered for each type of school. The number is the percentage of that group of schools reporting that aspect as a significant problem.

No entry has been recorded where no aspect was reported a significant problem by more than 10 percent of schools.

Table 7.8. Group Size for Practical Work in Year 9

State	Government	Catholic	Independent	Total
ACT	2.9	3.0	2.5	2.9
New South Wales	3.4	3.1	2.7	3.3
Victoria	2.4	2.8	2.2	2.4
Queensland	3.5	3.6	2.8	3.5
South Australia	2.5	3.1	2.6	2.5
Western Australia	3.1	3.2	3.0	3.1
Tasmania	2.9	2.9	2.8	2.9
Australia	3.0	3.1	2.6	3.0

Differences Between States in Teaching Science

Year 9 Science

Differences existed between the various school systems in Australia in aspects of teaching science. Firstly there were differences in the average size of groups in which Year 9 students did experimental work. In general students in Independent schools work in smaller groups than their peers in Catholic and Government schools. The data recorded in Table 7.8 show that as well as differences between school systems there were differences between States. Victorian and South Australian Year 9 students from government schools worked in smaller groups than those in other States. Presumably, as individuals, those students have greater opportunity to use apparatus during science practical sessions. The size of groups for experimental work would depend upon the size of classes, and the policy of the teacher, in addition to the availability of apparatus and bench space.

There were also differences between States in the proportion of time Year 9 students spent doing experimental work. Information on which the data in Table 7.9 were based was obtained from science co-ordinators. It therefore represents the formal allocation of time to this activity. Because the question referred to a particular time during the year, it was not possible to use the answers as an indication of the priorities of an individual school. Rather it was used as a measure of patterns between school systems. Using school systems in each State as the unit of analysis it appeared that working in smaller groups was associated with more experimental work. Based on the 21 school systems in the seven States and one territory the correlation coefficient between these two variables was -0.57. Using the States as units of analysis the rank order correlation coefficient

Table 7.9   Percentage Experimental Work in Year 9.

State	Government	Catholic	Independent	Total
ACT	60	32	89	58
New South Wales	46	44	52	46
Victoria	57	50	51	56
Queensland	40	37	52	41
South Australia	49	44	57	49
Western Australia	41	32	41	40
Tasmania	56	38	47	54
Australia	48	53	52	48

was -0.89. Victorian Year 9 students worked in small groups while doing a lot of experimental work. Their counterparts in South Australia worked in equally small groups but did a little less experimental work. Presumably this was because a larger proportion of science classes were not held in science rooms. Tasmanian and Australian Capital Territory students did a lot of experimental work but in groups of moderate size. However, in Queensland and New South Wales classes groups were larger and, in 1975, less time was spent doing experiments.

The fact that State differences in the amount of time allocated to experimental work were more marked than differences between school systems, is interesting. In examining the amount of time allocated to science, in Table 6.9, a similar result was obvious. It suggests that there were patterns of teaching science common to schools within each State regardless of whether those schools were Government schools, Catholic schools or Independent schools.

Senior School Biology

Data were provided, by the Director of the School Biology Project, about the number of laboratory exercises completed in schools using the BSCS Biology curriculum. That information was collected, as part of the School Biology Project, from schools across Australia. In these data there were also differences between States. For Year 9 Science there was no common curriculum across all States but this Biology teaching survey referred to the same curriculum materials used in all the States. Differences thus reflect different emphases in teaching patterns. The results of this survey are tabulated in Table 7.10.

Table 7.10 Number of Laboratory Exercises in BSCS Biology

	First Year	Second Year	Total
New South Wales	40.6	37.9	78.5
Victoria	35.9	36.8	72.7
Queensland	38.6	33.5	72.1
South Australia	37.9	30.8	68.8
Western Australia	41.5	34.3	75.9
Tasmania	36.4	39.7	76.1
Australia	38.6	36.0	74.6

(Number of Exercises shown for First Year and Second Year columns)

One interesting inference which could be drawn from these data was that State patterns of teaching junior Science were not necessarily the same as those for senior Biology. The correlations between State values of the percentage experimental work in Year 9 and number of BSCS laboratory exercises were, in fact, negative. This result was consistent with casual observation. For example in Queensland schools, the resources for experimental work were directed to senior rather than junior science subjects. In South Australia the extensive support for junior science may not have been matched completely in senior Biology. These propositions are mere speculation but the suggestion that there may be State traditions specific to particular subjects is at least worth pursuing in subsequent studies.

Summary

Two ways in which the effective use of science rooms may have been enhanced were the provision of sufficient apparatus and the existence of ancillary staff. It appeared that few schools regarded their apparatus as seriously deficient or that a lack of basic apparatus was a significant impediment to practical work. The only area of concern was the supply of major apparatus, the lack of which probably impeded demonstrations rather than student experimental work. In general a larger proportion of Government and Catholic schools reported deficiencies in major apparatus than did Independent schools.

Laboratory assistants were more generously provided in Government and Independent schools than in Catholic schools. In fact for many Catholic schools the lack of sufficient laboratory assistants appears to be a problem which prevents them making full use of the rooms and apparatus which are now available. However, in all schools lack of assistance and lack of time to prepare is the most generally reported impediment to practical work.

There was evidence that different traditions of teaching science subjects in each State may have affected the degree to which facilities were used. This remains an area to be investigated further.

CHAPTER EIGHT

THE IMPACT OF FACILITIES ON SCIENCE TEACHING AND LEARNING

It has been argued in the earlier sections of this report that the provision of good facilities was intended to have an impact on the form of teaching science. In this chapter use has been made of the views expressed by students in responding to the questionnaire which was described in Chapter Three. These students were all in Year 9 in 1976, but studied science under different circumstances. One other source of information has been used in this chapter. The opinions of non-government school Principals were obtained by analysing questionnaires which were returned to the Commonwealth Department of Education in 1970. Opinions held by this group of people complemented the impression gained from analysis of student views. Interviews with teachers, and case study visits to schools, which provided an additional perspective, have been reported in the next chapter.

The Views of Non-Government School Principals

The questionnaire, which was sent to all non-government schools in 1970 to assess outstanding needs for science facilities, contained a section seeking opinions about the effects of the new facilities. The questions were concerned with staff recruitment and retention as well as teaching practices. A simple 'Yes' or 'No' answer was requested to most questions. Those questions about staff retention allowed for three possible responses which would indicate an 'increase', a 'decrease', or 'no change' in teacher retention. Abbreviated forms of the questions and the responses to them are shown in Table 8.1.

The results summarized in Table 8.1 suggested that these Principals agreed about some of the possible effects of the new facilities. They were nearly unanimous in the view that improved facilities had affected the teaching and learning of science. More than 80 percent concurred that different methods were now used to teach science, that more experimental work was done, that teacher satisfaction was higher and that the efficiency of teaching was greater. It was also considered that many timetabling problems had been alleviated by the new rooms.

While views about the effects of the new facilities on student outcomes were not unanimous, there was some agreement. Increased student achievement in science was seen by 84 percent of the group as being attributable to better facilities, 70 percent ascribed a quickened interest in science to

Table 8.1 The Views of Non-Government School Principals about improved Facilities for Science[a]   (Percentages)

	Question[b]	Yes %	No %	Non Response %
1 (a)	Inducement to potential staff:			
	(i) Science teachers	47	46	7
	(ii) Laboratory assistants	27	29	44
2	Effect of New Facilities on Teaching			
	(a) Different science teaching methods	84	10	6
	(b) Additional Staff	49	44	7
	(c) More experimental work	93	2	5
3	Opinions about the Effects of Facilities			
	(a) Greater efficiency of teaching	93	1	6
	(b) Increased teacher satisfaction	90	4	6
	(c) Attracted students	55	34	11
	(d) Prevented student transfer	63	26	11
	(e) Increased student interest	70	22	8
	(f) Increased student achievement	84	3	13
	(g) Alleviated timetabling problems	83	7	10
4	Science Staff Resignation Rate [c]	Increase	Decrease	No Change
	(1) Teachers	0	17	83
	(2) Laboratory Assistants	0	8	92

Notes: a   N = 132 school returns representing all IEA Population II and Population IV schools.

b   These are abbreviated forms of the questions asked.

c   Three, rather than two answers were possible to this question.

their facilities, but only about 60 percent saw any effect in terms of discouraging students transferring from the school, and even fewer considered that new students had been attracted by the better facilities. As the latter two issues would apply only to those schools which had very poor facilities before the Program the response to those items does not mean a great deal for some schools. It is interesting that a significant proportion of Principals believed that improved facilities had an impact on students' achievement and interest in science.

No such agreement existed on those matters related to staffing. Respondents were evenly divided when asked whether good facilities were used as an inducement to potential staff and fewer than half considered the improved facilities attracted new staff. They were nearly unanimous that there had not been a noticeable change in the resignation rate of either science teachers or laboratory assistants.

The pattern which emerged from the opinions of this group of Principals was that improved facilities had an effect on the process of science teaching, may have had an effect on student outcomes, but had little effect on staff turnover or recruitment. One caveat needs to be stated. These opinions were collected using a questionnaire which also sought information about school science needs. That information was intended to be used in determining future funding. As school staff knew that the questionnaire was being returned to an agency which provided funds their answers may have been affected.

Student Views about Studying Science

Classes as the Unit of Analysis

The questionnaire which was used contained the three environment scales and the three activity scales described in Chapter Three. It was answered by students during the course of the Project Officer's visits to schools. For the reasons discussed in Chapter Three the questionnaire was developed for use with Year 9 classes[1]. It was given to intact Year 9 classes chosen at random in each school visited. Choosing classes was important because many of the attributes being studied were possibly more characteristic of classes than schools.

The class was considered to be the logical unit of analysis, and so the class mean seemed to be the appropriate statistic. Gardner (1972) in his study of attitudes to Physics, cited several studies which supported the proposition that class averages of students' ratings of Teachers' behaviour were congruent with those obtained from external observers. It seemed reasonable to expect that this would also be true for measures of class environment and learning activities. However, it also was considered important to assess the degree to which members of each class held similar views about the environment and activities which they experienced in Science. Following the suggestion of Lewis (1976) two approaches were used. The first was to calculate an F ratio to determine whether class membership was a significant factor in determining responses to the questions comprising each scale. Secondly, a ratio which indicated the proportion of the total variance on each scale which could be attributed to differences in class means was calculated.

---

1 See page 55

Table 8.2   Between and Within Class Variation in Responses to the Student Questionnaire[a]

Scale	F ratio	Significance Level	Eta-squared[b]
Involvement	7.5	0.001	0.18
Organization	12.2	0.001	0.26
Stimulation	11.2	0.001	0.25
Exploration	12.2	0.001	0.27
Textual	20.3	0.001	0.38
Practical	28.5	0.001	0.46

Notes: a The analysis has been reported for schools from two states only: New South Wales and Victoria.

b The ratio is the sum of squared deviations of class means from the grand mean to the total sum of squared deviations.

The F ratio was calculated using a one-way analysis of variance technique in which class was used as the independent variable. As is evident from the results, shown in Table 8.2, the F ratio was significant at better than the 0.001 level for every scale tested. This was interpreted as an indication that class membership was a significant factor associated with a student's response to the questionnaire. Therefore, it seemed legitimate to use class means in subsequent analyses.

Table 8.2 also contains values of the proportions of the total sums of squared deviations from the mean which were due to variation between classes. The ratio used to obtain these values, known as eta-squared (Kerlinger, 1964 : 203 ; Cohen, 1973 : 107), provided an indication of the unanimity among the members of each class. It can be seen that between 18 percent and 46 percent of the total variation was due to variations between classes. The residual proportion was due to variations within classes. Explaining similar results, obtained from a scale measuring the extent of teacher direction in Physics classes, Lewis (1976) distinguished between a 'personal' environmental press and a 'consensual' environmental press. Lewis assumed that the latter represented objective reality while the former was a result of each individual's perception of the environment. Students in the same environment and experiencing the same activities may either perceive, or report, differently. Alternatively, it is possible that students within each class actually experience different environments, and do different things in science lessons. It seems likely that both of these factors contribute to the within-class variation.

In this study the within-class variation was not examined further. Subsequent analyses were made using the class mean as a measure of the consensual environment. While the evidence justifies this approach it is important to remember that there were also differences of opinion among the students in each class.

Science Facilities and Science Learning : A Between-Class Analysis

Measures of the Availability and Quality of Science Facilities

On the basis of a previously reported factor analysis (Ainley, 1976), it had been decided that school science facilities could be considered in four dimensions. These were the availability of rooms, the quality of those rooms, the abundance of apparatus, and the number of laboratory assistants. In studying the effect of facilities on the views students held of their science learning, four variables corresponding to these dimensions were used.

1. The occupancy of science rooms was measured simply as the percentage of science lessons held in science rooms.
2. The quality of the science room most often used was assessed by the school science co-ordinator. The measure of 'quality' was a score obtained by summing the school science co-ordinator's assessment of the availability and accessibility of 14 key features[2]. The scores on that scale correlated well with an observer's rating (r = 0.83). The scale had been previously shown to discriminate between rooms considered to be of different quality, and to have a satisfactory internal consistency (α = .68)[3].
3. The abundance of apparatus in each school was represented as a composite score. Replies from science co-ordinators about the adequacy of major, minor and expendable apparatus did not correlate as expected with the criterion scores. Two possible explanations existed for this. Firstly,

---

2 See page 48
3 See page 141

most schools regarded their apparatus as sufficient, and secondly, the responses were the opinion of the science co-ordinator. Consequently those responses were possibly related to the program which the school conducted. A science co-ordinator, whose department was conducting a program which emphasized experimental work, may have regarded as inadequate a stock of apparatus which would have satisfied a peer at another school. The simple correlation coefficients suggested that answers to the question about expendable apparatus were more affected by this than those concerned with minor apparatus. By using a procedure described by Tukey (undated) and by Peaker (1975), a composite score based on these raw data was formed. A series of stepwise regression analyses of each scale against the apparatus variables was carried out. It appeared that by taking the rating for minor apparatus less the rating for expendable apparatus a satisfactory predictor could be obtained. This procedure was tantamount to using the expendable apparatus rating as a means of controlling for the bias introduced by the co-ordinator who gave the ratings. It assumed that the availability of minor apparatus was most important for junior science, and that different responses to the question about expendable apparatus reflected the attitudes of science co-ordinators.

4   The provision of laboratory assistants was represented by the number of laboratory assistants per 1000 students in the school. This was the simplest, and most direct, measure of the assistance provided by ancillary staff in the school.

The Regression Analyses

Each of the three aspects of the science learning environment and each of the activity dimensions were used as criteria in six separate regression analyses. In these analyses the four variables, which were used as measures of schools' science facilities, were considered to be potential predictors of the environment and activity scores. They were entered in the appropriate regression analyses in a predetermined sequence.

It was postulated that the first consideration ought to be the proportion of science lessons held in science rooms, because this seemed to be of paramount importance in the Program. Then, having controlled for the percentage of time in science rooms, the quality of those rooms was considered as a potential influence on the students' views of the environment and activities in Science. Having allowed for differences in the occupancy and quality of science rooms,

Table 8.3   The Impact of Science Facilities on the Science Learning Environment : Between-Classes Regression Analyses

Step	Variable	Involvement R	r	β	Organization R	r	β	Stimulation R	r	β
		.52			.59			.48		
1	Occupancy		.45	.26		.45	.10		.33	.11
2	Quality		.40	.22		.53	.45		.34	.18
3	Apparatus		.30	.22		.30	.22		.40	.31
4	Lab. Assistants		.01	.16		.03	.19		-0.16	.00

N = 105

the abundance of apparatus was considered as a potential predictor. In the final step, when the effect of the first three variables had been allowed for, the provision of ancillary staff was entered as a predictor. This stepwise procedure enabled each of the measures of the science facilities available to a class to be entered in a logical sequence, so that associations between the criteria and the first entered predictors were examined. The order in which the variables were entered corresponded to the priorities followed in the Science Facilities Program.

Science Facilities and Science Learning Environments

The results of the regression analyses, which were carried out using three aspects of the learning environment (involvement, organization and stimulation) have been reported in Table 8.3. Values of the multiple correlation coefficient (R), simple correlation coefficients (r) and regression coefficients (β) have been recorded. The magnitude of multiple correlation coefficients (R) was used to indicate the proportion of the variance (P), of each environment index, which was associated with variations in the facilities available. This proportion of the variance can be calculated from :

$$P = 100 R^2$$

As a generalization, it can be inferred from these results that between 23 and 35 percent of the variance in each criterion was associated with variations in the facilities available. In brief those classes which enjoyed better science facilities reported more favourably on the environment in which they learned about science.

An advantage of analysing the results using this form of regression analysis can be observed by considering the association between the provision of laboratory assistants and each environment index. Though the number of laboratory assistants per 1000 students was not significantly correlated with any index, after the effect of variations in room occupancy and quality and the availability of apparatus was controlled, it did contribute to the scores on involvement and organization.

From the relative size of the regression coefficients (β) it was possible to estimate the strength of the association between each facility variable and the environment indices. Keeves (1972 : 122) proposed that a change in a criterion score (ΔZ_y) could be related to a variation in a standardized predictor score (ΔZ_x) through the regression coefficient (β).

$$\Delta Z_y = \beta \Delta Z_x$$

Thus the regression coefficient (β) indicated the strength of the association between variations in the predictor (X) and the criterion (Y). Where more than one predictor was involved the equation could be expanded so that it became :

$$\Delta Z_y = \Sigma \beta_i \Delta Z_{xi}$$

where β_i = the regression coefficient of Y on X
and ΔZ_{xi} = the change in the standardized score for variable x_i

It was deduced from these data that classes whose science lessons were held in good quality science rooms, and who had sufficient apparatus available, reported that they had a greater opportunity to be involved in purposeful activity. The provision of laboratory assistants was also a component contributing to higher degree of involvement. The figures showed that room quality was the most powerful predictor of students reporting a well organized learning environment. As good quality science rooms were defined in terms of, <u>inter alia</u>, readily accessible services such a result was expected. Having sufficient apparatus, being frequently in science rooms and having enough laboratory assistants were also conducive to a well organized learning environment. As might have been expected, the availability of apparatus was the most powerful predictor of classes reporting a stimulating environment in which a variety of methods and materials were used. Such an environment was also supported by frequently being in good quality science rooms. In brief, good quality rooms were associated with class reports of good organization, abundant apparatus was associated with reports of a

Table 8.4   The Association between Facility Measures and Environment Indices : (Coefficient of Contribution - C)

	Involvement	Organization	Stimulation
Occupancy	12	5	4
Quality	9	24	6
Apparatus	6	6	12
Lab. Assistants	0	0	0
$100\ R^2$	27	35	23

N = 105

stimulating environment, and all four predictors combined were correlated with reports of an environment in which students were involved in purposeful activity.

An alternative way of presenting these data was to tabulate the coefficient of contribution (C) for each variable to each index. Keeves (1972 : 122) argued that this coefficient provided an estimate of the contribution each variable made to the total variance. This coefficient was calculated from the regression coefficients (β) and the simple correlation coefficients (r).

$$C = r\beta \times 100$$

Values of the coefficient of contribution have been recorded in Table 8.4 The sum of the values of C is equal to the total variance in the criterion which can be accounted for by the four predictors. Thus the total is equal to $100\ R^2$.

These values of C indicate the association of good rooms with class reports of a well organized environment and sufficient apparatus for an environment which is stimulating through the variety offered. They also indicate the fact that three variables, occupancy, quality, and apparatus have similar strength of association with reports of an involving environment.

Science Facilities and Science Activities

To examine the combined impact of various aspects of facilities on activities, an hierarchical regression analysis was again performed. The same conceptual framework, as for the environment scales, was used to determine the sequence in which variables were to be entered in the regression analyses. The results, which are shown in Table 8.5 for these analyses were less conclusive

Table 8.5 The Impact of Science Facilities on Activities in Learning Science : Between Classes Regression Analyses.

| | | \multicolumn{3}{c}{Exploration} | \multicolumn{3}{c}{Textual} | \multicolumn{3}{c}{Practical} |
Step	Variable	R	r	β	R	r	β	R	r	β
		.31			.26			.37		
1	Occupancy		.04	-.18		-.25	-.22		.30	.23
2	Quality		.17	.28		-.19	-.06		.21	.00
3	Apparatus		.16	.23		-.07	-.01		.30	.22
4	Lab. Assistants		.10	.23		-.02	-.06		-.12	.02
	N = 105									

than for the environment scales. However there was an association between the facilities used and the students' reported activities. The magnitude of the multiple correlation coefficients (R) indicated that between seven and fourteen percent of the variation in scores on these activity scales were associated with differences in the facilities available.

Once again the relative size of the regression coefficients were used to indicate the contribution of each facility variable to the total scores. Classes more frequently in science rooms and supported by abundant apparatus reported a greater emphasis on practical work. While good quality science rooms were positively correlated with a large amount of practical work, the regression coefficient indicated that this variable added nothing to the practical score if occupancy was allowed for in a prior step. Classes which reported a greater emphasis on textual learning were those classes which were less frequently in science rooms. Such classes were also those who occupied poorer quality science rooms. In brief the relative use of practical work and textual materials in teaching and learning science was associated with the proportion of lessons held in science rooms. Abundance of apparatus was also important for practical work while better quality science rooms were associated with less textual learning.

For the scale which was designated 'encouragement to explore' the results were more subtle. Only the quality of the room and the abundance of apparatus were positively correlated with that scale. However, the regression coefficients revealed a number of more interesting associations. Firstly, when a prior allowance was made for differences in rooms and apparatus, the provision of laboratory assistants made a contribution to the value of this index. Secondly, the regression coefficient for the variable occupancy was negative. At first glance this result was surprising as it indicated that when less time was spent in science rooms there was more encouragement to explore a range of phenomena. An explanation for this result would appear to be in the fact that many of the activities listed on this scale involved going out of the science room to locations such as the library. Moreover it did seem to be an act of choice on the part of the science teacher, or science staff, to use facilities in this way. Encouragement to explore was positively correlated with the total number of science rooms per 1000 students (r = 0.18) and the average quality of the schools' science rooms (r = 0.24). Apparently the choice to teach in a way which used resources outside the science room was made in the context of sufficient good quality science rooms being available in the school.

Correlations Involving School Facilities

In the regression analyses the facilities used by classes were related to class reports of their environment and activities. For the abundance of apparatus, and the provision of laboratory assistants it was assumed that that which was available to the class was also that which was available in the school. In the case of rooms it was considered desirable to examine the correlation between the data obtained from classes and school facilities. To do this two facility measures were used : the availability of dual purpose rooms (Q_2), and the average quality of school science rooms. The index Q_2, it will be recalled, was the percentage of dual purpose science rooms in excess of the assessed needs of the school : 'needs' being defined in terms of the amount of science taught.

Correlation coefficients between class reports of learning and measures of general facilities in the school have been recorded in Table 8.6. Of all the scales, only involvement was significantly correlated with the availability of dual purpose rooms (Q_2). The average quality of the school's science rooms was significantly correlated with most of the aspects of science learning about which students reported. It is worth noting that there was no significant association between the quality of school science rooms and the emphasis on textual learning. An assocation had existed between that activity and the quality of the class' science rooms. Conversely it can be observed that encouragement to explore was more highly correlated with the quality of school science rooms than of the class science rooms.

Table 8.6   Correlation Coefficients Between Facility Measures and Description of Learning (School Facilities)

	Correlation Coefficients	
	Availability (Q_2)	Quality
Involvement	.24	.42
Organization	.08 (ns) [a]	.34
Stimulation	.09 (ns)	.26
Exploration	.15 (ns)	.24
Textual	.08 (ns)	.09 (ns)
Practical	.08 (ns)	.17

Note   a (ns) = not significant at the .05 level
For N = 105 classes $r > .16$, $p < .05$
$r > .23$, $p < .01$

These results could be interpreted as an indication that reliance on textual learning is something which is a class, rather than a school, characteristic. One could postulate that more reliance was placed on textual materials in teaching a curriculum if a particular teacher was in a poor quality room. On the other hand it appeared from the results that encouragement to explore may have been a more general product of the science curriculum of the school and its teaching practices. As such the general quality of the school science facilities appears to be a formative factor shaping the curriculum and practice followed by the science department.

One cautionary note about a variable used in the regression analyses is warranted at this stage. The percentage of science lessons held in a science room was used as a measure of the opportunity which a class had to use science facilities, yet that variable may have reflected other facets of school organization. It was noted in Chapter Six that the proportion of science lessons held in non-science rooms was not significantly correlated with any of the indices of room availability. In this discussion it has been observed that room availability was significantly correlated with only one of the aspects of science learning reported. When conducting the regression analyses it was assumed that occupancy was a measure of the extent to which science facilities were available to the class being studied. The alternative possibility is that a high value for occupancy reflected good husbanding of resources, and that that also was evident in the curriculum followed. Because such similar results were found for room quality, about which teachers could do little, this alternative explanation has not been pursued. However, it is a competing hypothesis which should be borne in mind.

Table 8.7 The Association Between Reports of Science Learning and the Location of Science Rooms

	Correlation Coefficients	
	Proximity to Prepn. Area	Grouping of Science Rooms
Involvement	.34	.38
Organization	.45	.44
Stimulation	.22	.27
Exploration	.09 (ns)	.17
Textual	-.01 (ns)	-.05 (ns)
Practical	.40	.37

The Location of Science Rooms

Originally, it had not been intended to examine the location of science rooms as a component of the facilities in a school. Yet, a number of early visits to schools gave the impression that this aspect of science facilities was an important influence on what happened in schools. While the location of science rooms was not strictly part of either of the groups of variables concerned with quality or availability of science rooms, it was considered to be worth separate examination.

During the school visits, the proximity of each of the Year 9 science classrooms to the store preparation area was noted. So also was the general location of school science rooms in terms of whether the rooms were grouped closely together or widely scattered. Both of these measures were three point scales.

The results in Table 8.7 have been interpreted as indicating that it was valuable for Year 9 science teaching to be in rooms located near service areas. All the environment scales were positively correlated with this variable as was the amount of practical work reported by students. Apparently science teaching was less involving, stimulating and organized when a room was far from the supply area. Certainly one imagines it would be more difficult to arrange practical work under those circumstances.

Similar results were found using the general location of rooms as a predictor. In this case students in schools where science rooms were clustered together reported greater encouragement to explore a range of scientific phenomena, and in addition scored more highly on the environment and practical work scales. This was consistent with observations made during visits to schools that such an arrangement enabled greater cohesion of the department, and planning of teaching strategies and use of resources.

Conclusions

The main conclusion drawn from the results presented here was that the quality of the learning environment reported by students studying science was enhanced by good facilities. The proportion of time in science rooms, the quality of these rooms, the abundance of apparatus, the provision of laboratory assistants, and even aspects of the location of science rooms were associated with an enriched learning environment. In addition one is drawn to the conclusion that some activities used in teaching science were associated with the facilities available. Students from schools with sufficient good rooms reported more encouragement to explore scientific phenomena. Classes which had easy access to science rooms relied less on textual materials and, especially when apparatus was abundant, did more practical work. It appeared that good facilities enabled a more diverse range of activities in science lessons.

An explanation for the reported association between student views of learning science and the facilities available to them is probably complex. Possibly, the provision of good facilities removed limitations on certain activities, perhaps good facilities enabled teachers to do similar things more efficiently, or conceivably a more subtle explanation involving student reactions and perceptions would be appropriate. It is an issue which is beyond the scope of this report.

When this stage of the Science Facilities Project was conducted in 1976, the difference in the standard of science facilities between the best equipped and the worst equipped schools was less than the general change in facilities from 1964 to 1975. Necessity forced a cross sectional rather than a longitudinal study and this has resulted in examination of a smaller range of the 'independent' variable. Detecting the full impact of facilities on science teaching and learning was consequently more difficult.

The results obtained from student questionnaires did confirm the opinions of those non-government school Principals who replied to the Commonwealth Department of Education survey in 1970. They attributed different teaching methods, more experimental work, greater efficiency of teaching and greater teacher satisfaction, to the opportunities offered by the new facilities. While the effect of good facilities on these aspects of science learning was not large, it was significant. Good facilities may not dramatically alter science teaching practices but they can foster certain types of science teaching. Whitfield (1971) has argued that the place of science in the school curriculum was justified by its providing students with the experience of empirical enquiry. Developments in science teaching have assumed that this was best achieved by a variety of activity and enquiry methods involving students in first hand observation of scientific phenomena. Good facilities apparently assist these approaches to teaching science. That consideration ought to weigh heavily in judging the impact of the Science Facilities Program.

CHAPTER NINE

A CLOSER LOOK AT SOME SCHOOLS

Background to the Visits

The visits to schools served two purposes. One was to administer a questionnaire sampling students' views about learning science. The other was to use a wide range of techniques to find out the ways in which teachers considered their work was affected by the facilities available. This involved interviewing teachers, and other staff, as well as informally observing some of the activities in schools. The information gathered was used to identify some of the less quantifiable educational outcomes of having good facilities, as well as to provide background information which would assist in interpreting the results obtained from the student questionnaire. In this relatively unknown area of research it was considered important to use methods which allowed unexpected, or idiosyncratic, effects of facilities to be detected.

One example of an issue not explicitly explored through the student questionnaire was that of the introduction of new science curricula. In a study of the adoption of an integrated science curriculum in Scotland, Brown (1977) reported that teachers placed considerable importance on resource constraints when considering whether to use such curricula. She noted specifically that in schools with limited apparatus and scattered laboratories, the integrated course was viewed with disfavour. The integrated course placed greater demands on equipment than did separate science subjects. Brown (1977: 48) expressed the opinion that while such concerns may be less important than philosophical issues to those who develop curricula, they may assume paramount importance for teachers.

Hamilton (1975) has described the way in which the Scottish Integrated Science Scheme was implemented in two schools. In both cases he found that implementation was accompanied by a series of transformations of the intention of the scheme. One school had rather poor laboratory accommodation, a shortage of apparatus, and scattered science laboratories. In combination with other problems relating to lack of communication between science staff, patterns of school organization, and teacher absence, these factors resulted in a teaching program at variance with the vision of the Integrated Science Scheme.

> Instead of support materials the worksheets had become the
> syllabus; and, as teacher demonstrations were often substituted
> for pupil practical work, class teaching had become the dominant
> activity. (Hamilton, 1975 : 187)

Both these studies suggest that the way in which schools and individual teachers implement new curricula may be influenced by the resources available to them. The observations made by Hamilton (1975) also are a reminder that the form of the implementation is often a product of a variety of interacting factors. Therefore in this study it was decided to look at some schools in detail to examine the way in which facilities were utilized in science teaching.

While Chapter Eight made use of comparisons between classes on selected dimensions this chapter is concerned with detailed consideration of a small number of schools. The schools concerned were the same 29 from which student data were collected. In addition to these schools one matriculation college was visited, and a few less formal visits were made to schools which were notable for recently acquired, or very good, facilities. Clearly it was not possible to report in detail all the school visits. Instead, a few schools have been described with a view to illustrating some important issues. The reports have been chosen for that purpose. Schools described are not intended to be representative of States or systems. They are examples in which some important issues are most clearly evident.[1]

The descriptions of the schools have been collated from information obtained through interviews with science teachers, science co-ordinators, laboratory staff and others, and by personal observation. Use was made of loosely structured interview and observation schedules so that comparable information was obtained from each school. Goodlad and Klien (1974) used a similar general approach in a study of primary schools. Parsons (1976) has recently urged the use of theoretically based guides to interviews and observation in illuminative studies.

---

1 The names of the schools described in this Report are fictitious.

The Context of the Schools Visits

Most teachers of junior science supported the conventional wisdom of Australian science teaching in recent times: students should personally participate in scientific activities. Within that framework teachers differed in the emphasis they placed on pupils doing experiments themselves and upon the purpose which that activity served. As a broad generalization many teachers wished students' experimental work to be supported by some direct teaching, and other activities. Consider the view of one science co-ordinator.

> I place a high emphasis on activities. I think the kids participating in experimentation whether they're learning methods or handling equipment, or just seeing how to do things is very important. They gain confidence in their motor control, in addition to learning work. Of course it has all got to be followed up ... I think the kids have a tendency if there is not some structuring to just go holus bolus and not get as much out of it.

Pupils experiments were seen as serving a number of purposes. Some were extrinsic in that they related to either reinforcement of other learning or motivation for further learning (either of the particular topic or of the discipline over a longer term). Others were intrinsic in that they involved pupil experimental work as the principal vehicle through which to develop skills closely dependent on that work. Such aspects as 'problem solving' skills, hypothesis testing, reasoning from empirical data, and manipulating apparatus were included in this category. As most science teachers indicated a desire to accommodate many of these elements, differences in their intentions arose from the relative emphasis placed on each.

As an indication of the sort of balance which might be reached, and the way in which that may alter with time, consider the case of Highland High School. A program which was previously directed exclusively towards providing experience in scientific method has altered so that greater emphasis is now placed on acquisition of knowledge. The twin reasons for this change were a reconsideration of the capabilities of most students below Year 10, and a desire that students should acquire certain knowledge of relevance to environmental issues. A statement prepared by the science coordinator indicated:

The science staff at this time (when general aims were reviewed) rejected the idea that we should have a single major aim. One such aim which had been considered was to train students in the patterns and processes of Science so that they will be able to use the "Scientific Method" to solve new problems.

Our experience was that the student's ability to use the "Scientific Method" (formulate hypotheses, design experiments, etc.) was closely linked to their stage of mental development. After extensive training in the "Scientific Method" it was found that less than half of Form four students could apply it successfully to the solution of real problems. It may be that the ability to formulate hypotheses and to design controlled experiments requires formal thinking which has been shown to be relatively undeveloped in many students at form four level.

Thus, while accepting that the development of mental skills in students should be one aim, we felt that this should not dominate our teaching to the extent where content or knowledge is considered to be of secondary importance.

At this time, there was also an increasing community awareness of the consequences of the growth of science and technology and we felt that one of our important aims should be to develop the student's understanding of, and concern for, the impact of human activities on the environment.

It can be noted in passing that several of the schools visited were embarking on similar changes.

It was clear that science departments were continually choosing from a range of options the sort of science curricula which would be taught and the way in which it would be taught. Within departments, individual teachers had continually to decide upon methods to be used in science teaching. The mere presence of good facilities did not appear to automatically result in a particular form of teaching. Nor did the absence of good facilities preclude student experimental work being conducted in an improvized setting. What was visibly affected by the facilities available was the convenience and efficiency with which science could be taught. Many teachers who rejected the propostion that the facilities at their disposal determined the way they taught mentioned that convenience and efficiency were influenced. Other teachers, especially those in schools with poor science rooms, or those who could remember having taught in very poor science rooms, were more inclined to attribute stronger effects to the conditions under which they taught.

There was also evidence that new facilities were of greatest benefit when other circumstances favoured their effective use. Ruraton High School was a school where such circumstances were favourable: staff retention was high, suitable curriculum materials were being introduced, and two key people had been involved in extended in-service education. New science rooms were provided at a time of fortuitous circumstance.

Ruraton High School : Fortuitous Circumstance

Background

Ruraton High School was one of two government schools in a country town of about 8000 people. It enrolled 700 students. Eight of its fifty-three teachers taught science.

Ruraton High was a school in which the potential of its science facilities was exploited in full. The four science rooms now in use were first occupied in 1969. Surrounding circumstances seem to have enhanced the impact which they made. Most importantly, the new facilities were built at a time when there was interest in some new curriculum materials produced by the Junior Secondary Science Project. The new facilities dramatically contrasted with the old and thereby exaggerated the possibilities within them. In addition the school retained its science staff so that there was continuity of development and as a school, it was generally favourably disposed towards active forms of learning.

Its four rooms were part of an attractively designed building. This building also housed the administrative offices, the geography department, a matriculation centre, and some general teaching rooms. A private architect specifically designed the building to suit the site and it was set adjacent to an attractive garden of native shrubs. Other facilities of the school were in stark contrast to this. One building still being used was built for the original school sixty-five years ago. It was supplemented by an annexe which was formerly part of another school across a road, and several rows of demountable classrooms. Science subjects were previously taught in one poorly equipped science room in the old building. An adjacent room was modified with a few extra fittings so that it also could be used for science. In the words of the science co-ordinator, 'this meant that junior classes didn't get a look in [and] senior classes were there just for their prac. classes'. Teaching often involved going to a room 'with a bucket of water and a portable burner and that was science'.

The new curriculum materials, which became available at the time the new building was being erected were designed for a science syllabus which placed more emphasis on student activity and which had been introduced in the State a few years earlier. Science teachers at Ruraton were apparently keen to use the new methods and the new materials. Thus the new rooms were provided at a most opportune time. Perhaps with the wisdom of hindsight, the science co-ordinator recalled that:

> '... moving to the new building where there are four science rooms meant all classes could have all of their science in a science room, and in a particular room. Activity based programs which we run now would not have been possible under the old situation'.

The new methods were not entirely based on new curriculum materials from outside. Original material developed in the school was also used. The science co-ordinator had been at the school since 1960 except for a few years at other schools. He recalled that:

> 'Since (moving to) the new rooms we started writing our own programs. Now some of these programs we think are very good indeed. And we may perhaps use them in preference to ASEP material because they've been written by people here, suit our needs and so on. But the kids have been doing ASEP-type activities since the first full year we moved into the new building.'
>
> Q: Are you suggesting that the new rooms were a stimulus to writing original material?
>
> 'Certainly; there was no point otherwise.'

The strong impression gained from the science co-ordinator was that the provision of new rooms had removed a barrier to the teaching methods they had wished to adopt. It was a view shared by the acting Principal, himself a science teacher, who came to the school not long after the new block was occupied.

Science teachers stayed in Ruraton longer than is usual in government schools in country towns. In 1975 the science teachers had been at the school for an average of six years. This allowed teachers to follow ideas through their implementation period. It also allowed a good informal communication network to be established and for the teachers to be familiar with all the resources in the department. In 1976 there was a valuable blend of youth and experience on the staff. An additional valuable aspect of the staff was the period which two key members spent on part-time study leave in the early seventies. This involved moving to city schools temporarily and studying at a tertiary institution. On returning to Ruraton they not only brought new ideas but were sufficiently familiar with the school to be able to implement them.

Not only the science department of the school was active. A range of interesting developments reflected a general liveliness in the school. Many of these developments originated in the late sixties which suggested that there was a general atmosphere conducive to the sort of changes which occurred in science. Among the innovations which remained were:

(a) a series of short courses for Year 11 students which were intended to further and enrich their experience (e.g. pottery, ethics, journalism, energy resources),

(b) a matriculation centre for senior students,

(c) an activity program which provided for diverse leisure activities (canoeing, bushwalking, photography) as well as traditional sports,

(d) an improvized open plan Form 1 complex which was used for English and Social Studies, and

(e) a contribution from staff and the school resources to a community education program.

Science Facilities

The science rooms which were in use in 1976 were modern and adaptable. They were arranged in two pairs: one pair on each level of the new building. In three of the rooms services were provided on 'elongated pillars' while the fourth had all its gas, electricity and water outlets at the perimeter of the room. In each room the tables could be easily rearranged. Provision for storage in the rooms was good. Each was set out identically so that students could obtain items of basic apparatus easily. Between rooms there was a spacious preparation room on each level and associated with each room was a storage room. One fortuitous benefit arose from the arrangement of the rooms in pairs. Given the easy access from each room to the preparation room, and the wide adjacent corridor, there could be fluid movement between the rooms. In fact two rooms could sometimes function as an almost unified larger teaching space.

Four science rooms were almost precisely the number which would have been specified by the Commonwealth Standards Committee for the number of science periods taught in this school. In practice however, the use of two rooms by non-science classes for 25% of the time meant that the rooms were vacant less often than would be desirable. Notwithstanding this, the basic facilities for teaching science in the school were good. All science classes were held in good quality rooms. Indeed, each class had all its science lessons in the same room. Moreoever, the presence of a full-time laboratory assistant meant that the strain of maintaining and preparing apparatus was relieved. The only deficiencies were the ancillary provisions. There was no special provision for staff offices - corners of preparation rooms were being used - the school lacked a plant or animal room, there was no science reading room and there was no research laboratory.

Science Curricula and Science Teaching

It has been mentioned that ASEP and JSSP units were used extensively, and especially in Years 7 and 8. However, the science co-ordinator pointed out:

> 'We try not to just run through a unit as is ... we punctuate this with rather more formal demonstration lessons, discussion lessons if a unit is not available for an area of the course which we think is important or more importantly because we feel that every now and again the kids respond better to a change in treatment.'

Two younger teachers involved with Year 9 students voiced the same opinion. Commenting on the need for varied approaches one observed that 'kids get tired of activity lessons all the time'. The comment contained just a trace of disappointment from a person who earlier had expressed a leaning towards the philosophy of Rousseau as presented in Emile. Both were aware of student boredom with activities which interested them as teachers. Similarly, while both enjoyed using ASEP 'in a free spirit' (allowing individual progression through units) they felt pressure from problems of classroom management of resources, and of giving sufficient attention to students. Even given good laboratories, abundant apparatus and a laboratory assistant, basic educational problems remained to be solved.

Staff worked in close proximity to each other. Most had been more than one year at the school. Therefore communication about curriculum matters was assumed to occur informally. Certainly there was co-ordination

of the curricula. At each year level a common 'core' of units was studied
by all classes. Detail was not specified other than through resource
materials which were indicated. Within the 'core' individual teachers
decided the emphasis on different aspects of the unit. In addition to the
'core' there was an element of the years work which was entirely at the
discretion of each teacher and which was not common to every class. In this
way the department believed it could provide a planned sequential development
over the Years 7 to 10 and yet allow each teacher a degree of autonomy.
Within such a small staff it seemed to work. No one expressed dissatisfact-
ion.

A similar approach applied to assessment in Years 7 to 10. Teachers were
able to choose their own methods of assessing student progress but all arrived
at a five point letter classification. In practice all teachers used topic
tests, projects, and judgments about classwork in similar proportions. No
formal attempt at moderation was made but close informal collaboration was
hoped to remove major discrepancies between classes.

In Year 11 and 12 science subjects were a little more popular than in other
schools in the State and rather more popular than in other government schools. It
had 1.03 science subject enrolments per student while the State average was
0.94. Biology was especially popular accounting for 51 per cent of the Year 12
students against the State average of 41 percent. Only Physics, Chemistry and
Biology were offered in Year 11 and Year 12. Geology was once offered to
Year 11 students until the staff member whose interest this was left the
school. The school was considering making Physical Science available to
Year 12 students but it was limited, not by facilities, but by its size.
It was considered that such a subject may jeopardize the viability of Physics
and Chemistry which are important 'tool' subjects in tertiary studies.

As a rural high school Ruraton had the additional resource of the
surrounding bush. Biology made use of this. In a city school, field studies
involve time consuming and administratively difficult excursions. Biology at
Ruraton often included cycling to a nearby location for field work in
addition to longer field study camps. Strangely, such informal excursions
were less easily arranged for Years 7 to 10. More administrative requirements
needed to be fulfilled. One of the younger Year 9 science teachers commented
that while facilities in his previous school were poorer, the administrative
barriers to using the surrounding bush were fewer. This partly compensated
for poor facilities.

Teachers' Responses to the Facilities

Teachers in Ruraton differed in their opinion of the importance of the good
facilities. The science co-ordinator who remembered teaching under the old
conditions considered them useful.

> 'I don't necessarily think that to do worthwhile science you
> have to have a great amount of material but I think it nice
> to be able to draw on material if need be. Just to quote an
> example. Not being a physicist I don't know much about cathode
> ray oscilloscopes. But with the help of the Physics people,
> when I was doing some work on nerves we set up a good
> demonstration. If it didn't exist I wouldn't get upset. I'd
> survive but it's better to have it. And its better to have a
> room with a few taps in it, a spacious room, a quiet room, a
> room where desks can be moved into any shape that's required.'

The younger teachers who had not experienced the poorer conditions which previously existed, were rather less certain of the value of good facilities. They were more inclined to mention 'faults' such as the unsuitability of perimeter services in one room, a lack of trolleys and an unnecessarily large demonstration bench. The main value in the school science department was not the facilities but the staff atmosphere. In their view, the physical plant of the science department would not be a major factor in a decision to stay at the school.

Other Aspects

There were interesting aspects of the school's science teaching which are partly related to the facilities available. Previous mention was made of the use of the surrounding bushland. The science co-ordinator's comment was relevant as a contrast to the view that one problem of good laboratories was that they make science an indoor subject. He said that

> "it mightn't be a direct result but by the atmosphere created by new courses and new rooms, more use is made of the bushland around the school.'

This assertion needs to be tempered by considering the opinion of one of the younger science teachers that arranging for such excursions was rather difficult. Perhaps the difference arose from the different age levels the two teachers were dealing with or perhaps it may have resulted from the different experiences they had had.

School science facilities were used at odd times by photography and 'film making' groups. While rooms were kept locked, teachers did arrange to be present when students wanted to do extra work. The offer was more than nominal. The science co-ordinator claimed that

> 'In Year 7 teachers often have lunch in the room so that students can work in the lab. We make a lot of demands on staff time here.'

Yet while this extra activity was real it was also limited. The same spokesman conceded that 'perhaps we don't go far enough'.

The circumstances in which new rooms were provided at Ruraton High have helped ensure the successful use of those rooms. Coming at the right time in the right circumstances they have been used rather effectively. Students in Years 7 to 10 experience a stimulating and active program of science teaching.

A contrast was provided at Riversdale High School where similar ambitions for the teaching of junior science were not able to be implemented. Riversdale had inadequate science accommodation: even that available in the school was reserved almost exclusively for senior students. The conditions under which junior science was taught at Riversdale were similar to those which prevailed more widely before 1963.

Riversdale High School : Enthusiasm Frustrated

Riversdale High School was located in an established and affluent suburb. Its students constituted a slightly more heterogeneous population than this would suggest as there were pockets of poorer housing in surrounding areas. The school's grounds were spacious and attractive. Its buildings were a mixture of older main structures supplemented by recent additions. While it lacked the modern appearance of newer schools it appeared, by conventional standards, an attractive environment in which to teach. This superficial judgment was confirmed by a reportedly low loss of staff each year.

Science accomodation was not good. Too few science rooms were available to house all science lessons. In 1976 the school had six science rooms. Ideally it needed eight to satisfactorily house its 180, 50-minute science lessons each week.

When the quality of the six rooms was considered the situation appeared to be even worse. Only three of the six rooms could be considered to be of adequate quality. One of the remaining three was a converted library used mainly for teaching Geology. It had only a teachers' demonstration bench by way of special services. Two other rooms were built in the mid-fifties but not as science rooms. They were located a considerable distance from the main science block, they were too small (24 feet by 24 feet) for a normal class of 30 to 35 pupils, and were in poor repair. In each room only three sinks were functional, gas leaks were a problem and many stools - all of which appeared to be uncomfortable - needed to be fixed. Even had the repairs been effected the room design was poor. The problems of cramped working conditions were compounded by large fixed island benches too close together, and some hazardous plumbing arrangements. Water and gas pipes were laid just above floor level and, though protected by wooden covers, presented a real hazard to movement. In addition the chalk board was small, and there was no teachers' bench. The Fire Department had declared these two rooms to be unsafe as only one exit existed.

The three satisfactory science rooms were designed for the special science subjects of Physics, Chemistry and Biology. They were spacious and well designed if somewhat inflexible as a result of long fixed benches. They were located, with the previously described seminar/Geology room, in the special science block where they were close to the service and storage areas. In addition to the teaching rooms this block housed a science staff office, a subject masters office, and several preparation and storage areas. The whole complex was provided under the Science Facilities Program. A plaque attached near the entrance testifies to its opening in 1967.

Only students in Years 11 and 12 used the better rooms. Fewer than eight Science lessons for lower secondary school students were held there each week. As a consequence most Year 11 and Year 12 science lessons were reasonably accommodated but only the two dilapidated science rooms were available for the 90, 50-minute science periods in the lower secondary school each week. Mute testimony to the state of these rooms was provided by the fact the rooms were often unused, even when they were available. Teachers regarded them as unsafe for science.

Apparatus was plentiful. Senior Biology was especially well supplied with material. Even junior science had ample stocks of apparatus, but it was located in the science block. Hence it was not readily accessible to

the rooms in which junior science was held. Lack of secure storage adjacent
to those rooms precluded material being kept there. As the science co-
ordinator noted, there was not much loss due to breakage. Little wonder, as
the apparatus was rarely used. In addition to the adequate stocks of
apparatus there were two laboratory assistants to help prepare material.
They worked very effectively in the senior science subjects and could easily
have managed additional work in junior science if that had been required.
The laboratory assistants managed the records and maintenance of apparatus
supply. The school had effective laboratory assistants so that this did not
limit the use of experimental work.

Courses in junior science were formal, given to didactic teaching and
somewhat repetitive. The science co-ordinator observed:

> We teach a very theoretical type of course here. In fact they
> (State authorities) changed the science syllabus here about three
> or four years ago. We should have implemented that, but because
> of lack of facilities we virtually still use the old syllabus.
> The trend these days is to a lot more activity in courses. We
> would dearly love to be on to that, but because of the lack of
> facilities we follow a theoretical course ... They're lucky to
> do prac. once a week ... We did try some ASEP courses in Year 8
> for two years with one class which was lucky to be able to use
> one of the senior laboratories to do it. We did also try it with
> other classes and try to run it in classrooms but it was just not
> effective; mainly because of equipment losses, management and
> interference from other classes etc.

The school's stock of JSSP curriculum materials remained unused as witness to
the inhibition which facilities in the school placed on teaching methods.
Problems created by the poor facilities were more than self perpetuating:
they were self exacerbating. The syllabus had been devised to suit the poor
facilities and was formal and content specific. It was determined
unilaterally by the science co-ordinator. Assessment was by a common
examination (80 percent), teacher tests (15 percent), and project work
(5 percent).   The result was that teachers felt obliged to cover the large
amount of content, with the effect that project and practical work were
accorded low priority. At class level the fact that students were rarely
able to work in a laboratory resulted in a lack of familiarity with
procedures. Class management was therefore a problem, activities were
closely directed, and time was wasted in housekeeping on those occasions
when laboratory work was held.

The teachers involved in Year 9 science teaching agree about what they
would like to do. One said:

> Well, we don't do enough prac. work. I'd like to see a
> laboratory based course, not wholly experimental work, but
> at least that type of course. I took ASEP, actually the
> final year that was here, in my room but it wasn't satisfactory.
> You don't have water. You can't heat anything up. We did Mice
> and Men but there was nowhere to keep the mice. We had to run
> and get the mice at the beginning of every lesson (sic).

A colleague expressed a similar view asserting that if good laboratories were
available:

> I'd like to run a science course which was practically based.

A third teacher echoed these views seeing the course being taught as less student oriented and less interesting than desirable. The teaching about density, which was observed during the visit provides an illustration of the general pattern. Not once did students take measurements or make observations themselves. The concept was taught using a formal mathematical approach supplemented by computational exercises from a textbook.

When laboratory work was conducted it was done in isolation from theory. The laboratories were unsuitable for normal teaching because of the seating arrangements. Laboratory work was formal and recorded in a separate book according to a standard format. One of the teachers described lessons held in the laboratories this way:

> We can't have any individual work at all. We haven't got any space to store any experiments set up where we can say to the students take this and proceed. You have to do it step by step with them because there's no chance to organize it that (the former) way. There's not enough space so you have to be very careful, you can't have students moving around from place to place. They're fairly depressing places to work in.

Another found that the only means of compensating was to conduct demonstrations in the normal classroom. Outside this room was a drinking tap from which buckets of water could be carried into the room.

Teachers perceived that student enthusiasm was affected by the environment in which they worked. All expressed the view that one aim in teaching science, and especially of the experimental work, was to generate interest in scientific phenomena as well as to help students acquire some basic cognitive skills. The science co-ordinator was aware of the problem of facilities in this regard:

> I can remember going back to the Grade 8 in which we were running ASEP, where they were actually doing experiments in good conditions, and the enthusiasm of those Grade 8 students for science was amazing; Whereas our present Grades 8, 9 and 10 don't show enthusiasm as one of their finer points.

It was a view reiterated by other teachers. Students, it was felt, lost interest both because of the conditions and the course which had to be taught. And, because they lost interest, they did not work as well.

Teachers felt frustrated by their conditions. When asked what effect the poor conditions had on teachers, one replied:

> Frustrating! It takes a lot of time to organize and carry equipment from one place to the other .. it's a nuisance ... I guess frustration is the main thing ... at not being able to teach the way that you'd like to.

The co-ordinator was aware of the effect on the morale of staff.

> The number of complaints I get about those terrible junior laboratories is large. Lots of aspects affect teacher morale.

One aspect, in fact, was the preferential use of good facilities in senior science. Teachers in junior science felt envious and said that students held similar views. The area of hope in the school science program was a new Year 8 program. A course based on a more activity-directed book (Concepts of Science) was being introduced. Some effort had been made to have laboratories available for this course with the result that an estimated 60 percent of time was spent in the laboratory. A science levy of $1 per student per science subject generated about $1000 annually and this was used to buy material for the course. The teacher responsible felt that brighter students might miss some rigour but;

> the slower kids seem to benefit by doing more practical work and not being told things but having to find out ... They enjoy it, they maintain their interest in science, which is something usually they've begun to lose by this stage. I'd like to be able to say that they're better in the laboratory but this morning I had a disaster.

The program was still truncated by having to specifically schedule laboratory sessions rather than have mixed activities in any lesson. Its extension into Years 9 and 10 was dependent on more laboratories being available.

Teaching science at Riverside High seemed very much an experience of enthusiasm frustrated, and opportunity curtailed by lack of suitable science rooms.

At Ruraton High School the science co-ordinator regarded the new facilities as having had considerable impact by removing an obstacle to the sort of course which they wanted to teach. Science teachers at Riversdale High were in a contrasting situation. Especially those who taught junior science felt that the lack of good facilities impeded their teaching. Teachers at Petrin High School did not feel the privations of their poor facilities to be quite so important. All the teachers at Petrin were young. As it was their first school they had no experience of conditions elsewhere. In addition they were imbued with an enthusiasm for teaching which led them to improvise in order to teach activity courses. This they did in the certain knowledge that they would occupy new science rooms as the school was built. At Petrin it was possible to speak to science teachers both before and after they had the benefit of new facilities.

Petrin High School : Subtle Changes

Petrin High School was a new school in an old suburb. Its establishment was in response to a new wave of settlement in the area by younger families. These families were mainly migrant families. In economic terms it would be described as working class for most employment was in a nearby area of heavy industry. The most specific general problem for the school was that the students had reading difficulties. As a result teachers of most subjects, including science, had to take greater cognizance of the readability of the textual materials which they used.

The school began in makeshift accommodation. In 1975 most of the school had occupied new premises though considerable work on the school grounds needed to be done. Science was, in that year, still taught in poor conditions. When a first visit was made to Petrin, science accommodation was one modestly equipped portable classroom, and two other portable classrooms with no special equipment. The direct impact of these privations was that some units were not able to be offered, some activities in other units were omitted and generally the range of choice was restricted. One teacher expressed the problem this way:

> They (the poor facilities) don't affect the way you teach but rather the topics which you can teach. For example, I wanted to do Polymers but without a fume cupboard I felt it was too dangerous. When I first arrived I had to teach magnetism because magnets were all we had.

When asked about anticipated difference when a new suite of science rooms was occupied, the same teacher suggested subtle rather than major differences.

> Firstly I'll have more contact with the other science teachers. At the moment we're isolated from each other. I think things will be more readily available and I'll spend less time sending kids back and forth from one room to another. It will probably be more efficient.

It was an interesting adaption to curtail content areas rather than modify methods. Activity methods were considered to be of central importance. Content was included if the school had the facilities to teach it appropriately. In most other schools it was content areas which were first specified and then methods were used in accord with available facilities. The youthfulness and enthusiasm of the staff resulted in a perseverance with the course which they wished to follow.

When a return visit to the school was made one year later staff were able to reflect on the difference that occupying a new suite of four modern well-designed science rooms made to their teaching. The new rooms were not only fine teaching rooms but they had the advantage of adjoining a spacious well-designed preparation area. There was no dramatic change reported. The general approach to teaching was as before and was described by one teacher as:

> To make students aware of the use of science, the value of science, the relevance of science without becoming too specific. We try to steer away from very straight formal chemistry for example. We have no prerequisite for Year 11 studies except that they (the students) have an awareness about handling apparatus, they can use things, they can reason deductively but they need not know such specifics as how many electrons are in atoms of different elements. The main reason being that from 120 to 130 Year 10 students we have 14 in Year 11 Chemistry. I can't see that we could justify a curriculum suited only to those students when the rest should have a much more general approach.

Adopting this framework did not mean neglecting factual knowledge. Consider the same teacher's view of experimental work.

> We place a high emphasis on experiments because they learn
> and it keeps their interest going. With the ASEP units half
> the time they enjoy it but they learn nothing. But if you're
> able to back up the experiment with some teaching that experiment
> becomes quite meaningful. Now I add a fair bit of explanation.

While the general approach to teaching had not dramatically changed some subtle changes had taken place. One comment was that:

> My ninth year units are either ASEP units or derived from ASEP
> units so the equipment is very simple. I haven't found myself
> doing anything different to what I did in the units last year.
> I found a great time-saving though. It saved time because I've
> got things in the room. I don't have to carry them from room to
> room. I've got hot water on tap and ice here ... Last year for
> hot water I had to send a thermos to the staff room to be filled
> from an urn. Well that takes 10 minutes or so. Now we just run
> a tap.

The same teacher continued to comment on the students' reactions in a view echoed by colleagues:

> The kids are better in class because they feel they're in a
> science room and having everything you need is important ...
> They seem more responsive. They look after equipment better.
> They're interested. You can get them into a pattern of knowing
> where to put things away and what to do. They know where
> things are, whereas they don't when you bring in five trays
> to the portable rooms. They forget what came off which tray
> and you have bedlam at the end.

There were also some changes in teaching methods reported. Two teachers, who had been at the school previously remarked upon the use of impromptu demonstrations:

> I would have done more demonstrations this year simply because if
> I want material I've got it handy. Quite a few more demonstrations
> actually.

The demonstrations were not just of grand experiments but of simple graded experiments to introduce an investigation and to save time. Even audio-visual aids such as the overhead projector and slide projectors were more readily used in the new rooms.

While this description of Petrin High School suggests relatively small effects of the new facilities, three other factors need to be considered. One is that the science teachers who had been at Petrin in 1975 and 1976 had not taught at other schools. They had therefore developed appropriate strategies to cope with poor facilities. A second is that during 1975 the effects of poor facilities were mitigated by a very efficient laboratory assistant who managed apparatus very well. Thirdly, the interview questions concerned junior science. As one teacher remarked:

> Your questions have been aimed at ninth Year. With 11th Year
> I can't compare but I can observe that with the exception of
> about two, I would have been struggling to do any of the
> experiments I've done this year. I don't think I could have

>   taught Year 11 Chemistry ... I could exist in portables for
>   Year 9 Science but I couldn't exist that way for Year 11
>   Chemistry.

This suggests that the strategy of avoiding content areas requiring special facilities, could not be applied to Year 11 Chemistry. Content in that subject was apparently much more immutable.

An additional point could be made concerning a previously quoted comment about contact with other science teachers. At Petrin as at many schools there were conflicting views about the degree to which each class at a given Year level should follow a common course, and the extent to which one Year should build on the previous Year. In short the conflict was between school autonomy in curricula and teacher autonomy in curricula. It was an important issue if only because students were not held in the same class within their Year, from each Year to the next. An extreme view of teacher autonomy seemed likely to contain the seeds of a confused experience of science for many students.

It would be naive to attribute this problem to the scattered facilities before 1976. The debate occurs in many schools. Yet it seemed possible that the lack of an identifable science area, with consequent lack of contact between staff, contributed to a habit of separateness. The poor facilities didn't create the problem: they merely made it harder to solve.

There were schools which had an apparent abundance of science rooms which were not fully used and in which rather haphazard and inactive science courses were followed. The visit to one such school at Casterbridge revealed that while it had ample rooms it had little else. The science department and its equipment had deteriorated so that it was no longer as useful as it ought to have been.

Casterbridge High School : Rooms but Little Else

Casterbridge High School was located in a low socioeconomic area of a large city. Gradual changes in the age distribution of the surrounding community have resulted in a decline in the school enrolment. Some years ago the school had nearly 1500 students on roll. Now a few more than 800 attend the school. Facilities, which were provided when the school was large, now serve the smaller number of students. The surplus of facilities was accentuated in Science subjects by the surprisingly large proportion (more than one quarter) of students in Years 9 and 10 who did not study Science at all. In addition the retention of students from Year 10 to Year 11 was low. Fewer than 40 percent of the Year 10 students proceeded to Year 11. Thus even though four of the 12 science rooms were equipped with nothing more than a demonstration bench the school had an abundance of rooms. All science classes could be held in laboratories. Surprisingly few science classes were actually held in laboratories.

While the school had sufficient rooms many were of poor quality. In fact they could be considered to form three groups: six were built as part of the school before 1964, two were built outside the Science Facilities

Program in the mid-sixties and four were built in the early stages of the Science Facilities Program. The six older rooms were particularly shabby. Room D was so small (24 ft x 24 ft) that it could really only accommodate 20 students. It was expected to hold 30. While it was the smallest, all the old rooms were cramped. Island benches were so crammed in the rooms that movement in classes was difficult, even hazardous. Two of these six rooms were demonstration rooms and therefore had no services at student benches but two others intended as laboratories had no taps or sinks at those benches while the two properly serviced rooms had many inoperable and broken sinks. The benches were chipped and partly corroded and in no room was hot water available. The adjacent store-preparation rooms were useless because they were not stocked with basic apparatus. This was especially a problem because the rooms were so scattered around the school that to provide apparatus from the central store was nearly impossible. None of these rooms had any provision for using visual aids, all lacked display board space and even the area of the chalkboard was meagre. The two more recent non-commonwealth rooms were similar. They only differed in that, being of more recent construction, they were in slightly better repair.

A special science block was provided under the Science Facilities Program at the beginning of that scheme. It contained rooms of infinitely better quality, good storage provision and a science staff room. Yet it had faults. The Chemistry room was a single purpose laboratory. The superstructure above the runnels was intended to store reagent bottles. If they were still used for that purpose they would be an even greater obstacle to teaching than at present. The Biology room was of fairly rigid design while the Geology room had no student work benches and was therefore unsuited to anything but formal lessons. The Physics room was a well-equipped and well-designed room. It was noted that this block was reserved exclusively for senior classes.

The quality and the design of the science labs resulted in lack of use. One teacher of considerable experience offered a reason for the lack of use made of laboratory facilities.

> I would say the poor quality of the labs ... It looks good. When you walk around the grounds you see all the labs. and everything. It really doesn't look too bad until you walk in there and you start trying to teach in the situation ... They look good and people who don't teach science think they are good. Well, I've taught in lab. D and I'll tell you that unless I really had my back to the wall I wouldn't go back in there. I avoid D lab. I don't mind other labs in terms of size but I don't like the arrangement of the seats, the lack of power points, the lack of sinks for them (the students) to wash and clean their equipment, an inability to get to a sink and push them under if there's been an accident. There's no accident shower at all.

The teachers of junior science suggested that the type of rooms available forced them to teach practical and theory in separate lessons, and also to use less activity than desired. The general pattern was to take a class to the laboratory when necessary, otherwise science was taught in classrooms. Another teacher commented on the laboratories he used.

> There are only six sinks and three are leaking all the time. I've been at the administration for two and a half years to get them fixed up ...

The room is physically too small for thirty kids. The amount
of equipment that is stored in it is inadequate, the glassware,
the general equipment that doesn't have to be moved from the
laboratory, or shouldn't be moved from the laboratory, is
simply not there. The normal things that I don't think should
be moved from a laboratory get moved from class to class
depending upon who wants them ... If you're setting up a prac.
you have to specifically outline everything that you might need.
Everything includes even bunsen burners and matches for example,
tapers everything.

The science co-ordinator who was new to the school in 1976 observed that the school administration did not organize the timetable to enable laboratories to be fully used.

Actually we're well off here for lab. hours. Of course even
though we've got the lab. hours to put them in all the time,
because of the way the timetable is based we can't do it ...
But then of course a lot of teachers don't like to teach in
the laboratories because they are so small.

If you've got 33, 34, or 35 students in these junior laboratories
then it is very very difficult to do any work; because you've
got to spend a lot of your time disciplining so that they'll do
what you want them to do when you want them to do it.

The poor quality of the science rooms and school organization were two reasons why the rooms were not fully utilized. Two other reasons were management difficulties in the science department and the nature of the syllabus being followed in the school.

Difficulties in the science department seem to have resulted in a poor stock of apparatus and lack of organization of laboratory staff. The school was poorly provided with apparatus. Twenty-four bunsen burners cannot be considered adequate. Only five of the 25 microscopes in the school were in proper working order. A lack of pyrex test-tubes resulted in the use of soda glass tubes for heating. There was of course considerable damage. The science co-ordinator mentioned the difficulties which this situation presented for the introduction of ASEP units.

To do ASEP you need plenty of lab. hours but you also need plenty
of equipment. Now you don't need very sophisticated equipment but
you do need a very very large number of beakers, test-tubes, and
all sorts of rubbish, which we don't possess - as I was telling
you earlier about the pyrex test-tubes. The fact that we don't
have any pyrex test-tubes means that when you do an experiment
which involves the heating of some substance you ruin your test-
tube and you can't use it again. Our soda glass stocks are also
going down. Now there are two reasons for this. One is that we
only get a small grant and the other one is that the time span
between ordering and delivery is so long.

The science co-ordinator was new to the school. He was attempting to rectify the depletion of non-consumable stock which had occurred over previous years. There had been three science co-ordinators in the three previous years. Orders had not been diligently placed or followed up and repairs had not been made. Nor had rooms been renovated.

The stock of apparatus also affected Year 11 and 12 teaching in science subjects. While schools had nominal autonomy in these areas the co-ordinator observed:

> The equipment that's put on these books (lists of equipment) is really say PSSC for Physics and Chem Study for Chemistry. Now if you want to change your course you've got to change your equipment as well and you've got to make sure its available. ... There are chits on which you can write in equipment you would like but whether you'd get it is another matter. I've never done that. I'll never be game to try that ... By the time you get your equipment a year later and they say 'not obtainable' or 'refused' then, a year later, you've got to start looking for alternative sources.

All three laboratory assistants were young and inexperienced. They would have been of greater value to the science department had more direct supervision been provided. Lack of continuity of leadership had resulted in too little direction of their work. Often they seemed to have too little to do. The widely scattered location of science rooms meant that their task would have been difficult anyway.

The fairly formal and didactic pattern of science teaching in Year 10 and below followed a syllabus developed in the school. In theory the school science department was responsible for its development. However in practice the document had been devised by the previous science co-ordinator It was best characterized as a listing of chapter headings and sub-headings from a single textbook (<u>Science for Secondary Schools</u>). Even where the book had been written for use in another State (Geology) no adaption had been made. Moreover this text is generally regarded as better suited for students with well developed reading skills. It therefore seemed an inappropriate choice for Casterbridge.

The resulting work program had the expectation that all classes would cover a large amount of content. As a consequence teachers felt that the pressure of time was on them and that they could not afford to allow students to do many experiments. One teacher saw it desirable, especially in Chemistry and Biology topics, for students to gain understanding through doing experiments which would be followed by a consolidating theory discussion. However,

> there is just no time for this. Time is the major factor in our science course at the moment. You are really pushing to cover material.

The new science co-ordinator was aware of the problems and could see various means to reform. He was supported by a recently appointed energetic Principal. It was intended to reconstruct the junior science syllabus in consultation with the science teachers, to use some new curriculum materials such as ASEP, and to improve contact between staff through regular meetings. However for the new methods to be applied it was recognized that the school's stock of apparatus needed to improve dramatically and the old science rooms needed renovation.

While Casterbridge High School had an adequate number of science rooms but little else some schools had made most concerted efforts to make the maximum possible use of their facilities. One such was Western College.

However, even the best intended efforts were curtailed by some aspects of the facilities available.

Western College : Making Do

Not all non-government schools were completely adequately supplied with rooms. Western College was a boys school in an industrial area of a major city. It enrolled 900 students but its retention to Year 11 was 60 percent and to Year 12, 43 percent.

Four science rooms were provided at Western College under the Science Facilities Program; two were completed in 1967 and two more in 1971. In addition some $8000 was allocated from the Program for the purchase of apparatus. With 125 50-minute periods to be accommodated the school just did not have sufficient science rooms. Given a 30-period teaching week the school ought to ideally have six, or at least five, rooms. It was not recommended for additional science accommodation in 1971, though it was included on a list of schools likely to develop needs for additional accommodation.

The rooms were of good quality if of an older design. All except the 'Physics' room had long fixed benches across the room. The Physics room had fixed pillars with movable benches thus allowing great flexibility of arrangements. Since the rooms were all located close to each other it was relatively easy for apparatus to be shifted between rooms when necessary. This was especially important as Western College had no laboratory assistant.

Every effort had been made to ensure that classes were in science rooms as much as possible. The school timetabled separately for Years 7, 8, 9, and 10 and Years 11 and 12. As a result there were no lunch and recess breaks common to all classes. At almost every available time all science rooms were used: there were but two times each week when one science room was not used. Even so two-thirds of the Year 7 science lessons were not able to be held in science rooms.

The school made considerable efforts to engage its junior students in active science learning. ASEP units were used extensively, though not exclusively, in Years 7 to 10. A number of JSSP units were also available but these were not used as much. Generally a good range of basic equipment was available for this teaching though there were specific shortages of such instruments as microscopes.

In spite of the school's attempt to fully use the facilities available to it some problems existed. There were apparently difficulties which were hard to overcome in this situation. For Year 7 students the lack of access to science rooms affected the way science was taught to them. One teacher, in response to a question of whether this made a difference to teaching science, expressed the view that:

> It does really. With Form One, I find it much harder to take a period of all theory. I prefer most lessons to be fairly practical and it is a bit difficult getting equipment from a science room down to an ordinary classroom. I do less practical with them.

His colleague concurred. Teaching Year 7 was very difficult but even teaching Year 9 was difficult because the rooms were in such constant use. The excessive use of the rooms meant that it was hard to prepare.

For preparation its difficult. We've also a broken timetable: the junior school, intermediate school and senior school work on different timetables so that in my lunch time I can't get into a science room to prepare for my lesson coming up. However we're well-equipped with trolleys in the preparation rooms and I put the equipment on the trolleys.

The trolleys were extensively used but because no laboratory assistant was employed some store rooms became a little disorganized. An arrangement which the school called 'team teaching' was employed in Years 9 and 10. In practice this meant that teachers specialized in Biology, Physics, and Chemistry and classes rotated each term. It allowed rooms to be set up for those respective sub-disciplines. Such an arrangement was convenient for teachers who had heavy teaching loads. It also helped obviate some of the problems of having too few science rooms and no laboratory assistant. Whether it was an ideal arrangement for students was arguable. The pattern of organization in Years 9 and 10 was consistent with the observation made by Brown (1977): when facilities were scarce it was easier to organize the teaching of separate science subjects than to teach science as an integrated study of a discipline. This school appeared to regard it as a compromise. At Year 7 and Year 8 a general science teacher took classes through the whole year.

The other problem was that staff were often rushed. Lack of adequate space in which to prepare exacerbated the difficulties created by heavy teaching loads and lack of laboratory assistance.

Given a situation with insufficient science rooms it took considerable effort to organize so that the maximum use was gained from them. It was also indicative of a general purposefulness in the teaching program that the school was attempting to teach the type of course that was considered appropriate. The enthusiasm of at least some staff was evident in the strong electronics club at the school. Physics materials and the Physics laboratory were used by this group which had been organized by a teacher who was an amateur radio enthusiast. At the time of the visit to the school an attempt was being made to construct an electric car. The Friday evening meetings of the electronics club even involved many parents.

The program of science teaching at Western College was one in which concerted attempts were made to teach active, involving science courses. In teaching that program throughout the school teachers were hampered by a shortage of rooms and a lack of laboratory assistants. They were forced to make do with what was available.

The Schools : A Resumé

In the studies made of the schools described in this chapter, differences in the approach to teaching science were observed. Many of these differences seemed to be best attributed to differences in staff, the influence of State authorities, the need to take account of local conditions, and skill of the science co-ordinator. However, the facilities available for teaching science were also influential. The standard of facilities affected the range of options available to science teachers when planning courses. In addition, the morale of science teachers, and the organization of science departments seemed to be influenced by the facilities available.

The influence of the standard of science facilities on the range of choices available to teachers was illustrated by the contrast between Ruraton and Riversdale High Schools. Ruraton High School had an adequate number of good science rooms. Teachers chose to promote active forms of learning in science through enquiry methods. By contrast at Riversdale High this option was not available. Lack of appropriate accommodation circumscribed teaching methods. Didactic approaches to teaching science were unavoidable in these circumstances. Casterbridge High provided another contrast to Ruraton. It had an abundance of science laboratories, though many were of poor quality, but it had chosen not to use enquiry-based teaching methods. Casterbridge differed from Ruraton in having both a high staff turnover and a rather disorganized science department. It had received very little encouragement to embark on more stimulating courses of science.

Western College persisted with modern science curricula in spite of inadequate science accommodation. However, the lack of sufficient accommodation prevented adequate preparation of lessons and restricted opportunities to maintain rooms. Petrin High was observed before and after it occupied new science rooms. Even though the courses it offered did not change dramatically, and teachers maintained similar intentions with regard to science teaching, some subtle changes occurred. Teachers reported that they were better organized, that they made more use of impromptu demonstrations, and that their students were more responsive. In brief it seemed that while the formal curriculum had not altered, there appeared to have been changes in the science lessons which students experienced.

It appeared that good science facilities were of definite assistance to science teachers. Teachers working under poor conditions expressed frustration at the restrictions they faced. Where facilities were either insufficient or of poor quality teachers were frustrated in their attempts to implement the courses they thought desirable. Their counterparts in schools with good facilities were able to teach more easily and waste less time on organizational aspects of science teaching. Several experienced members of Science Teachers Associations expressed the view that an important effect of the Science Facilities Program was an increased sense of professionalism amongst science teachers. This view was illustrated during visits to Valley and Orchard High Schools. Both had recently been provided with new science accommodation. The new accommodation was of notably better quality than what had been at the school previously. It was interesting that at these schools older rooms were being renovated to make them more comparable with the new ones. New and better storage facilities had enabled more effective organization of school resources. A more co-ordinated use of new curriculum materials in junior science had been introduced. Presumably these observations were manifestations of some undefined change within the science department. Things which had not been of high priority now seemed worth doing.

The visits to schools provided evidence that the standard of science facilities did influence the teaching of science. Of course good facilities were not the only factor in shaping the science teaching patterns in schools. But, they did set limits within which choices could be exercised. When those limits were too narrow, choice was limited and frustration was apparent.

CHAPTER TEN

TEACHER RETENTION AND STUDENT ENROLMENTS

Introduction

Two anticipated effects of the Science Facilities Program which have not yet been discussed concern the retention of teachers and the enrolment patterns of students.

It was noted in Chapter Two that an enduring criticism of the Science Facilities Program was that it lavished funds upon material facilities without devoting similar attention to the retention of better qualified science teachers. However, it has also been observed that some people associated with the Program hoped it would break the self-perpetuating cycle in science teaching : poor facilities, low morale, high staff loss and unsuitable curriculum materials. Specifically it was hoped that an improvement in facilities would lead to better qualified scientists being attracted to teaching, and remaining longer in schools.

When the Science Facilities Program legislation was first introduced to the Federal Parliament, mention was made of the need to attract greater numbers of young people to scientific and technical careers. It was assumed that improved facilities would serve that end. In fact in every State the proportion of senior students enrolled in physical sciences has declined over the period of the Program. This in spite of the improved facilities. Yet, superimposed on this general trend, there were perturbations: differences existed between States, school systems and schools. It is possible that the provision of good facilities influenced such fluctuations.

Science Teachers in Australian Schools

The Qualifications and Sex of Science Teachers

The teachers about whom the information used in this section of the report was obtained were all teachers of science in the sample schools during 1975. A teacher of science was defined as a person who taught a science subject on a regular basis in that year. The term science subject included Science (multistrand, combined or general), any one or more of Physics, Chemistry, Biology, Human Biology, or Geology, Agricultural or Rural Science, Environmental Science, or science included in a General Studies Program. It did not

Table 10.1 Percentage of Science Teachers with a Completed Tertiary Qualification in Science (Survey Sample of Schools, 1975)

	Government	Catholic	Independent	Total
ACT	83 (73)	70 (59)	100 (100)	82 (74)
New South Wales	80 (61)	66 (49)	81 (73)	77 (59)
Victoria	90 (62)	72 (56)	89 (68)	87 (61)
Queensland	67 (53)	61 (45)	71 (63)	67 (52)
South Australia	81 (61)	64 (43)	74 (67)	79 (60)
Western Australia	66 (55)	75 (61)	80 (63)	68 (56)
Tasmania	86 (60)	44 (40)	92 (80)	79 (57)
Australia	80 (58)	67 (40)	83 (69)	78 (59)

Notes :   The Figures in parentheses are the percentages of teachers who held Bachelor or higher degrees.

The number of teachers involved was 3127.

include Domestic Science or Geography. Defined in this way the teachers concerned would have constituted those staff normally considered to form the science department of a school.

The sample used in the survey of science facilities was a sample of schools, not teachers. However, because the schools were selected with a probability proportional to size it was considered appropriate to use the school as the unit of analysis. Data were aggregated by school and then the school means were used to estimate values of the various parameters for States and systems. Since the schools were selected with a probability proportional to size, this method avoided any bias which would have emphasized schools with only a few teachers.

At the time the Science Facilities Program began it was difficult to staff secondary schools with teachers qualified in science. As noted in Chapter One, more than one teacher in three lacked any scientific qualification. The data which are recorded in Table 10.1 indicate the percentage of science teachers in the group surveyed who were qualified in science. Qualified in science was taken to mean a completed tertiary science qualification. A narrower view would include only those teachers holding a Bachelor or higher degree in science or a related field. Because of the diversification of tertiary education in recent years it was considered more appropriate to encompass all tertiary science qualifications. However, the proportion of teachers who held Bachelor or higher degrees has been included in parentheses.

Table 10.2 Percentage of Science Teachers in 1975 who were Female
(Survey Sample of Schools, 1975)

	Government	Catholic	Independent	Total
ACT	42	55	64	49
New South Wales	29	42	58	32
Victoria	29	45	33	32
Queensland	20	36	33	23
South Australia	26	45	39	29
Western Australia	21	32	34	24
Tasmania	22	33	32	33
Australia	26	41	40	30

A one way analysis of variance suggested that the difference between school systems was significant ; Catholic schools had fewer qualified science teachers than Government or Independent schools. Also significant was the difference between States, with fewer science teachers from Queensland and Western Australia having completed tertiary qualifications in Science.

While it appears that the supply of qualified science teachers in Australian schools is now much better than in the early sixties, it would be naive to attribute this to improved facilities. Far more likely contributors to this change have been a decline in other employment opportunities for scientists, increased salaries for teachers and expanded teacher training programs.

It is interesting to note, in passing, that the profession of science teaching still contains a majority of males. In 1961, when the Science Teachers Association survey was conducted, 30 percent of science teachers were female (Keeves, 1961). Data collected by Rosier (1973a) in 1970, suggested that some 36 percent of science teachers were then female. The information collected in 1975 indicates a national average of one third of science teachers were females. As the samples from which these data were derived were not strictly comparable, the figures should not be taken to indicate trends. Rather, they do suggest that the proportion of science teachers who were female has remained relatively stable over the years. Table 10.2 records the percentage of science teachers who were female, for each State and school system. The differences between school systems were significant : there was a smaller percentage of female science teachers in government schools. It is also interesting to note the difference in the government school systems of each State. A different balance of sexes in the Australian Capital Territory is particularly noticeable.

Table 10.3 Number of Years Teaching Experience of Science Teachers
(Survey Sample of Schools, 1975)

	Government	Catholic	Independent	Total
ACT	7.0	6.7	4.6	6.5
New South Wales	7.3	9.2	11.5	7.9 (8.5)[a]
Victoria	6.1	8.1	12.4	7.0 (8.7)
Queensland	6.0	11.7	11.2	7.3 (8.8)
South Australia	5.7	10.9	9.1	6.4 (7.0)
Western Australia	6.9	11.2	10.1	7.7 (8.6)
Tasmania	7.6 (6.7)[b]	14.9	12.3	8.4 (10.2)
Australia	6.6	9.6	11.2	7.4 (8.5)

Notes : a Figures in parentheses are for 1970 as reported by Rosier (1973a).

b This includes teachers in Matriculation Colleges. If they were not included the value recorded would be 6.7. This value agrees with that reported by Butler (1977).

The Experience and Mobility of Science Teachers

Other characteristics of the science teaching profession about which data was collected in 1975 were the years of teaching experience and mobility of teachers. The only data from the early sixties which was available was that presented in the report of the Australian Science Teachers Association survey (Keeves, 1966). On the basis of information tabulated in that report it was possible to estimate that teachers in the sample had been teaching for an average of ten years. Further information, which referred to 1970, was published as a result of the IEA study of science achievement (Rosier, 1973a). This suggested an average teaching experience of some eight-and-one-half years. The results of the survey conducted in 1975 have been recorded in Table 10.3. On average science teachers in that year had been teaching for seven-and-one-half years.

Butler (1977), in an examination of the experience of Tasmanian science teachers between 1970 and 1975, found results which paralleled this national change.

In 1975, the differences between States were not significant but those between school systems were. Science teachers in Independent schools were more experienced than their counterparts in Catholic or Government schools.

Table 10.4   Number of Years at Present School
             (Survey Sample of Schools, 1975)

	Government	Catholic	Independent	Total
ACT	2.2	3.0	3.1	2.6
New South Wales	3.2	3.3	7.2	3.3
Victoria	3.2	3.1	7.0	3.5
Queensland	3.1	3.9	6.5	3.4
South Australia	2.9	4.0	5.0	3.1
Western Australia	2.6	2.9	4.7	2.8
Tasmania	3.2	3.1	6.3	3.3
Australia	3.1	3.3	6.4	3.3

The mobility of science teachers is probably even more important than the length of their teaching experience. Rosier and Williams (1973 :19) noted that :

> For a teacher of science coming to a new school, time is also needed to gain familiarity with the equipment available in the school laboratories, and with the ecology of the local environment.

The problems associated with high mobility extend further. Rosier and Williams (1973 : 17) commented on the difficulties created in relation to school-based assessment procedures. Even greater difficulties would be created for school-based curricula. If innovations are to be soundly implemented they would need to be followed through and modified by those responsible for their introduction.

Rosier and Williams (1973) made a longitudinal study of the IEA sample of teachers from 1970 to 1972. From those results it was possible to estimate that some 65 percent of the teachers sampled in 1970 were still at the same school in 1971 and some 45 percent remained for at least one further year. This corresponded to an average time in a school of a little less than four years (Rosier, 1973). Rosier and Williams (1973) also found that while Government and Catholic schools had similar levels of staff stability, the Independent schools had much more stable staffs. This was attributed to their greater autonomy in appointing staff.

The average number of years the science teachers sampled had been at their present schools in 1975 can be seen in data which are recorded in Table 10.4. No suggestion of a greater stability could be inferred from that data.

The pattern of lower stability in Government and Catholic schools and greater stability in Independent schools was repeated and the differences between States were not significant. In fact the data in Table 10.4 suggest that the mobility of science teachers in 1975 was a little greater than it had been in 1970. It ought to give cause for concern that this situation prevailed at a time when there was considerable devolution of authority for the science curriculum to schools.

Factors Associated with High Stability of Staff

An AID analysis was used to examine the differences between schools in the mobility of science staff. In particular this analysis was used to test whether better facilities were associated with greater staffing stability. The principles underlying the AID were discussed in Chapter Six. In the present application the criterion being analysed was staffing stability measured as the mean number of years science staff had been at their present school. State, school system, location, coeducational status, and type of school were entered as non-monotonic (nominal) variables. The availability of science rooms (Q_1), the availability of dual purpose rooms (Q_2), average room quality, the abundance of apparatus, the provision of laboratory assistants, the proportion of rooms built under the Science Facilities Program, the proportion of science lessons not in science rooms, and the sex composition of the school were entered as monotonic (ordinal or interval) variables. The splitting pattern which resulted has been recorded in Figure 10.1.

As expected the first split, which was that accounting for most difference between schools, was between Independent and either Government or Catholic schools. Consistent with Table 10.4, Independent schools had more stable staffs. Among Independent schools the next division was between boys schools and those schools which were either coeducational or girls schools. Science teachers at boys schools had been at their present school for longer. For both boys and other Independent schools the final split was made on the basis of State. Victorian and Tasmanian schools of both categories had longer retention of their staffs while Queensland Independent schools of both groups had more mobile science staffs.

For Government and Catholic schools the pattern of splitting was more complicated. This group of schools split initially between those with 75 percent or more of their science rooms having been provided since 1964 and those with less than that proportion of new rooms. At first glance it

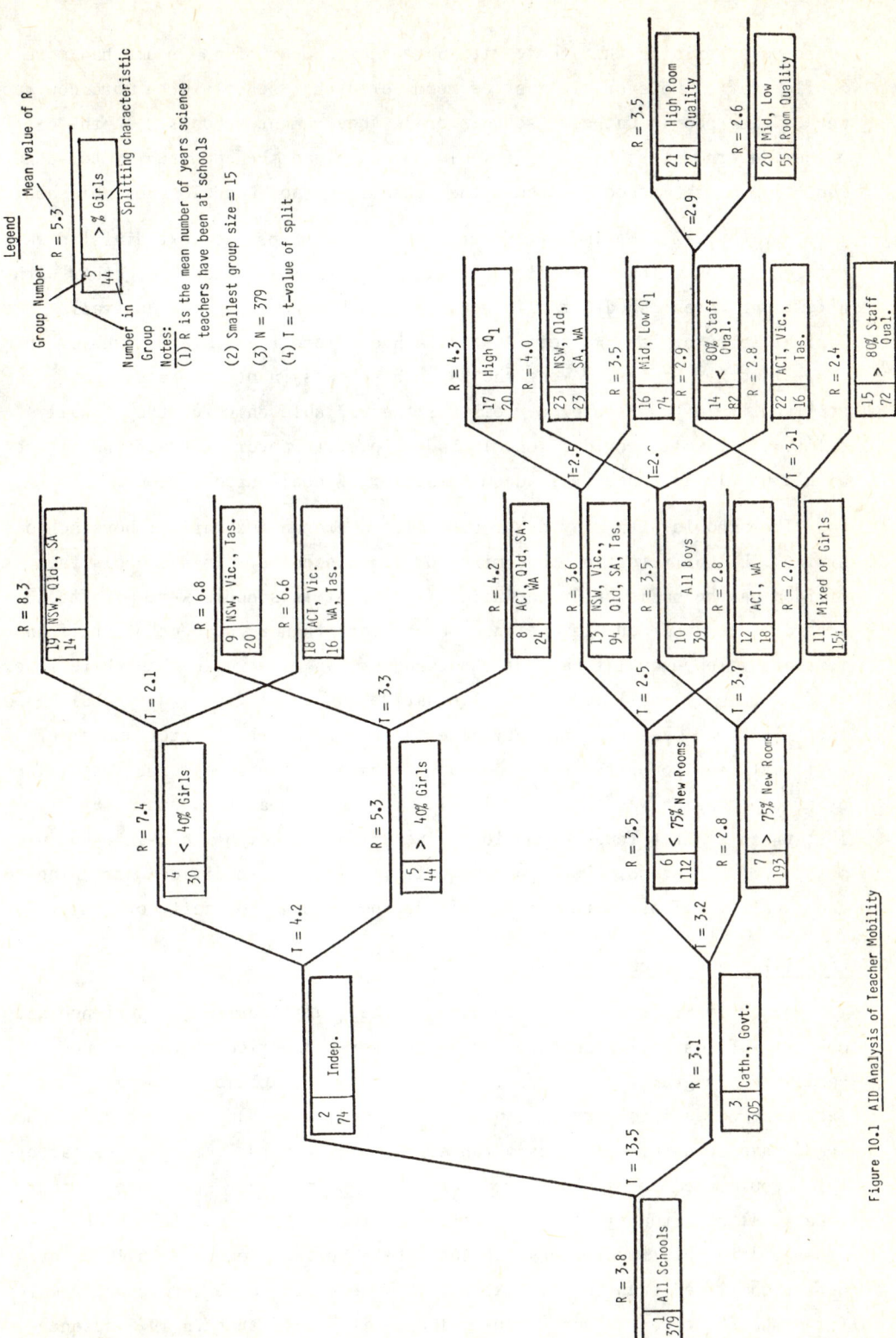

Figure 10.1 AID Analysis of Teacher Mobility

appeared surprising that those with a greater number of new rooms had more mobile staff. However, it must be remembered that schools with more new rooms were either poorer Catholic schools or new Government schools. In the case of new Government schools staff would not have had the opportunity to spend much time at the schools because the schools had not been long established.

For the 112 schools with fewer new science rooms the next division was between States. Those schools were mainly Government schools together with a few long established Catholic schools. Such schools in the Australian Capital Territory and Western Australia had a more rapid staff turnover than those in other States. Among the 94 such schools in other States the availability of dual-purpose rooms was the variable on which they finally split. Very well provided schools had a lower turnover of staff than those with a barely adequate or inadequate number of dual-purpose rooms.

The schools with many new rooms split again on sex ratio : boys schools having a higher retention than mixed or girls schools. Boys schools then divided on the basis of State while mixed or girls schools were partitioned according to staff qualifications. Where more than 80 percent of staff had tertiary science qualifications the turnover was more rapid than where fewer staff were well qualified. Two alternative interpretations were possible for this. One was that the very newest schools had the greater number of well qualified young teachers who had not been at the school for long. The other explanation was that schools with more well qualified staff may have lost those staff through promotion. The 82 relatively new non-Independent, mixed or girls schools with some unqualified staff were divided according to room quality. Those with better science rooms retained staff for longer.

Facilities and Teacher Mobility

It was not possible to relate changes in the qualifications, experience and mobility of Australian science teachers, over the period of the Science Facilities Program, to changes in the standard of facilities. Apart from the fact that no satisfactory initial data existed, any changes which had occurred would have been influenced by a range of other factors. Among those factors which would need to be considered were changes in salary structures, other vocational opportunities, and promotion policies. In fact, the evidence presented in this report suggests that while science teachers in 1975 were better qualified than in the sixties, they were less experienced and remained for a shorter time in each school. Indeed it seemed that in 1975 science teachers were less experienced and more mobile than in 1970.

The AID analysis of teacher mobility in a sample of schools in 1975 suggested that facilities were not a major factor associated with the propensity of science teachers to move from one school to another. However, in two sets of circumstances aspects of facilities were associated with teacher mobility. Firstly, among older non-Independent schools a few schools very well provided with science rooms were distinguished by having low teacher mobility. Secondly, better quality science rooms were associated with less staff mobility in the relatively new non-Independent schools which were either coeducational or for girls. Even though the standard of science facilities did not appear to be a major influence on staff mobility, in general these cases are worth noting. In interviews with science teachers differences of opinion emerged. The standard of facilities in a school were a factor considered by some teachers when they contemplated changing schools; but for other teachers such matters were not considered important.

Teachers Attitudes to Science Teaching

The possibility existed that teachers in schools with good facilities had a different attitude to science teaching than those who had poor facilities available. Such a proposition is akin to that postulated by Englehardt (1968); facilities influence teaching methods not just by limiting some activities but by suggesting other possibilities. While no data was collected as part of the Science Facilities Project about this aspect it was possible to use some of the data collected during the IEA study of science achievement (Comber and Keeves, 1973).

As part of the IEA study science teachers completed an attitude-to-science-teaching scale. A copy is included in Appendix I. This 10-item scale attempted to measure the degree to which teachers regarded enquiry based learning as important in science. Very little information about facilities in schools was obtained during the IEA study. However, it was possible to use the variety of sources described in Chapter Three to find out the number and type of science rooms in the schools at that time. This data was merged with the IEA Population IV (Year 12) data and then aggregated by school. The reliability of the scale was calculated using the school means for each item. A value for the coefficient alpha of 0.78 was obtained. This seemed to indicate a satisfactory internal consistency.

It was possible to obtain data from which to calculate room availability for science periods taught, room abundance per 1000 students, and the proportion of new commonwealth rooms in the school (as a surrogate for room quality). These were used in a correlation analysis, the results of which

Table 10.5 Teachers Attitudes to Teaching Science - A Correlational Analysis (IEA Population IV Sample, 1970)

Facilities Variable	Correlation Coefficients with Teacher Attitude[a]	N (Schools)
Q_1 - Science Rooms for Science Periods	-12	161
Q_2 - Laboratories for Science Periods	-09	161
L_1 - Science Rooms/1000 students	-13*	193
L_2 - Laboratories/1000 students	-15*	193
Proportion Commonwealth rooms	-14*	193

Notes: a Decimal points have been omitted.
       * $p < .05$

are reported in Table 10.5. The correlation coefficients in that table are either not significantly different from zero or barely significant. This suggests that teachers attitudes to science teaching were not strongly associated with the facilities available. If anything it seems that teachers in schools with fewer, and older, science rooms were more favourably disposed to enquiry teaching which involved students actively. This may have been due to the frustration of being restricted increasing the desire to do what was not possible. The most plausible interpretation of these data was that the provision of new rooms probably enabled teachers to do what they felt to be appropriate, rather than changed their attitude to science teaching.

Student Enrolments in Science Subjects

Changes Over Time

One early expectation concerning the Science Facilities Program was that improved facilities would attract an increased number of students to the study of science. Since that Program began there has been a much publicized decline in the proportion of Year 12 students choosing to study the physical sciences (Fensham, 1970; Lee Dow, 1971; White, 1973). It would appear that the changing subject choices of senior students in Australian schools reflects, though in diminished intensity, the swing from science which the Dainton Report (1968) documented in Britain. However, the changed pattern of subject choice should not be characterized as simply a swing from science; for Biology has become an extremely popular subject. It is interesting to note that both White (1973) and Lee Dow (1971) suggested that the swing in popularity was not to the humanities but to such social sciences as economics. The improvement of material facilities through the Science Facilities Program was not associated with an increase in the popularity of the physical sciences, though Biology did become more popular over this time.

A recent British review (Entwistle and Duckworth, 1977) of students choice of science subjects in senior secondary school concluded that the swing from science was at least partly due to changes in the composition of the senior secondary school. This may also be the case in Australian schools.

> It thus appears that at least part of the swing away from science may be attributed to the changing nature of the sixth form. More girls, more less-able pupils and a greater variety of subjects and subject-combinations will all reduce the proportion of scientists without any necessary change in pupils attitudes to science. (Entwistle and Duckworth, 1977:67).

The relative proportions of Year 12 students studying particular subjects have often been taken as an indication of the popularity of those subjects. Brenton (1976) argued that changes in the composition of the Year 12 population need to be considered when interpreting changes in such indices over time. The retentivity of schools had increased since the sixties and many more girls than previously now completed a full secondary education (Rowlands, 1976). Brenton was concerned with enrolment trends in Victoria and used both the relative proportions of Year 12 in each subject and the absolute numbers enrolled in those subjects. The combination gave a clearer picture of trends than either by itself. These data have been recorded in Table 10.6. While the decline in the relative popularity of Physics and Chemistry was apparent, so was the fact that absolute enrolments had not declined dramatically. A decline in absolute enrolments would represent a marked fall in popularity.

White (1973) argued that an appropriate index of changes in subject enrolments was the proportion of the relevant population who enrolled in that subject. The relevant population was the grade cohort which began secondary school together. As there was not sufficient data available White (1973) used the Year 10 enrolments from two years earlier as an approximation to the size of the grade cohort. Since losses from the school system had already occurred before Year 10 that figure was not equal to the grade cohort. An alternative approach used in the present study was to estimate the proportion of the grade cohort in each subject (G) by using the relative proportion of Year 12 (P) in that subject and the retentivity of the system (R).

$$G = PR$$

Table 10.6   Enrolments in Science Subjects from 1964 to 1975 in Victoria

Subject	1964 N	1964 P	1964 G	1968 N	1968 P	1968 G	1972 N	1972 P	1972 G	1975 N	1975 P	1975 G
Biology	2100	20	4.0	3700	25	6.5	7300	36	11.9	9700	42	14.7
Chemistry	4100	38	7.6	5300	36	9.4	6000	30	9.9	6400	28	9.8
Physics	4100	40	8.0	5400	37	9.6	5800	29	9.6	5600	24	8.4

Notes :   N = Total number of students taking subject for Higher School Certificate.

P = Percentage of Higher School Certificate students taking subject.

G = Percentage of Grade Cohort from Year 7 taking subject in Higher School Certificate.

Source : Brenton (1976)

The data presented by Brenton (1976) for Victoria was able to be used in this way and values of G, for four years between 1964 and 1975, have been recorded in Table 10.6. Over this period of time Physics and Chemistry attracted a little less than 10 percent of those who entered secondary school. While in the case of Physics there was a small decline between 1972 and 1975, the proportion of the grade cohort enrolled in Chemistry has been remarkably constant. Apparently these physical sciences have consistently attracted a little less than one-tenth of the grade cohort. The decline has been relative : enrolments in these subjects have not increased as rapidly as school retentivity. By contrast Biology has grown very rapidly. Over the decade it has enrolled an increasing proportion of the grade cohort. It was the most popular Year 12 subject in Victorian schools during 1976 (Brenton, 1976).

The data in Table 10.6 referred only to Victoria. Comparable data for Western Australia have been recorded in Table 10.7. A similar pattern is apparent. Biology had increased its popularity substantially in both a relative and absolute sense. Physics and Chemistry were maintaining an enrolment of about one-eighth of the secondary school intake, though there was a slight decline between 1972 and 1975.

McKenzie (1976) has reported a decline in the absolute number of students enrolled in Physics and Chemistry at Year 12 level in Queensland. Though data were not available from which to calculate the proportion of the

Table 10.7　Enrolments in Science Subjects from 1965 to 1975 in Western Australia.

	1965			1968			1972			1975		
Subject	N	P	G	N	P	G	N	P	G	N	P	G
Biology	1366	45	8.9	2045	51	12.4	3483	62	18.5	4419	65	22.0
Chemistry	1405	46	9.2	1863	47	11.3	2513	44	13.3	2507	37	12.5
Physics	1708	57	11.2	2081	52	12.6	2487	44	13.2	2459	36	12.2
Human Biology	-	-	-	-	-	-	538	9	2.9	1788	26	8.9

Notes : N = Number of students enrolled in subject.

P = Percentage of Year 12 students enrolled in subject.

G = Percentage of grade cohort enrolled in subject.

Source : Education Department of Western Australia (1975)
Waddy (1976)

grade cohort which this represented it seems reasonable to assume that this also had declined. Accordingly Queensland showed a rather greater decline in physical science enrolments than Victoria or Western Australia. It also showed the similar remarkable growth in Biology.

On the basis of the analysis of enrolment trends in Western Australia and Victoria it is tempting to suggest that the swing from science would be better characterized as a failure of Physics and Chemistry to grow at the same rate as retentivity. The Queensland figures suggest a more substantial decline in that State. A more complete analysis of science enrolments in each Australian State is needed before a firm conclusion could be reached. A more complete analysis would take account of changes in sex ratio of enrolments in physical sciences (Rowlands, 1976) and the combination of other subjects which are taken with Physics and Chemistry. In Victoria the subject grouping which includes Physics, Chemistry and Mathematics is by far the most popular combination of subjects (VUSEB, 1975).

Differences Between Schools

An alternative approach to an examination of subject choices was to use a cross-sectional, rather than a longitudinal, analysis. The Science Facilities Project obtained data about student enrolments in science subjects in 1975. It was apparent that there were differences between school systems, and between schools within systems, in the propensity of students to enrol in science subjects. The percentage of Year 12 students enrolled in the main

Table 10.8 Percentage of Year 12 students Enrolled in Science Subjects
(Survey Sample of Schools, 1975)

	Biology	Chemistry	Physics	Other	- (Main Subject)
ACT[a]	41	23	23	24	Unit 2A Science[c]
New South Wales[a]	37	28	25	28	Unit 2A Science
Victoria	41	29	24	2	Ag. & Env. Science
Queensland	51	37	33	7	Zoology/Geology
South Australia	68(59)[b]	26	25	11	Earth Science
Western Australia	62	34	36	24	Human Biology
Tasmania	50	27	24	18	Geology

Notes : a   For the ACT and New South Wales only one-half of the schools were offering separate science subjects in 1975. The figures recorded refer to those schools and not those following Wyndham Science.

b   The figure in parentheses is the official figure (Sullivan, 1976). The difference is probably due to non-examination subjects.

c   Unit 2A Science is a multistrand course for non-science specialists.

science subjects in each State have been recorded in Table 10.8. These data have been derived from enrolment statistics obtained from the 1975 survey sample of schools. In this way some of the problems associated with using examination statistics (Lee Dow, 1971) have been avoided. As the differences between school systems were not significant, values for each school system within States have not been recorded. Differences between States were significant.

From the data in Table 10.8 it could be seen that there were differences in the pattern of enrolments between States. While Biology was the most popular science subject in every State it was extremely popular in South Australia and Western Australia. In Queensland and Western Australia, Physics and Chemistry attracted a greater proportion of students than elsewhere. Perhaps the greatest differences between States were in science subjects other than the big three. In Western Australia considerable numbers of students studied Human Biology while in Victoria very few students studied sciences outside the three main subjects. The smaller school size in Victoria probably restricted the range which could be offered to students. Half the schools in New South Wales were following the trial science syllabus which allowed choice between science sub-disciplines. As those schools had chosen to use this new approach, before it became universal in 1976, they

217

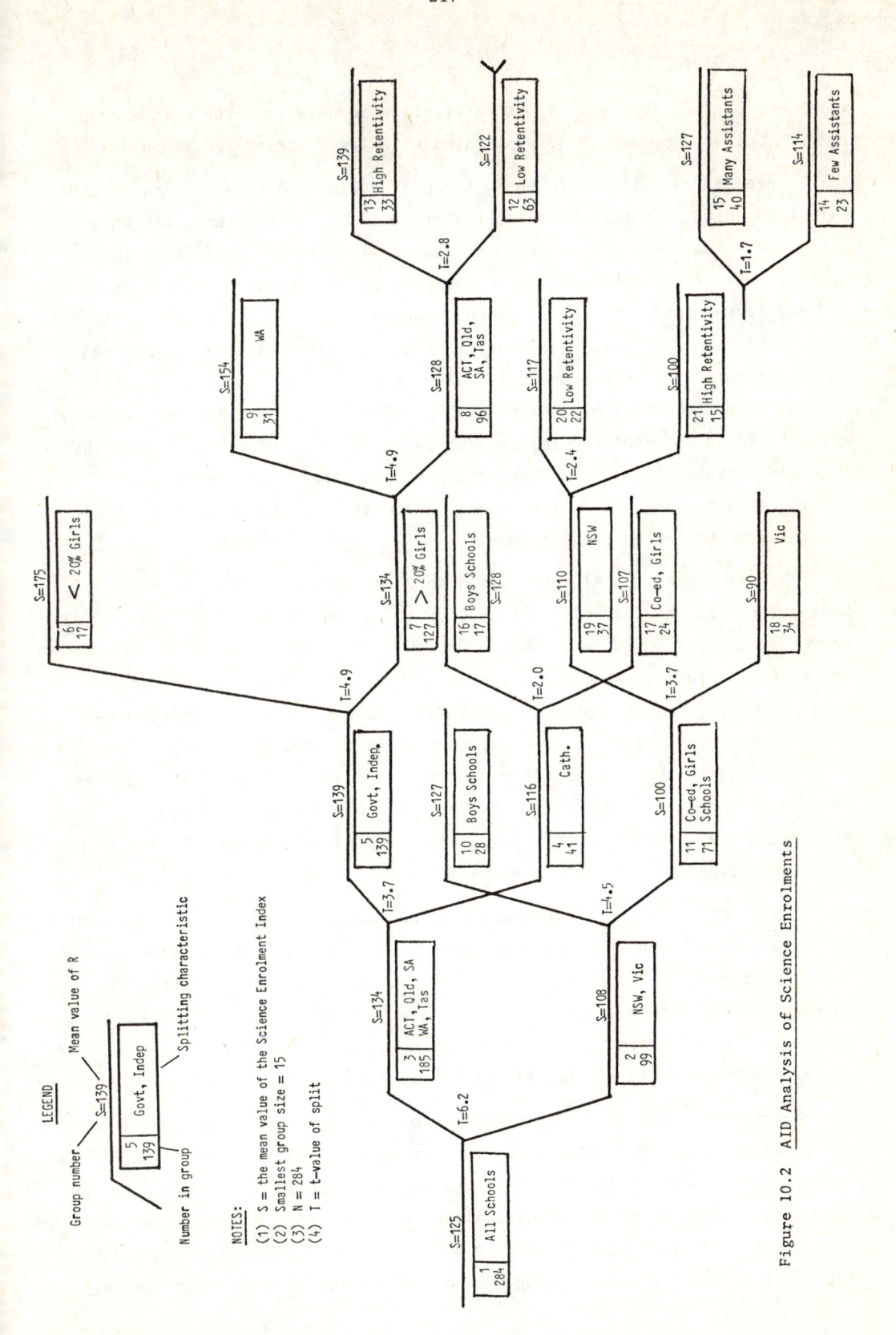

LEGEND

Group number ─── Mean value of R
           ╲   ╱
            S=139
          ┌───┬──────────────┐
          │ 5 │ Govt, Indep │
          ├───┼──────────────┘
          │139│
Number in group ──╯   ╲── Splitting characteristic

NOTES:
(1) S = the mean value of the Science Enrolment Index
(2) Smallest group size = 15
(3) N = 284
(4) T = t-value of split

Figure 10.2 *AID Analysis of Science Enrolments*

(Tree diagram contents:)

Group 1: All Schools, 284, S=125

T=6.2

Group 3: ACT, Qld, SA, WA, Tas, 185, S=134
Group 2: NSW, Vic, 99, S=108

T=3.7 (from group 3)
Group 5: Govt, Indep., 139, S=139
Group 4: Cath., 41, S=116

T=4.5 (from group 2)
Group 10: Boys Schools, 28, S=127
Group 11: Co-ed, Girls Schools, 71, S=100

T=4.9 (from group 5)
Group 6: < 20% Girls, 17, S=175
Group 7: > 20% Girls, 127, S=134

T=2.0 (from group 4 area)
Group 16: Boys Schools, 17, S=128
Group 17: Co-ed, Girls, 24, S=107

T=3.7 (from group 11)
Group 19: NSW, 37, S=110
Group 18: Vic, 34, S=90

T=4.9 (from group 7)
Group 9: WA, 31, S=154
Group 8: ACT, Qld, SA, Tas, 96, S=128

T=2.4 (from group 17)
Group 20: Low Retentivity, 22, S=117
Group 21: High Retentivity, 15, S=100

T=2.8 (from group 8)
Group 13: High Retentivity, 33, S=139
Group 12: Low Retentivity, 63, S=122

T=1.7
Group 15: Many Assistants, 40, S=127
Group 14: Few Assistants, 23, S=114

were probably not typical. It is interesting to note that the existence of Unit 2A Science appears to be associated with lower Biology enrolments.

Since States differed in the pattern of subjects available, and in the extent to which students chose particular subjects, further analyses were conducted using the Science Enrolment Index. This index was defined in Chapter Six. It was the weighted sum of all science subject enrolments divided by the total Year 12 enrolment. Hence it was equal to the average number of science subjects taken per Year 12 student. This index was used as the criterion in an AID analysis. The predictors entered included some non monotonic (nominal) variables - State, system, location and coeducational status - and some monotonic (ordinal or interval) variables - room availability, laboratory availability, room quality, apparatus abundance, provision of laboratory assistant, staff experience and qualifications and the sex composition and retentivity of the student body.

The results of the AID analysis have been represented in Figure 10.2. Most salient is the observation that facilities available did not account for many of the splits which were made. The variables which did account for the main split were State, sex and school system. The first split was made on the basis of State; Victoria and New South Wales having lower science enrolments than other States. This lower group then split according to the sex composition of the schools with boys schools having higher science enrolments than other schools. Finally, schools other than boys schools differed between the two States. Those in Victoria enrolled fewer students in science subjects than their counterparts in New South Wales.

In the other States, Government and Independent schools had significantly higher science enrolments than Catholic schools. Subsequent splits were made on the basis of the sex composition of the school, State and retentivity. Measures of facilities did not enter the analysis until the last split when, for a small group of schools with low retentivity, the provision of laboratory assistants was associated with higher science enrolments.

Since State differences in the Science Enrolment Index were significant and because State differences accounted for several splits made in the AID, a further analysis was made. States, rather than schools, were used as the unit of analysis, and the amount of time allocated to science in the junior secondary school was correlated with the values of the Science Enrolment Index. As Keeves (1976) points out by using such a unit of analysis many confounding

Table 10.9　A Between States Analysis of the Association Between Time Allocation to Science and Science Enrolment Index.　(Rank Order Correlation Coefficients)

	Time in Year 8	Time in Year 9	Time in Year 10	Science Enrolment Index
Time in Year 8		52	62	54
Time in Year 9			71	98
Time in Year 10				73

Note : Decimal points have been omitted.

influences can be controlled. For example differences in the retentivity to Year 12, and the sex composition of Year 12, are much smaller between States than between schools. Under these conditions the association between the amount of time allocated to junior science and the Science Enrolment Index at Year 12 was quite strong. Correlation coefficients have been reported in Table 10.9. The association with Year 9 science has been represented in Figure 10.3

Correlations, no matter how large, do not imply causality. It is possible that those States in which junior secondary science was emphasized were also those which provided encouragement for senior students to enrol in science subjects. However this result was consistent with some literature concerned with science interest and choice of subject. Ormerod and Duckworth (1975) cite evidence of the early age of arousal of interest in science and particularly identified an age corresponding to early secondary. The same authors mention that the perceived difficulty of science subjects was a deterrent to studying those subjects in senior secondary schools. Given Keeves (1976) conclusion that the amount of time spent in learning science was strongly correlated with science achievement, one is tempted to interpolate that students who spend little time in junior science do not acquire confidence in their ability to handle reputedly difficult science subjects.

Though this interpretation has been stated tentatively it does suggest that patterns of senior enrolments are as much influenced by science teaching in the junior school as by senior school curricula. It was shown in Chapter Six that the facilities provided under the Science Facilities Program were used more frequently by senior science subjects than junior science classes. Perhaps, if the facilities had been more generally made available to classes in Years 7 to 10, an impact on science enrolments might have been more noticeable.

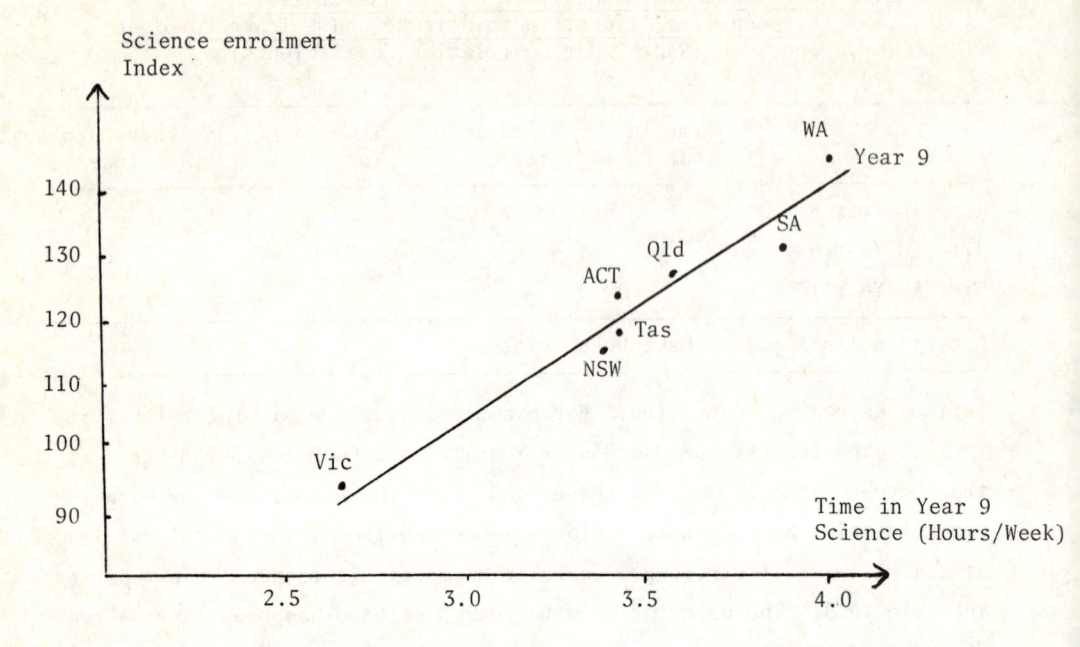

Figure 10.3. The Association between Science Enrolments and Time Allocated to Science

Summary

In brief there was only a little evidence found to support the proposition that the provision of facilities had diminished the mobility of science teachers. Nor was there much evidence to support the view that better facilities increased the propensity of students to study science subjects in the final year of secondary school.

Concerning the characteristics of the science teaching profession it was observed that though science teachers were now better qualified they were also less experienced than in the early sixties. The mobility of teachers appeared to have increased between 1970 and 1975. Considering schools in 1975 there was little association between the standard of their science facilities and the length of time which science staff had been at the school. Only in the case of a few schools was an association observed.

A between-schools analysis using the Science Enrolment Index as criterion failed to find any evidence to suggest that high science enrolments were associated with good facilities. However, a between-States analysis led to the suggestion that one reason for this may have been that new facilities were generally used more frequently by senior rather than junior students.

CHAPTER ELEVEN

IN   RETROSPECT

It would be rather difficult, and probably lead to an oversimplification, to make a single unequivocal judgment about the Australian Science Facilities Program. The context in which it operated was so varied and its aims were sufficiently broad to make a cautious analysis necessary. Consider the context of the Program. It applied in government and non-government schools in each State. As the governments of the States had the constitutional responsibility for the provision of education within each State there were differences in the educational milieu in which the Science Facilities Program was implemented. In addition, over the 11 years of the Program's duration many other educational and social changes occurred. A larger and more diverse range of students remained at school until Year 12, there was more extensive devolution of authority for curricula and management of schools, and the Commonwealth government was making additional forms of assistance available to schools. These, and many other changes, meant that the context in which the Science Facilities Program operated was not only different in each State but also changed with time.

The primary objective of the Science Facilities Program was clear. More, and better quality science facilities were to be provided in schools. It was the secondary aims expected to follow from the provision of good facilities, which were more ambiguous. As was argued in the early chapters of this report it was necessary to examine the statements of those implementing the Program to clarify what was meant by those who initiated the program. It was believed, by the Commonwealth government's consultants, that good science teaching should be well organized, involve pupils actively in learning science and be stimulating in the variety of experience it provided. Pupils' experimental work was regarded as an important aspect of science education which would be facilitated by making available good science rooms and sufficient apparatus. Hence it did appear that science teaching was expected to improve as a result of having better facilities. Furthermore it was believed that this would be manifested in changes in students' interests and achievement.

This report has attempted to examine the extent to which science facilities in schools were improved under this Program and some of the influences of the Program upon science education in Australia.

The Provision of Science Facilities

Science Rooms

As a broad generalization science accommodation was substantially improved during the course of the Science Facilities Program. Schools were provided with more science rooms and better quality science rooms.

Considering specifically those schools which already existed when the Program began, some three fifths of their present science rooms were added after 1964. Moreover the rooms provided under the Science Facilities Program were considered by teachers to be of better quality than other rooms in which science was taught. While not all science rooms built between 1964 and 1975 were provided under the Science Facilities Program a majority was so funded. Certainly most new science rooms in non-government schools were assisted, while nearly two-thirds of those built in government schools were provided under the Program. This included the new schools which were established during the period.

At the conclusion of the Science Facilities Program some deficiencies remained. About one school in ten had a deficiency of science rooms with an additional one in ten having a moderate deficiency. A deficiency was defined as having too few science rooms to accommodate every science lesson. Moderate deficiencies were such as would have necessitated too much use of science rooms if every science lesson was properly accommodated. Thus, most schools appeared to have adequate Science accommodation at the conclusion of the Program.

This conclusion cannot be presented without some qualifying comments. Some of the rooms included as science rooms were not fully equipped for students to do experimental work: often they had only a teacher's demonstration bench. If such rooms were not counted as science rooms then one in five schools would have to be considered deficient. The proportion would have been even larger if some of the poor quality science rooms in Queensland government schools were excluded. It would have been bigger still if Victorian schools devoted a similar amount of time to junior science as do other States.

A consequence of having sufficient science rooms available was that most science lessons were able to be conducted in science rooms. Only one in eight junior science lessons and one in twenty of the lessons in senior science subjects were not actually held in science rooms during 1975. In a few cases this was not so much because rooms were not available but because a choice had been made to use other school resources. However, not all of those rooms were necessarily of good quality. Sixteen percent of science co-ordinators regarded the laboratory facilities in their school as a significant impediment to practical work.

On a number of indicators government schools were less well provided with science accommodation than non-government schools at the conclusion of the Science Facilities Program. More government schools had insufficient science rooms for the lessons they taught, and more of them used demonstration rooms rather than fully equipped dual-purpose rooms. In addition science teachers in the older government schools were still using more of the rooms which had been present in 1964, than their counterparts in the non-government system. Specifically, while 90 percent and 73 percent of the science rooms in Catholic and Independent schools of this vintage had been added or renovated since 1964, the corresponding figure for government schools was only 59 percent. This condition was reflected in the opinions of science co-ordinators. Only three percent of those in Independent schools regarded laboratory facilities as a significant impediment to student experimental work. In Catholic schools 11 percent of the co-ordinators were of that opinion but 18 percent of those in government schools expressed that view.

It was difficult to use any objective measures to compare the conditions between States because of differences in the amount of science taught. States in which schools were among the best provided with laboratories appeared to have a shortage of laboratories for the amount of science taught. Hence, in South Australia a significant number of science lessons was not held in science rooms, even though the schools were well provided with rooms. By contrast, in Victorian schools few science lessons were held in non-science rooms even though a smaller number of science rooms was available to the school population. Different reasons appear to be behind the large number of science lessons held outside science rooms in Queensland. Resources appeared to be unevenly distributed between schools and more of the rooms available were of poor quality. It was the science co-ordinators of Queensland government schools who were most critical of their laboratory facilities. In 40 percent of the schools those facilities were regarded as an impediment to practical work.

In conclusion it appeared that while the Science Facilities Program had made a significant impact on the provision of science accommodation there remained some areas in which the task was not complete. The remaining problems would appear to be best solved by the expenditure of relatively small sums of money on the upgrading of demonstration rooms at present used for science teaching, and improving the quality of existing science rooms.

Apparatus

Between eight and 14 percent, depending on the school system, of the total money available under the Science Facilities Program was spent on the purchase of apparatus. It was even more difficult to identify what had come from the Facilities Program in the case of apparatus than buildings. For this reason it was only possible to comment on the provision of apparatus at the time the Program concluded.

Very few schools (five percent) reported frequent deficiencies in the supply of either 'expendable' or 'minor' apparatus. Rather more schools reported deficiencies in 'major' apparatus. Major apparatus was noticeably deficient in one fifth of the schools. However, lack of apparatus was not often regarded as a significant problem in practical work. Only eight percent of schools regarded it as a problem.

While this suggests a rather satisfactory picture a few reservations seem appropriate. The first is that the apparatus supply in schools was sometimes very specifically geared to a particular syllabus, thereby limiting the options available to the school. Secondly, some deficiencies in major apparatus caused great difficulties in particular fields of study. Microscopes were a notable example of this, for the study of some aspects of Biology was something made difficult by a shortage of these instruments. Thirdly, the apparatus stocks of schools may deteriorate quickly if supplies of expendable apparatus are not maintained and if other apparatus is not able to be maintained. While the Science Facilities Program enabled schools to build up a basic stock of non-consumable apparatus, any decline in funding below levels needed to maintain stock would be likely to have a deleterious effect on science teaching. Finally, while few schools reported frequent deficiencies a much larger number reported deficiencies some of the time. A possible method of handling such episodic deficiencies would be for schools in close proximity to each other to loan or share some items of equipment. Such a system has been suggested by the State Education Department to schools in South Australia.

One further need regarding science apparatus in schools is that for special items which are not available commercially. The Science Equipment Centre in Tasmania provides such a service for schools in that State. It develops apparatus for special purposes in schools, as well as for industry, and simultaneously provides training for skilled precision engineers. The portable laboratory benches which it constructs could provide a possible solution for those schools with immediate and pressing needs for better science rooms.

It seems that by 1975 most schools reported a good basic stock of minor apparatus for which replenishment and maintenance, rather than large additions, were needed. Lack of basic apparatus was the least frequently mentioned impediment to practical work. However, the lack of major items of apparatus continued to present a problem to a significant proportion of schools.

Other Aspects of Facilities

The Science Facilities Program was restricted to the provision of rooms and apparatus. It was not concerned with providing laboratory assistants who might have ensured that those facilities were fully utilized. Increasing numbers of laboratory assistants have certainly been employed by schools over the time of the Science Facilities Program but were acquired through other sources of finance. Catholic schools were not able to do this so extensively as Government and Independent schools. More than half of the Catholic schools in Australia reported that lack of assistance was an impediment to practical work. By contrast this was true of only 18 percent of the Government schools and 29 percent of Independent schools. The actual level of provision of laboratory assistance was lower in Catholic schools than in either Government or Independent schools. Government and Independent schools had approximately the same level of provision of laboratory assistance.

Assistance with the employment of ancillary staff would appear to be an important way of ensuring that expensive facilities were fully utilized. Such assistance seems particularly important in schools with limited financial resources. From the impressions gained during visits to schools it would appear that the mere employment of laboratory staff is not enough by itself. It needs to be supported by appropriate training programs, and by the development of management skills in science co-ordinators. The provision of laboratory assistance should not be restricted solely to the employment of relatively unskilled people to assist with routine work. In addition, there needs to be some staff with special technical skills, who are able to perform more difficult maintenance, repair and apparatus construction tasks, available to groups of schools. The type of planned, structured team of ancillary staff available to schools in Western Australia is one means by which this might be achieved.

It is interesting to note that lack of assistance was the most frequently reported impediment to practical work in Catholic and Independent schools. Lack of storage space and unsuitable laboratories were more frequently reported problems by government schools, though lack of assistance was still a widespread problem.

The Influence of the Science Facilities Program

The Influence on Educational Systems

Though the Australian Science Facilities Program was largely intended to assist the teaching of science in schools by providing better facilities in schools, it also influenced wider developments in science education. It was one factor influencing a number of changes which took place in educational systems over this time. These changes can be classified as either management changes or curriculum changes. Since the Program was applied in different educational systems in each State it is hard to generalize about this influence. Clearly other influences were also important and the degree to which the Science Facilities Program was important varied from one State to the other.

One general change which occurred in most government school systems was to allow schools more choice in the apparatus with which they were supplied. While this was a necessary adjunct to allowing schools more autonomy in curricula it was probably assisted by the Science Facilities Program. By making available more money, it enabled apparatus other than bare essentials to be provided. Early experiences resulted in the realization that schools were in the best position to make decisions about priorities in apparatus. A variety of different approaches was used across States but all had the common element of increasing the school's choice of apparatus. The Science Facilities Program was the first area in which many of these schemes were tried, though now they are often associated with general aspects of school funding.

A great deal more attention has been paid to the design of science rooms since the Science Facilities Program began. Not only have designs been improved, but in most States science educators have been involved in the planning process.

This probably has been the most widespread influence of the Program, even though it was the hardest to document. By making available large sums of money for science rooms, the Program enabled greater attention to be paid to designing science rooms which would suit modern science curricula.

The Science Facilities Program assisted the implementation of new science curricula in two ways. The first was the most direct and obvious. In several States money was made available from this source to provide schools with apparatus to trial and implement new courses such as PSSC Physics, Harvard Project Physics, Chem. Study Chemistry, and BSCS Biology. The assistance was probably not crucial, but it was certainly helpful. The second was a less direct influence. The existence of better science rooms and more abundant basic apparatus altered the context in which curriculum development could occur. Many curricula which were adopted in the late sixties and early seventies explicitly assumed that schools had good science facilities.

While the fact that funds were used to assist in the implementation of new curricula was beneficial, it does raise another issue. Recognition of the need to provide funds for curriculum development and implementation had come too late and provided too little. The ad hoc use of funds was welcome but a more formal and co-ordinated allocation of resources would have been better. The very fact that the Facilities Program was used in this way was an indication that insufficient attention had been paid to the total needs of science education.

The Influence on Science Teaching in Schools

From the study which was made of Year 9 science teaching in schools with varying standards of science facilities it seemed that better facilities were associated with an enriched learning environment and more active forms of science learning. An enriched learning environment was one in which there was greater involvement in purposeful activity, better organization and more stimulation in the variety of methods and materials used. Good quality rooms were most strongly associated with student reports of better organization, and more abundant apparatus was associated most strongly with students perceiving a more stimulating environment. Being frequently in science rooms, using rooms of good quality and having sufficient apparatus were all associated with a reported greater involvement of students in learning activities. Student reports of active forms of learning, defined as more experimental work, less textual learning, and greater encouragement to explore were also associated with better science facilities.

Observations made during visits to schools were consistent with the results of the statistical analysis of students' views. The standard of science facilities did influence the way in which science was taught. Even though changes were not dramatic they were observable. Science teachers certainly found it more convenient and efficient to teach actively when they had good facilities. While good facilities were neither a determining nor major factor shaping the science teaching patterns in schools, they were a component which set limits within which choice could be exercised. Schools made different uses of the facilities available to them. Rooms and apparatus were used most effectively when supported by skilled laboratory assistants, modern curriculum material and energetic science teachers.

It is necessary to exercise caution when generalizing from a cross sectional study to changes which occurred over time. However it did appear that the provision of good facilities through the Science Facilities Program generally facilitated the development of enriched learning experiences in science and nurtured more active forms of science learning. The extent to which such developments occurred also depended on other factors : good laboratory staff, good teachers and suitable curricula.

Other Influences

Two other possible influences of the Science Facilities Program were studied in this Report. One was the potential influence of facilities on students' propensity to enrol in science subjects while the other was the influence of facilities on the mobility of science teachers.

Facilities available in schools did not appear to be a major determinant of school science enrolments in Year 12. This result is not surprising as the propensity of students to enrol in science subjects is more likely to be associated with other factors, such as the extent to which students acquire the confidence to study difficult subjects. In so far as such choices can be influenced by schools, it seems likely that the amount, and quality, of science teaching which occurs in the lower secondary school is important.

Teacher mobility was not generally affected by the facilities available in schools though a few exceptions were noted. For some teachers it appeared that the standard of science facilities was an influence upon their decision to remain at a particular school. However, because so many other factors were also important the association observed was neither general nor strong.

In summary the Science Facilities Program appeared to influence some concomitant developments in science education across school systems. Good science facilities in schools were found to be associated with an enriched experience of science learning for students. In that respect the Australian Science Facilities Program enhanced the quality of science education in Australian schools.

The Origins of the Program

The Australian Science Facilities Program was not based upon the findings of a report which had identified the needs of science education. Rather, it arose as a response to a number of political developments. As Smart (1975) suggested, it was a response to three groups of demands, made in the context of long term changes in constitutional interpretation and short term political circumstance. Only one of the three groups of demands was concerned with special assistance for science teaching. The other two were more general requests for the Commonwealth to become involved in secondary education and for governments to assist non-government schools.

The absence of an initial investigation hindered the Program in several ways. The most fundamental was that insufficient analysis had been made of the nature of the plea for assistance to science teaching. Only a general area of concern had been identified. The response of government may have been more effective had some prior investigation been conducted. It was argued in Chapter One that improved facilities were but one aspect of the needs of science education in the early sixties. Certainly it must be recognized that, because the Program was the first Commonwealth venture into non-tertiary education, to provide facilities was politically safer. Yet, had the complementary needs of science education, which the Australian Science Teachers Association identified as involving curriculum development and teacher training, been formally recognized subsequent developments may have been better co-ordinated.

Even within the context of providing facilities some more detailed initial planning would have helped to guide priorities between different areas of school science. For example, it was noted earlier that there were two strands within the plea for special assistance to science teaching. One was utilitarian and concentrated upon the supply of scientific and technical manpower, while the other emphasized the role of science in a modern liberal education. The extent to which these two strands possessed common elements and the degree to which they were opposed were never explored. Furthermore, the emphasis and priority which ought to be given to each was not explicitly examined. By default the early endeavours of the Science Facilities Program were largely devoted to providing facilities for Physics and Chemistry classes in Year 12.

A more prosaic deficiency can be seen in the fact that the Program began without adequate information about the needs of schools for science facilities. While it was agreed that generally science was taught under parlous conditions, neither the relative needs of each school system in each State, nor the needs of individual schools were accurately known. Such information had to be accumulated as the scheme progressed. There were differences in the standard of science facilities between school systems in each State when the Program began. For non-government schools those differences which remained in 1971 were taken into account when the final quadrennium of the Program was being planned. The differences between government school systems were never officially acknowledged.

Not only did too little initial planning occur, but the opportunity for a formative evaluation was neglected. Several suggestions for formative evaluation were made during the mid sixties. There was support for some formative evaluation from both the Commonwealth Standards Committee and from officers in the Department of Education. It is regrettable that the Minister did not agree to make funds available for this purpose at a time when the resultant information would have been valuable in guiding the final stages of the scheme.

The Administration of the Program

Different administrative arrangements were made for government and non-government schools. In the case of government schools, funds were provided for each State Education Department who applied them to the secondary schools in that State. Each State authority was responsible for administering the scheme in regard to its government schools, subject to a number of constraining conditions. For non-government schools the general administration of the Program was carried out by Commonwealth government departments. The Commonwealth government was advised by two State Advisory Committees from each State, which advised on priorities for the allocation of funds, and a Commonwealth Advisory Committee on Standards for Science Facilities in Independent Secondary Schools. This latter committee advised the government on appropriate standards and assisted schools in the development of plans.

This administrative structure was a consequence of the constitutional provision that States were responsible for the provision of education. Therefore money had to be provided to schools through State governments. For non-government schools the State authorities merely transmitted money from the Commonwealth to schools; the effective administrative agency was the Commonwealth. The money allocated for government schools was administered by State Education Departments. As State governments jealously guarded their authority in this area, any attempt by the Commonwealth to circumvent that authority would have met opposition. It would have been politically unrealistic for the Commonwealth to act as an administrative agency for the Program with respect to government schools.

This bifurcated administrative structure had wider ramifications. Common standards were not applied to all schools, detailed information about the needs of government schools was not available to Commonwealth authorities, and the wisdom accumulated during the course of the Program was not readily shared. Relations between State and Commonwealth authorities with respect to provision in government schools were not always smooth. At the beginning of the scheme States were not fully consulted, during the Program they were obliged to operate within constraints determined by the Commonwealth, and they had to provide great detail about how money had been spent. Equally State authorities were unnecessarily reticent about providing the Commonwealth with information which would have helped in planning. In brief there was too little communication between the various authorities.

Government schools suffered as a result of these problems. In particular, the effect of the lower level of funding to government schools was never made obvious. The needs of government schools were not assessed by the same procedures as those of non-government schools. Hence, those needs were never clearly apparent to the Commonwealth. Since State Education Departments were not asked to assess needs according to common guidelines suitable information was not provided.

In retrospect some administrative structure which facilitated co-operation between State and Commonwealth authorities, and which helped the exchange of information between government and non-government systems, might have alleviated some of these problems. Any alternative structure would have to have been compatible with constitutional provisions and the established areas of responsibility. Within these limitations, a national policy advisory group, with a wider membership and broader terms of reference than the Commonwealth Standards Committee, would have been useful. If such a group had its members drawn from State Education Departments, as well as from non-government schools it could have assisted the Program greatly. That group could have recommended standards, monitored progress, and advised on policy for all schools. It could also have been responsible for conducting formative evaluations of the Program. Executive bodies could have implemented the Program in the light of guidelines suggested by the national advisory group. It need not have usurped the authority of State Education Departments, yet it could have provided for a more co-ordinated implementation of the Program.

At the State level two administrative reforms can be envisaged. The first concerns the involvement of government schools in the planning of science accommodation. In non-government schools the involvement of science staff and the Principal in the planning of new science facilities was a valuable exercise. It meant that those people were obliged to consider the ways that science subjects were being taught and also their planning of future developments. This reassessment occurred in the context of the immediate and practical task of planning a science teaching facility, and in consultation with an adviser who also visited many other schools. As a consequence the planning procedure proved to be a valuable in-service education exercise. Many State Education Departments now also consult school staff in planning facilities. It is a development which ought to be encouraged. The second administrative reform at State level concerns the degree to which co-operation might be achieved between school systems. In each State there were two State Advisory Committees, who determined priorities for non-government schools. It might have been possible for a single State Advisory Committee to involve representatives of non-government schools and the Education Department. Recommendations on priorities could then have been made to the State Minister for Education in the case of government schools and to the Commonwealth for non-government schools. Under such an arrangement there would have been an increased probability of an exchange of information and the potential for some shared use of expensive resources in rural locations.

A discussion of the administrative arrangements for the Science Facilities Program would not be complete without mentioning the method of allocating finance. Firstly, there was no justification in terms of the needs of schools for providing money to non-government schools at double the per capita rate as to government schools. Evidence presented in Chapter Four showed that State governments were not able to compensate for the difference. Secondly, the method of allocating funds between States and systems up to 1971 was inappropriate. This method divided funds first between government and non-government schools, on the basis of secondary enrolments, and then between States according to gross population. Such a method failed to take account of the differences between States in the proportion of students in each school system, the different Years at which secondary school commenced, the different retentivity and differences in the age structure of the population. If funds are to be divided between States and systems it should either be according to enrolments or the first division should be between States followed by division between systems.

A Concluding Comment

The Science Facilities Program had a considerable impact upon the resources available for teaching science. Within the limitations imposed upon the Program, it improved the standard of accommodation for science teaching in schools, and the abundance of basic scientific apparatus. Criticisms of the Program in this respect are mainly restricted to the observations that it was too narrowly limited to material facilities, and that less attention was given to meeting the needs of government than non-government schools.

As the cost of specialist facilities in school buildings continues to increase it will be necessary to demonstrate that those facilities have been well used. A recent report to the Commonwealth government stated its concern in a more general context.

> The relationship between resource levels and the quality of schooling as it is experienced by students and as it is manifested in measurable outcomes among them is another essential concern of the Commission (Schools Commission, 1975 : 16).

The present study has been concerned with material facilities and science education. On the basis of the evidence presented it is argued that while the provision of good facilities is unlikely to dramatically change school practices, it can foster better quality science learning. Such effects may be subtle but they are not trivial. The place of science in the curriculum, according to Whitfield (1971), is justified by its providing students with the experience of empirical enquiry. Developments in science teaching assumed that this was best achieved in an enriched learning environment, one which was well organized, involving and stimulating, with a variety of activities in which students participated in the direct observation of scientific phenomena. Good facilities, apparently, assisted these approaches to teaching science.

A brief conclusion could well be expressed by paraphrasing a statement from a recent report to the Commonwealth government (Schools Commission, 1975 : 13). Additional resources alone do not make good science teaching but adequate resources are a helpful condition for improvement. In so far as it went, the Australian Science Facilities Program assisted the development of science education in Australia. It would have been more effective had greater attention been given to other needs of science education.

References

Ainley, J.G. 'The Australian Science Facilities Program : A Study of Its
1976   Impact on Schools'. Bulletin of the Victorian Institute for Educational Research, 36, 17-39 (June).

Anders, D.J. 'The Necessity for General Science'. Australian Science
1959   Teachers Journal, 5, 1, 63-66.

Anderson, G.J. and Walberg, H.J. 'Assessing Classroom Learning Environments',
1974   in K. Marjoribanks, (ed). Environments for Learning. Slough, Britain : National Foundation for Educational Research.

Angus, M.J., Evans, K.W. and Parkin, B. An Observation Study of Selected
1975   Pupil and Teacher Behaviour in Open Plan and Conventional Design Classrooms. The Australian Open Area Schools Project, Technical Report No.4, Perth : Education Department of Western Australia.

Anthony, B.C.M. The Identification and Measurement of Classroom Environment
1967   Process Variables related to Academic Achievement. Unpublished Doctoral Dissertation, University of Chicago.

Arkansas State Department of Education. Science Guidelines for the Secondary
1966   Schools of Arkansas. Little Rock, Arkansas. ED 023 276.

Australian Academy of Science. Scientific and Technological Manpower Supply
1957   and Demand in Australia. Canberra : AAS.

Australian Science Education Project (ASEP). Guide to ASEP : Unit 401.
1974   Melbourne, Victoria : ASEP.

Australian Science Teachers Association. Australian Science Teachers Journal,
1955   1, 1.

Australian Science Teachers Association. Statement of Changes and Developments
1962   : The Effect of Our Teaching Upon Our Pupils. Melbourne:ASTA.

Australian Science Teachers Association. 'The Needs of Science Education in
1964   Australian Schools'. Australian Science Teachers Journal, 10, 1, 41-42.

Australian Science Teachers Association. Minutes of Federal Council Meeting;
1967   Held by M.J. Rosier (Secretary) at ACER.

Australian Science Teachers Association. Summary of Correspondence Regarding
Undated   an Australian Science Education Foundation. Mimeo, Prepared by J.P. Keeves, circa. August 1964.

Baas, A.M. Science Facilities. Educational Facilities Review Series No.11,
1973   ERIC Clearing House on Educational Management. ED 071 144.

Barker, E. 'A New Science Course in New South Wales'. Australian Science
1963   Teachers Journal, 9, 1, 39-48.

Basset, G.W. 'Towards a National System of Australian Education'.
1965   Australian Science Teachers Journal, 11, 2, 9-15.

Berndt, K.L. 1957. 'The Relation between Business and Industries and Science Teachers'. *Australian Science Teachers Journal*, 3, 2, 18-19.

Best, E.D. 1967. 'The Adaption of BSCS Biology in Australia'. *South Australian Science Teachers Association Journal*, March, 29-30.

Betjeman, K. 1974. 'Science Facilities in Western Australian Secondary Schools'. *Australian Science Teachers Journal*, 20, 3, 23-32.

Betjeman, K. 1975. *Design Brief for Senior High Schools - Flexible Area Secondary Schools for the 80's.* Perth, Western Australia : Education Department.

Bourke, J.E. 1969. 'Australian Catholic Schools into the Seventies'. *Quarterly Review of Australian Education*, 3, 2. Hawthorn, Victoria : Australian Council for Educational Research.

Bourke, J.E. 1974. 'Roman Catholic Schools'. In D.A. Jecks (ed). *Influences in Australian Education.* Perth : Carrolls Pty.Ltd.

Brenton, A.M. 1976. 'Senior Secondary Science Courses : Victoria'. *Australian Science Teachers Journal*, 22, 2, 102-106.

Britain, Council for Scientific Policy. 1968. *Enquiry into the Flow of Candidates in Science and Technology into Higher Education*, (The Dainton Report). London : HMSO, Cmnd 3541.

Brown, S.A. 1977. 'A Review of the Meanings of, and Arguments for, Integrated Science'. *Studies in Science Education*, 4 (1977), 31-62. Centre for Studies in Science Education, Leeds.

Butler, J.N. 1977. 'A New Statistical Picture of Tasmanian Science Teachers'. *Australian Science Teachers Journal*, 23, 1, 43-49.

California State Department of Education. 1964. *Science Curriculum Development in the Secondary Schools.* Report of the Statewide Advisory Committee on Science Instruction in the High School. California State Department of Education : Sacramento, California.

Carter, D.P. 1965. 'The Teaching of Physical Sciences in Girls Schools'. *Australian Science Teachers Journal*, 11, 3, 66-68.

Cohen, J. 1973. 'Eta-Squared and Partial Eta-Squared in Fixed Factor ANOVA Designs'. *Educational and Psychological Measurement*, 33, 107-112.

Coleman, J.S. et al. 1966. *Equality of Educational Opportunity*, Volumes I and II. Washington, D.C. : U.S. Government Printing Office.

Comber, L.C. and Keeves, J.P. 1973. *Science Education in Nineteen Countries.* Stockholm and New York : Almqvist and Wiksell and John Wiley and Sons.

Commonwealth of Australia, Committee on Australian Universities (Chairman : K.M. Murray). 1957. *Report.* Canberra : Government Printer.

Commonwealth of Australia, Commonwealth Advisory Committee on Standards for
1964-1975   Science Facilities in Independent Secondary Schools. <u>The Design of Science Rooms</u>. (Editions 1 to 5) Canberra : Australian Government Publishing Service.

Commonwealth of Australia. <u>Final Report of the Commonwealth Advisory</u>
1976   <u>Committee on Standards for Science Facilities in Independent Secondary Schools</u>. Canberra : Department of Education.

Commonwealth of Australia, Department of Education; <u>Files</u> :

64/917	Annual Grant for Science Buildings and Equipment in Secondary Schools in Queensland.
64/1006	Annual Grant for Science Buildings and Equipment in Secondary Schools in Western Australia.
64/1081	Annual Grant for Science Buildings and Equipment in Secondary Schools in Tasmania.
64/1083	Annual Grant for Science Buildings and Equipment in Secondary Schools in South Australia.
64/8924	Minutes of Commonwealth Standards Committee. Sixth Meeting. 16 July 1965.
64/8930	Minutes of Commonwealth Standards Committee. Fourth Meeting. 14 November 1964.
64/8946	Minutes of Commonwealth Standards Committee. Second Meeting. 1 August 1964.
64/8961	Minutes of Commonwealth Standards Committee. First Meeting. 6 May 1964.
65/10157	Minutes of Commonwealth Standards Committee. Seventh Meeting. 21 January 1966.
67/1571	Minutes of Commonwealth Standards Committee. Eighth Meeting. 30 June 1967.
67/1855	States Grants (Science Facilities) : Administration and Finance- New South Wales.
67/1857	States Grants (Science Facilities) : Administration and Finance- Queensland.
67/4951	Minutes of Commonwealth Standards Committee. Ninth Meeting. 30 June 1967.
68/337	States Grants (Science Facilities) : Administration and Finance- Tasmania.
68/2764	Science Facilities Scheme - Proposals for Extension Beyond 1971. Four Parts.
69/3376	States Grants (Secondary Science Facilities) : Administration and Finance - Tasmania.
70/1390	Minutes of Commonwealth Standards Committee. 14th Meeting. 4 July 1970.
70/6081	Minutes of Commonwealth Standards Committee. 15th Meeting. 27 February 1971.
71/2233	Minutes of Commonwealth Standards Committee. 16th Meeting. 10 May 1971.

72/1296   Minutes of Commonwealth Standards Committee. 17th Meeting. 24 June 1972.

72/1547   Science Facilities Scheme - Information Provided for the Minister 1972-5.

74/1547   Minutes of Commonwealth Standards Committee. 21st Meeting. July 1974.

Commonwealth of Australia. <u>Parliamentary Debates : House of Representatives</u>.

26 July 1945	Menzies, R.G.	Vol.	pp.4618-
7 May 1964	Menzies, R.G.	Vol.44,	pp.1639-1641.
18 May 1965	Menzies, R.G.	Vol.46,	pp.1587-1589.
20 May 1965	Calwell, A.A.	Vol.46,	pp.1732-1736.
27 March 1968	Fraser, J.M.	Vol.58,	pp.514-517 and pp.986-989.
1 May 1968	Cairns, J.F.	Vol.58,	pp.972-975.
1 May 1968	Cairns, K.	Vol.58,	pp.983-986.
9 May 1968	Barnard, L.	Vol.58,	pp.1261-1266.
29 May 1969	Fraser, J.M.	Vol.65,	pp.2508-2510.
5 May 1971	Fairbairn, D.	Vol.72,	pp.2665-2667.
5 May 1971	Beazley, K.	Vol.72,	pp.2814-2817.
5 May 1971	Reynolds, L.	Vol.72,	pp.2825-2829.

Commonwealth of Australia. <u>Parliamentary Papers</u>.

States Grants (Science Laboratories and Technical Training) Act 1964, Act No.50 of 1964.

States Grants (Science Laboratories) Act 1965, Act No.40 of 1965.

States Grants (Science Laboratories) Act 1967, Act No.9 of 1967.

States Grants (Science Laboratories) Act 1968, Act No.12 of 1968.

States Grants (Science Laboratories) Act 1971, Act No.65 of 1971.

Cooley, W.W. and Lohnes, P.R. <u>Evaluation Research in Education : Theory, Principles, and Practice</u>. New York : John Wiley.
1976

Coxhead, P. <u>An Empirical Study of Some Aspects of Secondary School Science involving 11 to 13 Year-old Pupils</u>. Unpublished Ph.D. Thesis, Cambridge University.
1974

Coxhead, P. and Whitfield, R.C. 'Some Problems of Measurement Concerned with Science Practical Work for 11 to 13 Year Old Pupils'. <u>Research in Science Education</u>, <u>4</u>, 45-54. Australian Science Education Research Association.
1975

Cull, R.G. 'Report on Small Practical Classes'. Report presented to the New Deal for School Science Conference organized by the New South Wales Teachers Federation, mimeo.
1961

Cull, R.G. 'The New Deal for School Science Conference'. *Australian Science*
1962   *Teachers Journal*, 8, 2, 59-62.

Dale, L.G. 'An Australian Innovation in Curriculum Construction'.
1966   *Australian Science Teachers Journal*, 12, 3, 43-48.

Dark, H.G.N. and Squires, A. 'A Survey of Science Teaching in 9-13
1975   Middle Schools'. *School Science Review*, 56, 196, 464-478.

Dawson, J.R. 'The Impact of New Curricula on Facilities for Biology'.
1964   *The American Biology Teacher*, (December).

Department of Education and Science (Britain). *Designing for Science*.
1967   Oxford School Development Project. London : HMSO.

Dettrick, G.W. 'Impressions of CHEM STUDY'. *Australian Science Teachers*
1966   *Journal*, 12, 3, 88-94.

Drew, C.J. 'Research on the Psychological Behavioral Effects of the Physical
1971   Environment'. *Review of Educational Research*, 41, 447-465.

Dyer, H.S. 'School Factors and Equal Educational Opportunity'. *Harvard*
1968   *Educational Review*, 38, 1, 38-56.

Dyer, H.S. 'Towards Objective Criteria of Professional Accountability in
1970   the Schools of New York City'. *Phi Delta Kappan*, 52, 4, 206-211.

Englehardt, D.F. *Space Requirements for Science Instruction in Grades 9-12*.
1966   Harvard University, Graduate School of Education. ED 022 353.

Englehardt, D.F. *Aspects of Spatial Influence on Science Teaching Methods*.
1968   Doctoral Dissertation, Harvard University, Graduate School of
        Education. ED 024 214.

Entwistle, N.J. and Duckworth, D. Choice of Science Courses in Secondary
1977   School. *Studies in Science Education*, 4, 63-82.

Fensham, P.J. 'The Place of Science in Australian Education'. *Search*,
1970   1, (1970), 28-33.

Field, T.W. 'Science Facilities in Independent Schools : A Decade of
1974   Australian Government Involvement'. *Australian Science Teachers*
        Journal, 20, 3, 33-39.

Fish, G. 'Secondary School Science Facilities in New Schools in Tasmania'.
1974   *Australian Science Teachers Journal*, 20, 3, 41-45.

Fitzgerald, R.T. *The Secondary School at Sixes and Sevens*. Hawthorn,
1970   Victoria : Australian Council for Educational Research.

Fitzgerald, R.T. and Mathews, J.K. 'Educational Policy and Political
1975   Platform : The Australian Labor Government'. *Australian Education*
        Review, 7, 4. Hawthorn, Victoria, Australian Council for
        Educational Research.

Fitzpatrick, G.S. and Angus, M.J. Through Teachers Eyes : Teaching in an
1974   Open Space Primary School. The Australian Open Area Schools
          Project, Technical Report No.1. Perth : Education Department
          of Western Australia.

Gardner, P.L. Attitudes to Physics. Unpublished Ph.D. Thesis, Monash
1972   University, Clayton, Victoria.

Getzels, J.W. and Thelen, H.A. 'The Classroom as a Unique Social System'.
1960   National Society for the Study of Education, Yearbook - Part II,
          59, 53-   Chicago : University of Chicago Press.

Gill, P.N. 'The Federal Science Grant : An Episode in Church and State
1965   Relations, 1963-1964', in E.L. French (ed). Melbourne Studies
          in Education 1964. Melbourne, Victoria : Melbourne University
          Press.

Goodlad, J.I. and Klien, M.F. Looking Behind the Classroom Door.
1974   Worthington, Ohio : Charles A. Jones Publishing Company.

Gordon, C.E.S. The Independent Schools of Australia. Current Affairs Bulletin.
1957   (December), University of Sydney.

Gorton, J.G. Letter to Non-Government School Principals. January.
1965   (CDE, File 64/8927).

Gorton, J.G. 'Foreword', in Commonwealth of Australia, The Design of
1966   Science Rooms. op.cit.

Guthrie, J.W. 'A Survey of School Effectiveness Studies', in J.W. Guthrie
1970   (ed). Do Teachers Make a Difference. Washington, D.C. : U.S.
          Government Printing Office.

Hall, I.M. 'Victoria : Science Labs in State Post Primary Schools'.
1974   Australian Science Teachers Journal, 20, 3, 105-106.

Hamilton, D. 'Handling Innovation in the Classroom : Two Scottish
1975   Examples', in W.A. Reid and D.F. Walker (eds). Case Studies
          in Curriculum Change. London : Routledge and Kegan Paul.

Heffernan, M.L. et al. 'Matriculation Chemistry : The New 1966 Course'.
1964   Lab Talk, 7 (June) 4-5. Science Teachers Association of
          Victoria.

Holt, H.H. Federal Election, 1966 : Policy Speech. Canberra : Liberal
1966   Party of Australia.

Hudspeth, K. 'Changes in High School Design'. Tasmanian Education Gazette,
1973   7, 7, 11-13.

Hughes, P.W. 'Mathematics and Science in the School Curriculum'. Australian
1963   Science Teachers Journal, 9, 2, 45-52.

Industrial Fund for the Advancement of Scientific Education in Schools.
1957a   The Planning of Science Laboratories. London : Industrial Fund.

Industrial Fund for the Advancement of Scientific Education in Schools.
1957b   Apparatus Brochure. London : Industrial Fund.

Institute for Social Research. OSIRIS II MANUAL. Ann Arbor, Michigan :
1971   University of Michigan.

Johnson, P.G. Science Facilities for Secondary Schools. Office of
1956   Education Misc. No.17. Washington : U.S. Government Printing Office.

Keeves, J.P. 'The Case against General Science'. Australian Science
1959   Teachers Journal, 5, 2, 35-41.

Keeves, J.P. Seven Years - Lean or Bountiful. Report of the Survey
1966   conducted by the Australian Science Teachers Association in 1961. Mimeo.

Keeves, J.P. The Home, the School, and Educational Achievement. Unpublished
1971   Ph.D. Thesis, Australian National University : Canberra.

Keeves, J.P. Educational Environment and Student Achievement. Stockholm :
1972   Almqvist and Wiksell.

Keeves, J.P. Curricula Factors Influencing School Learning : Time and
1976   Opportunity to Learn. IEA (Australia) Report 1976:2. Hawthorn, Victoria : Australian Council for Educational Research.

Kelly, A. Scales of School Learning Conditions. IEA Data Bank.
1975   Form 8-751117 (November).

Kelly, P.J. 'Evaluation Studies of Nuffield A Level Biology Trials :
1972   Part 4.' Journal of Biological Education, 6, 2, 197-205.

Kelly, P.J. and Monger, G. 'The Evaluation of the Nuffield O-Level Biology
1974a   Course Materials and their Use - Part I'. School Science Review, 55, 192, 470-482.

Kelly, P.J. and Monger, G. 'The Evaluation of the Nuffield O-Level Biology
1974b   Course Materials and their Use - Part II'. School Science Review, 55, 193, 705-715.

Kelly, P.J. and Nicodemus, R.B. 'Early Stages in the Diffusion of the
1973   Nuffield A Level Biological Science Project'. Journal of Biological Education, 7, 6, 15-22.

Kerlinger, F.N. Foundations of Behavioral Research. New York : Holt,
1964   Rinehart and Winston.

Kerr, J.F. Practical Work in School Science. Leicester, Britain :
1964   Leicester University Press.

Kevin, Br. 'Subject Matter and Teaching Methods'. Australian Science
1956   Teachers Journal, 2, 2, 30-33.

Layard, R., King, J. and Moser, C. The Impact of Robins. London :
1969   Penguin.

Lee Dow, Kwong. Teaching Science in Australian Schools. Melbourne :
1971   Melbourne University Press.

Lewis, R. 1976. *The Effect of Selected Teacher and Student Behaviour on the Cognitive and Affective Objectives of PSSC Physics.* Unpublished Ph.D. Thesis, Monash University, Clayton, Victoria.

Lovegrove, E. 1974. *Recent Trends in Secondary Schools with Particular Reference to the South Australian Open-Space High Schools.* Adelaide : Research and Planning Branch, Education Department of South Australia.

Lovegrove, E. 1975. *Secondary Open Space Teachers Study 1975.* Adelaide : Research Branch, Education Department of South Australia.

Lucas, K. 1975. 'The Supply of Physics Equipment in High Schools in Three Australian States'. *Australian Science Teachers Journal,* 21, 2, 118-120.

Maling-Keepes, J.M. 1978. *Educational Evaluation : Key Characteristics.* Hawthorn, Victoria : Australian Council for Educational Research.

Martin, W.E. 1960. 'Facilities, Equipment and Instructional Materials for the Science Program', in N.B. Henry (ed). *Rethinking Science Education.* The Fifty-ninth Yearbook of the National Society for the Study of Education - Part I. Chicago, Illinois : University of Chicago Press.

McKenzie, S. 1976. 'Senior Secondary Science Courses : Queensland'. *Australian Science Teachers Journal,* 22, 2, 97-98.

Menzies, R.G. 1963. *Federal Election, 1963.* Policy Speech of the Prime Minister (the Right Hon. Sir Robert Menzies) delivered in Melbourne on November 12, 1963, Canberra : Liberal Party of Australia.

Menzies, R.G. 1970. *The Measure of the Years.* Cassell Australia : Melbourne.

Merrilees, D. 1958. 'Conference on Science in Schools'. *Australian Science Teachers Journal,* 4, 3, 52-54.

Merrilees, D. 1956. 'The Role of the Science Teacher in Expanding Scientific and Technical Manpower'. *Australian Science Teachers Journal,* 2, 2, 22-24.

Messel, H. et al. 1964. *Science for High School Students.* Nuclear Research Foundation, Sydney, University of Sydney.

Messel, H. et al. 1966. *Senior Science for High School Students.* Nuclear Research Foundation, University of Sydney.

Mississipi State Department of Education. 1962. *Science Facilities for Mississipi Schools.* Jackson, Mississipi : Mississipi State Department of Education.

Morgan, D.G. 1964. 'BSCS Biology'. *Lab Talk,* 8 (November) 10-11. Science Teachers Association of Victoria.

Morgan, D.G. (ed). *Biological Science : The Web of Life*, together with
1967   *Students Manual : Laboratory and Field Investigations* and
          Teachers Guide. Canberra : Academy of Science.

Morgan, R.L. 'Biological Education in Senior Secondary Schools in Australia'.
1970   *Australian Science Teachers Journal*, 16, 3, 79-84.

Moser, C.A. and Kalton, G. *Survey Methods in Social Investigation*. London :
1971   Heinemann.

National Science Teachers Association. *Conditions for Good Science Teaching*
1970   *in Secondary Schools*. Recommendations of the Commission on
          Professional Standards and Practices of the NSTA. Washington,
          D.C. : NSTA.

New South Wales, Education Department. *Science Notes*, 8. Sydney :
1972a   Education Department. Mimeo.

New South Wales, Education Department. *Science Notes*, 9. Sydney :
1972b   Education Department. Mimeo.

New South Wales, Education Department. *Science Notes*, 11. Sydney :
1973   Education Department.

New South Wales, Education Department. *Public School Architecture in*
1975   *New South Wales*. Sydney : Education Department.

New South Wales, Education Department. *Files* :

70/4471   Commonwealth Science Grant.

71/25623   Commonwealth Science Grant.

New South Wales Teachers Federation. *New Deal for School Science,*
1961a   *Conference Papers*. Mimeo.

New South Wales Teachers Federation. *Letter to Conference Participants*.
1961b   Mimeo.

New South Wales Teachers Federation. *Space Age Problems Can't be Solved by*
1962   *Horse and Buggy Methods*. Sydney : New South Wales Teachers
          Federation.

Nie, N.H. et al. *Statistical Package for the Social Sciences*. New York :
1975   McGraw Hill.

Northfield, J.R. Private Communication.
1976

Novak, J.D. *Facilities for Secondary School Science Teaching : Evolving*
1972   *Patterns in Facilities and Programs*. Washington, D.C. :
          National Science Teachers Association.

Nunally, J.C. *Psychometric Theory*. New York : McGraw Hill.
1967

Olsen, F.J. 'Practical Requirements of a Scientific World and Our Teaching
1955   Response'. Australian Science Teachers Journal, 1, 2, 23.

Ontario Department of Education. Science Laboratories for Secondary Schools.
1968   Toronto, Canada : School Planning and Building Research Section, Ontario Department of Education. ED 085 905.

Oppenheim, A.N. Questionnaire Design and Attitude Measurement. London,
1966   Britain : Heinemann.

Ormerod, M.B. and Duckworth, D. Pupils Attitudes to Science. Slough,
1975   Britain : National Foundation for Educational Research.

Owen, J.M. The Effects of Schools on Achievement in Science. IEA (Australia)
1975   Report 1975:1. Hawthorn, Victoria : Australian Council for Educational Research.

Owen, J.M. The Impact of the Australian Science Education Project on Schools.
1977   Hawthorn, Victoria : Australian Council for Educational Research.

Parlett, M. and Hamilton, D. Evaluation as Illumination : A New Approach
1972   to the Study of Innovatory Programs. Occasional Paper No. 9. Centre for Research in Educational Sciences : University of Edinburgh.

Parsons, C.A. 'The New Evaluation : A Cautionary Note'. Journal of
1976   Curriculum Studies, 8, 2, 125-138.

Peaker, G.F. An Empirical Study of Education in Twenty One Countries :
1975   A Technical Report. Stockholm and New York : Almqvist and Wiksell and John Wiley.

Pfitzner, E.N. 'Qualities of High Level Students : Their Recognition and
1956   Encouragement'. Australian Science Teachers Journal, 2, 2, 24.

Prosser, B. and Woolley, T. 'Open Plan Science in South Australia'.
1974   Australian Science Teachers Journal, 20, 3, 57-64.

Purves, A.C. and Levine, D.V. Educational Policy and International
1975   Assessment. Berkley, California : McCutchan Publishing Corp.

Ramsey, G.A. 'Curriculum Development in Secondary School Science. Part 1'.
1972a   Quarterly Review of Australian Education, 5, 1. Hawthorn, Victoria : Australian Council for Educational Research.

Ramsey, G.A. 'Curriculum Development in Secondary School Science. Part 2'.
1972b   Quarterly Review of Australian Education, 5, 2. Hawthorn, Victoria : Australian Council for Educational Research.

Ramsey, G.A. Some Reflections on the Australian Science Education Project.
1974   Transcripts of a talk given at the Regional Centre for Science and Mathematics, Penang, Malaysia : Mimeo.

Ramsey, G.A. and Howe, R.W. 'An Analysis of Research on Instructional
1969   Procedures in Secondary School Science'. The Science Teacher, 36, 3, 62-70, and 36, 4, 72-81.

Randhawa, B.S. and Fu, L.L.W. 'The Assessment and Effect of Some Classroom
1973   Environment Variables'. Review of Educational Research, 43,
          3, 303-321.

Richards, A.H. 'Assistance by Business and Industry to ASTA'. Australian
1957   Science Teachers Journal, 3, 2.

Richardson, H. 'Shortage of Trained Scientists in Australia'. Australian
1957   Science Teachers Journal, 1, 2.

Robertson, W.W. A Critical Survey of Laboratory Work in Science in NSW
1962   Secondary Schools. Unpublished Master of Education Thesis,
          University of Sydney.

Robins, G. 'Science Facilities in Queensland State Secondary Schools'.
1974   Australian Science Teachers Journal, 20, 3, 5-8.

Rosenshine, B. Teaching Behaviors and Student Achievement. Slough,
1971   Britain : National Foundation for Educational Research.

Rosier, M.J. 'A Statistical Picture of Australian Science Teachers'.
1973a   Australian Science Teachers Journal, 19, 4, 27-39.

Rosier, M.J. Variation Between Australian States in Science Achievement.
1973b   IEA (Australia) Report 1973:5. Hawthorn, Victoria :
          Australian Council for Educational Research.

Rosier, M.J. and Williams, W.H. The Mobility of Teachers of Science in
1973   Australia 1970-1972. IEA (Australia) Report 1973:7. Hawthorn,
          Victoria : Australian Council for Educational Research.

Ross, K.N. Searching for Uncertainty : an empirical investigation of
1975   sampling errors in educational survey research. Occasional
          Paper No.9. Hawthorn, Victoria : Australian Council for
          Educational Research.

Rowlands, R.G. 'Are Girls a Disadvantaged Group?' Australian Journal
1976   of Education, 20, 1, 21-37.

Ryans, D.G. Characteristics of Teachers. Washington, D.C. : American
1960   Council on Education.

Savage, Sir Graham. 'Planning of School Science Blocks'. Australian
1958   Science Teachers Journal, 4, 2, 3-12.

Schlessinger, F.R. Science Facilities for Our Schools. Washington, D.C. :
1963   National Science Teachers Association.

Schonnel, F.J. 'Science Teaching and the Community'. Australian Science
1956   Teachers Journal, 2, 2.

Schools Commission. Report for the Triennium 1976-78. Canberra, Australia :
1975   Australian Government Publishing Service.

Schwab, J.J.   'The Teaching of Science as Enquiry', in J.J. Schwab and
1962   P.R. Brandwein (eds). The Teaching of Science. Harvard, USA.

Shaycoft, M.F.   The High School Years : Growth in Cognitive Skills.
1967   Pittsburgh, Pennsylvania : University of Pittsburgh, Project
              TALENT Office.

Sheldrake, P. and Berry, S. Looking at Innovation. Slough, Britain :
1975   National Foundation for Educational Research.

Sheperd, S.R.   'An Outline of Science Courses at Junior Secondary Level in
1970   the Australian States'. Australian Science Teachers Journal,
              16, 1, 83.

Smart, D.   The Industrial Fund for the Advancement of Scientific Education
1972   in Schools : Precursor to the Menzies Government's Secondary
            Schools Science Laboratories Scheme. Paper given at the
            Australian Association for Research in Education Conference,
            Canberra. Mimeo.

Smart, D.   'Origins of the Secondary Schools Libraries Scheme', in
1974   D.A. Jecks (ed). Influences in Australian Education. Perth :
            Carrolls Pty.Ltd.

Smart, D.   Federal Aid to Australian Schools : Origins and Aspects of the
1975   Implementation of the Commonwealth Science Laboratories and
            Libraries Schemes. Unpublished Ph.D. Thesis, Australian
            National University, Canberra.

Smart, D.   'Federal Government Involvement in Australian Education 1964-1975'.
1976   Journal of Educational Administration, 14, 2, 236-251.

Smith, R.A.   'The School Laboratory - Its Function and Design'. South
1967   Australian Science Teachers Association Journal (May).

Smith, R.A.   Private Communication.
1975

Spaull, A.D.   'Educational Policies of Australian Political Parties', in
1974   D.A. Jecks (ed). Influences in Australian Education. Perth :
              Carrolls Pty.Ltd.

Sonquist, J.A. and Morgan, J.N. The Detection of Interaction Effects.
1964   Monograph No.35, Survey Research Centre, Institute for Social
              Research, University of Michigan.

Stake, R.E.   'The Countenance of Educational Evaluation'. Teachers College
1967   Record, 68,   523-540.

Stanhope, R.W.   'Physical Science and Biology should replace other Junior
1959   Secondary School Sciences'. Australian Science Teachers Journal,
              5, 1, 47.

Stanhope, R.W.   'Science Courses in Australian Schools'. Australian Science
1961   Teachers Journal, 7, 3, 23.

Stanhope, R.W. 'Report of Proceedings of the ANZAAS Council'. Australian
1964 Science Teachers Journal, 10, 1, 43.

Stanhope, R.W. 'Developments in Senior School Science Curricula in Australia'.
1967 Australian Science Teachers Journal, 13, 1, 5.

Steele, J., House, E. and Kerins, T. 'An Instrument for Assessing Instructional
1971 Climate through Low-Inference Student Judgements'. American
Educational Research Journal, 7, 447-466.

Stenhouse, L. An Introduction to Curriculum Research and Development.
1975 London : Heinemann.

Stranks, D.R. 'Drifts from the Sciences'. Inserted in the South Australian
1969 Science Teachers' Association Journal (December).

South Australia, Education Department. Secondary Science Curriculum Committee.
1976 1976 Annual Report. Adelaide, South Australia : Government Printer.

Tannock, P. 'The Development of the Federal Government's Role in Australian
1976 Education', in G.S. Harman and C. Selby Smith (eds). Readings in
the Economics and Politics of Australian Education. Rushcutters
Bay, New South Wales : Pergamon.

Tasmania, Education Department. High School Buildings : Handbook of General
1975a Educational Specifications of Accommodation. Hobart, Tasmania :
Education Department.

Tasmania, Education Department. Secondary College Buildings : Handbook of
1975b General Educational Specifications of Accommodation. Hobart,
Tasmania : Education Department.

Tasmania, Education Department. File 8547, 'Commonwealth Secondary Science
Scheme'.

Taylor, P.H., Christie, T. and Platts, C.V. Factors Related to the Choice
1973 of Science among Able Fourth Year Secondary School Pupils.
University of Birmingham (Report available from the National
Lending Library for Science and Technology, Boston Spa, Yorkshire).

The Four Associations. 'The Provision and Maintenance of Laboratories in
1960 Grammar Schools'. School Science Review, 41, 145.

Tisher, R.P. 'Research in Science Education and the Australian Science
1965 Education Foundation'. Australian Science Teachers Journal,
11, 1, 19.

Tomlinson, D. The Liberal Party in Commonwealth Initiatives for Education,
1976 1949 to 1972. Unpublished M.Ed. Thesis, University of Western
Australia, Perth.

Tukey, J.W. Rosettes as Carriers of Regression. An unpublished paper from
Undated Princeton University and Bell Telephone Laboratories.

Turner, J. 'The Planning of Science Accommodation in High Schools'.
1974 Australian Science Teachers Journal, 20, 3, 9-22.

Victoria, Education Department. Board of Inspectors of Secondary Schools.
1966   Science Newsletter, 3. (A66/147).

Victoria, Education Department. Board of Inspectors of Secondary Schools.
1967   Science Newsletter. (September) (A67/1248).

Victoria, Education Department. Board of Inspectors of Secondary Schools.
1969   Science Newsletter, 3. (May) (A69/1015).

Victoria, Education Department. Board of Inspectors of Secondary Schools.
1972   Science Newsletter, 9 (May).

Victorian Universities and Schools Examinations Board (VUSEB). Papers
1963   relating to the School Science Conference, October.

Victorian Universities and Schools Examinations Board (VUSEB). Handbook of
1966-1971   Prescriptions and Directions. Victoria : Government Printer.

Victorian Universities and Schools Examinations Board (VUSEB). Supplement
1975   to Circular to Schools No.72. (August). Melbourne : Victorian Universities and Schools Examinations Board.

Waddy, R. 'Senior Secondary Science Courses : Western Australia'.
1976   Australian Science Teachers Journal, 22, 2, 99-102.

Walberg, H.J. 'Social Environment as a Mediator in Classroom Learning'.
1969   Journal of Educational Psychology, 60, 6, 443-448.

Walberg, H.J. and Anderson, G.J. 'Classroom Climate and Individual Learning'.
1968   Journal of Educational Psychology, 59, 6, 414-419.

Western Australia, Education Department. Science Report. Perth : Education
1969   Department. Mimeo.

Western Australia, Education Department. Science Report. Perth : Education
1970   Department. Mimeo.

Western Australia, Education Department. Science. Perth : Education
1972   Department.

Western Australia, Education Department. Science Report. Perth : Education
1974   Department. Mimeo.

Western Australia, Education Department. Survey of Upper Secondary Science
1975   Education in Western Australia. Perth, Western Australia : Education Department.

Western Australia, Education Department. Files :

1277/65   Commonwealth Grant for Secondary Science Equipment.

1968/73   Science Equipment.

White, R.T. 'From the Two Cultures to Money : Trends in Enrolment in HSC
1973   Subjects in Victoria'. Science Education Research 1973. Brisbane, Queensland : Australian Science Education Research Association.

Whitfield, R.C. *Disciplines of the Curriculum*. London : McGraw Hill.
1971

Wilson, A.F. *The Effects of Schools in Victoria on the Science Achievement*
1975 *of Junior Secondary Students*. IEA (Australia) Report 1975:2.
Hawthorn, Victoria : Australian Council for Educational Research.

Yaxley, M. 'A Case for an Australian Science Education Foundation'.
1964 *Australian Science Teachers Journal*, *10*, 2, 47.

APPENDIX A

A SUMMARY OF QUESTIONS ABOUT THE AUSTRALIAN

SCIENCE FACILITIES PROGRAM

A. School Effects
   Level 1   The Provision of Facilities
   1.1 To what extent were the needs of schools, in each system, for science rooms satisfied at the conclusion of the Science Facilities Program?

   1.2 To what extent did schools in each system gain additional accommodation as a result of the rebuilding program since 1963?

   1.3 Which classes within schools had greatest access to the new rooms?

   1.4 Were rooms provided under the Science Facilities Program considered to be more suitable for teaching science than the older rooms?

   1.5 What proportion of schools were adequately supplied with apparatus for science teaching at the conclusion of Science Facilities Program?

   1.6 Did schools have laboratory staff to assist in fully using facilities which were available?

   1.7 Which aspects of facilities were seen as impeding the conduct of practical work in schools?

   Level 2   Facilities and Teaching
   2.1 Were differences in the extent and standard of facilities in schools associated with differences in the way science was taught.

   2.2 Did patterns in the organization and planning of science in schools alter as a result of improved facilities?

   2.3 Did schools with extensive and good facilities retain science teachers for longer than other schools?

   2.4 Were the attitudes of science teachers toward practical work related to differences in facilities available to them?

A. School Effects (Contd)

   Level 3   Facilities and Outcomes of Science Teaching

   3.1 Are good facilities associated with high achievement in a better understanding of science?

   3.2 Do schools provided with good facilities have more of their year 12 students enrolled in science studies?

   3.3 In schools with good facilities for teaching science did students express a greater interest in science and different attitude to science than those in schools with poor facilities?

B. System Effects

   4.1 What developments in the design of science facilities occurred during the course of the Science Facilities Program?

   4.2 Was the employment of laboratory assistants stimulated by the provision of improved facilities?

   4.3 Were funds from the Science Facilities Program used to assist the development or implementation of new curricula?

   4.4 Have systems of supplying government schools with apparatus altered during the course of the Science Facilities Program? To what extent were these changes helped by the additional funds which became available?

APPENDIX B

THE SCHOOL QUESTIONNAIRE

AUSTRALIAN COUNCIL FOR
EDUCATIONAL RESEARCH

SCIENCE FACILITIES IN AUSTRALIAN SCHOOLS

SCHOOL QUESTIONNAIRE

(To be completed by the TEACHER IN CHARGE OF SCIENCE)

Information given in response to this questionnaire is confidential to ACER and will be used only in making statistical calculations or for deriving general statements. No individual school will be identified in reports of this study.

Copyright © ACER 1975
Published by the
Australian Council for Educational Research
Frederick Street, Hawthorn, Victoria, 3122.

NOTES FOR GUIDANCE IN COMPLETING THIS QUESTIONNAIRE

1. Different designations of grade or year levels of secondary school are used in the various States and Territories of Australia. In this national questionnaire it is necessary to use year descriptions throughout. The equivalent State or Territory designation currently in use is shown in the following table.

Name used in this study	A.C.T.	N.S.W.	VIC.	TAS.	QLD.	S.A.	W.A.
Year 7	Form 1	Form 1	Form 1	First yr	-	-	-
Year 8	Form 2	Form 2	Form 2	Second yr	Grade 8	First yr	First yr
Year 9	Form 3	Form 3	Form 3	Third yr	Grade 9	Second yr	Second yr
Year 10	Form 4	Form 4	Form 4	Fourth yr	Grade 10	Third yr	Third yr
Year 11	Form 5	Form 5	Form 5	Fifth yr	Grade 11	Fourth yr	Fourth yr
Year 12	Form 6	Form 6	Form 6	Sixth yr	Grade 12	Fifth yr	Fifth yr

2. Where reference is made to 'studying a science subject' it includes the study of Science (multistrand, combined or general), any one or more of Physics, Chemistry, Biology, Human Biology, or Geology, Agricultural or Rural Science, Environmental Science, or science taken as part of General Studies program. It does not include Domestic Science or Geography.

3. In answering some sections of the questionnaire you may need to consult
    (i)   enrolment details.
    (ii)   the school timetable.

4. In recording enrolment details use figures as 1 August 1975 if they are conveniently available.

5. Space is available at the end of many questions to enable you to comment if you wish. Space is also available at the end of the questionnaire for any general comments you wish to make.

6. Please return this questionnaire to
    Mr J. Ainley
    Science Facilities Project
    Australian Council for Educational Research
    PO Box 210
    HAWTHORN, VICTORIA, 3122.

257.

	Office use only
	1:1-4
	1:5
	1:6
SECTION 1 GENERAL INFORMATION	1:7
	1:8
1. Name of the school: _____	1:9
2. Name of person completing questionnaire: _____	1:10
	1:11
3. Was the school established since 1964? Yes/No ☐	1:12
	1:13
4. Does your school have a nearly uniform length teaching period throughout the week? Yes/No ☐	1:14

If YES

5. What is the length of a teaching period (in minutes)?   ☐   1:15,16

6. How many such periods make up the teaching week?   ☐   1:17,18
   (i.e. How many such periods comprise the timetable for the week's activities?)

If NO briefly describe the pattern of teaching periods which operates throughout the week.

_____
_____
_____
_____
_____
_____
_____

SECTION 11 FACILITIES FOR TEACHING SCIENCE

A SCIENCE ROOMS AND ACCOMMODATION

Items 7 to 11 refer to the rooms <u>equipped for and principally used for</u> science teaching. Other types of room are mentioned in subsequent items. Include temporary (portable) as well as permanent rooms only if they are equipped for science teaching.

In some of these items space has been allowed for a large number of science rooms. <u>Most schools will not need to use all of these spaces.</u>

Please enter your answers to items 7 to 9 inclusive in the table provided below. The space for room identification has been provided for your convenience only.

7. When was this room built or converted from an existing classroom?

    Key: A.   After 1970.

            B.   From 1964 to 1970 inclusive.

            C.   Before 1964.

8. What was the source of finance for the building/refitting of this room?

    Key: A.   Built under the Commonwealth Science Scheme.

            B.   Refitted under the Commonwealth Science Scheme.

            C.   Existed or built independently of the Commonwealth Science Scheme.

            D.   Built since 1964 but source of finance is uncertain. (This may apply to new government schools).

9. Please indicate whether in each of these rooms there is provision for:

    Key: A.   Pupil experimental (laboratory) work.

            B.   Teacher demonstrations only.

ROOM	1	2	3	4	5	6	7	8	9	10	11
Room Identity											
Qn. 7 (Date)											
Qn. 8 (Finance)											
Qn. 9 (Purpose)											

Office use only

1:19,20

1:21

1:22

1:23

1:24

1:25

1:26

1:27

1:28

259.

												Office use only

1:29-31

1:32-34

1:35-37

1:38-40

1:41-43

10. For each of the following features of each room indicate by placing the appropriate letter in the grid, whether it is:
   A. Adequate.   B. Barely adequate.   C. Inadequate.   D. Non-existent.

Note: 'Adequate' refers both to the quality and quantity of the services and where appropriate, to its accessibility for student use. Space for comment is available on page 16.

ROOM	1	2	3	4	5	6	7	8	9	10	11
Area of the room											
Provision of water taps and sinks											
Provision of gas outlets											
Provision of power points											
Provision of fume cupboards											
Provision of display boards											
Storage space in room											
Adjoining preparation and storage area											
Seating accommodation											
Working space for pupils laboratory work											
Writing space for pupils											
Demonstration bench											
Hot and cold washing up facilities											
Projection facilities											

-5-

11. How many periods per week is each room used for the following types of classes?

	1	2	3	4	5	6	7	8	9	10	11
Room Identity											
Chemistry (Year 11 & 12)											
Physics (Year 11 & 12)											
Biology (Year 11 & 12)											
Other science (Year 11 & 12)											
Other science (Year 7 to 10)											
Non-science classes											

12. How many rooms other than those mentioned in Items 7 to 11 are used for science classes?

13. How many science periods are taken in rooms not equipped for science teaching (i.e. non-science rooms)?

        (a) In years 7, 8, 9, and 10.

        (b) In years 11 and 12.

B.   SCIENCE APPARATUS

Items 14 to 19 refer to the science equipment available at your school.

For items 14 to 16, indicate your response by using the following key:

    A.   Yes.

    B.   Yes, but minor deficiencies at certain times.

    C.   No, generally deficient in some items at some times.

    D.   No, general deficiencies in many items occur frequently.

    E.   No, deficiencies occur most of the time.

261.

                                                                                                                   Office use only

14. Has your school a sufficient supply of "expendable" equipment (e.g. test tubes, beakers, stock reagents)?   1:68

Optional Comment: _____

_____

_____

15. Has your school a sufficient supply of minor science apparatus (e.g. bunsen burners, stands, magnets)?   1:69

Optional Comment: _____

_____

_____

16. Has your school a sufficient supply of essential major items of equipment (e.g. balances, electrical meters, microscopes)?   1:70

Optional Comment: _____

_____

_____

17. Each of the following statements represents a possible source of difficulty in arranging student experimental work. Place a tick in the appropriate column to indicate the degree to which each has been a source of difficulty at your school in 1975.

	Not a problem 1	Rarely a problem 2	Sometimes a problem 3	A significant problem 4	
(a) An insufficient supply of basic apparatus					1:71
(b) Inappropriate laboratory facilities					1:72
(c) Too much preparation time involved					1:73
(d) Too few laboratory assistants					1:74
(e) Difficult to store apparatus					1:75

Optional Comment: _____

_____

_____

18. For each of the following items of equipment indicate:
    (i) the approximate number possessed by the school.
    (ii) the frequency of use of the item (if any are possessed).

	NUMBER	USE (tick the appropriate column)			
		Never	Rarely	Occasion-ally	Often
Astronomical telescope					
Chemical semi-micro analysis kits					
Power operated vacuum pump					
Cathode-Ray oscilloscope					
Linear air track apparatus					
Substitution or top loading balances					
Anatomical models and skeletons					
Aquarium tanks (with aerator and heater)					
Micro projector					

19. ASEP Module Packs contain 10 student books, 10 record books, and in some cases, other assorted items.

    (a) How many ASEP Module packs were purchased by the school up to 31 December 1974?

    (b) How many ASEP Module packs were purchased in the period 1 January 1975 to 1 October 1975?

    (c) How many ASEP Module packs do you estimate will be purchased between 1 October 1975 and 1 February 1976?

Office use only

1:76-80

2:1-5

2:6,7
2:8,9
2:10,11
2:12,13
2:14,15
2:16,17
2:18,19
2:20,21
2:22,23

2:24,25

2:26,27

2:28,29

-8-

263.

Office use only

SECTION III   SCIENCE TEACHING PROGRAM

(i)   Years 7 to 10.

20. How many separate groups (classes) are taken for science subjects each of the following grade levels?

(a)	Year 7		2:30,31
(b)	Year 8		2:32,33
(c)	Year 9		2:34,35
(d)	Year 10		2:36,37

21. Tick the appropriate column to indicate the way students are allocated to classes in Science (or in separate science subjects) at the following year levels.

	All classes are structured so that they contain students with a wide range of abilities.	Some classes contain students with a wide range of abilities, other classes contain students of more similar abilities.	Classes are structured so that students of similar abilities are grouped together in any one class.	
Year 7				2:38
Year 8				2:39
Year 9				2:40
Year 10				2:41

22. For each separate class group at the Year levels 7 to 10, how many Science periods are taken each week?

Note: (1) If your school does not plan its timetable on a standard length teaching period enter the replies as the amount of time each week spent in science classes (in minutes to the nearest 10 minutes).

(2) Include any extra classes of science based elective studies held in addition to the normal science program.

CLASS GROUP	1	2	3	4	5	6	7	8	9	10	11
Year 7											
Year 8											
Year 9											
Year 10											

2:42,43
2:44,45
2:46,47
2:48,49
2:50,51
2:52,53
2:54,55
2:56,57

23. For this item refer to YEAR 9 science teaching only. Base your estimate on the average for the class groups in Year 9 over the last full teaching week. State your estimate as a percentage of the total science teaching time for that week.

    (a) What percentage of the science teaching time involved teacher demonstration?   2:58,59

    (b) What percentage of the science teaching time involved experimental work performed by students.   2:60,61

Optional Comment: _____
_____
_____
_____

24. When students in years 7 to 10 do experiments in the science laboratory in what size groups do they normally work? (Please tick the appropriate box).

    (a) Individually   2:62

    (b) In pairs

    (c) In groups of three

    (d) In groups of four or more

Optional Comment: _____
_____
_____
_____

(ii) Years 11 and 12.

25. In the tables on the following pages specify for each science subject taken at Grade 11 and 12 the number of separate class groups, and, the average number of periods taken by those class groups each week.

Notes: 1. Separate tables have been provided for N.S.W. schools.
       2. For Western Australian schools record information for "Web of Life" Biology in (d) and for "Human Biology" in (h) in each case.
       3. For Queensland enter "Zoology" and "Biological Science" information in (h) in each case.

Office use only

26.1 <u>Year 11.</u>

		Number of class groups	Av. number of periods/week
(a)	Science		
(b)	Physics		
(c)	Chemistry		
(d)	Biology [2]		
(e)	Geology/Earth Science		
(f)	Agricultural/Rural Science		
(g)	Environmental Science		
(h)	Other, specify: _____		

Office use only

2:63,64
2:65,66
2:67,68
2:69,70
2:71,72
2:73,74
2:75,76
2:77,78

For New South Wales Schools ONLY (Year 11)

2:78-80

		Number of class groups	Av. number of periods/week
(a)	Multistrand Science (4 Unit) - Enter only those classes which are taken separately from specialist 2 unit courses.		
(b)	Physics (2 unit)		
(c)	Chemistry (2 unit)		
(d)	Biology (2 unit)		
(e)	Geology (2 unit)		
(f)	Agriculture (All size units)		
(g)	Engineering Science (All size units)		
(h)	Multistrand Science (2 Unit A)		

-11-

26.2 Year 12.

	Number of class groups	Av. number of periods/week
(a) Science		
(b) Physics		
(c) Chemistry		
(d) Biology ^{2}		
(e) Geology/Earth Science		
(f) Agricultural/Rural Science		
(g) Environmental Science		
(h) Other, specify: _____		

Office use only

3:1-5

3:6,7
3:8,9
3:10,11
3:12,13
3:14,15
3:16,17
3:18,19
3:20,21

For New South Wales Schools Only (Year 12)

Science	Level	Number of class groups	Av. number of periods/week
(a)	1.		
(b)	2F.		
(c)	2S.		
(d)	3.		

3:22,23
3:24,25
3:26,27
3:28,29

SECTION IV   SCIENCE STAFF

27. (a) How many members of the school's teaching staff are teachers of science? (Note: A teacher of science is a person who has taught a science subject on a regular basis throughout 1975)

3:30,31

(b) How many teachers are there on the school staff?

3:32,33,34

28. How many full-time equivalent non-teaching assistants (e.g. laboratory assistants) are there on the science staff?

3:35

267.

	Office use only

29. For each teacher of science please supply the following details by entering the response in the grid provided.

    (a) Sex: M. Male.   F. Female.   3:36,37

    (b) Teaching Experience to the nearest year. (number of years)   3:38,39,40

    (c) Length of teaching at the present school. (number of years)   3:41,42,43

    (d) Teacher training. A. Teacher training qualification.   3:44,45

                        B. No teacher training qualification.

    (e) Science qualifications:

        A. Post-graduate degree in science or in a science related field.

        B. Bachelor degree in science or in a science related field.   3:46,47
           (including concurrent Science-Education degrees).

        C. Other completed tertiary science qualification.   3:48,49

        D. Incomplete tertiary qualification in science or no post-secondary   3:50,51
           qualification.

TEACHER	1	2	3	4	5	6	7	8	9	10	11	12
(a) Sex												
(b) Teaching experience												
(c) Years at present school												
(d) Teacher training												
(e) Science qualification												

TEACHER (contd)	13	14	15	16	17	18	19	20	21	22	23	24
(a) Sex												
(b) Teaching experience												
(c) Years at present school												
(d) Teacher training												
(e) Science qualification												

SECTION V   ENROLMENTS

Please indicate enrolments as at 1 August 1975 if this information is conveniently available. If precise information is hard to obtain please give an approximate figure.

30. How many students are enrolled in each of the Year levels listed below?

    (a) Year 7   3:52-54
    (b) Year 8   3:55-57
    (c) Year 9   3:58-60
    (d) Year 10   3:61-63
    (e) Year 11   3:64-66
    (f) Year 12   3:67-69

31. How many GIRLS are enrolled in each of the following Year levels?

    (a) Year 9   3:70-72
    (b) Year 12   3:73-75

32. How many students in each of the year levels listed below study a science subject? If all students at any Year level study a science subject write ALL.

3:76-80
4:1-5

    (a) Year 7   4:6-8
    (b) Year 8   4:9-11
    (c) Year 9   4:12-14
    (d) Year 10   4:15-17
    (e) Year 11   4:18-20
    (f) Year 12   4:21-23

33. How many GIRLS in each of the following Year levels study a science subject?

    (a) Year 9   4:24-26
    (b) Year 12   4:27-29

34. Please indicate the number of students in <u>Year 12</u> studying each of the following areas.

		Males	Females	
(a)	Physics			4:30-35
(b)	Chemistry			4:36-41
(c)	Biology[1,2]			4:42-47
(d)	Science			4:48-53
(e)	Geology/Earth Science			4:54-59
(f)	Agricultural/Rural Science			4:60-65
(g)	Environmental Science			4:66-71
(h)	Other, specify: _____			4:72-78

Note: 1. For Western Australian schools, enter numbers for "Web of Life Biology" in (c) and "Human Biology" in (h).
2. For Queensland schools enter numbers for "Zoology" and "Biological Science" in (h) and numbers for "Biology" in (c).

4:79-80

<u>For New South Wales schools only</u>: Please indicate the number of students studying science at each level in YEAR 12.

5:1-5

Science		Level	Males	Females	
	(a)	1			5:6-11
	(b)	2F			5:12-17
	(c)	2S			5:18-23
	(d)	3			5:24-29

SECTION VI   COMMENTS

35.   If you would like to make any additional comments about any of the aspects covered by the sections of this questionnaire, write these comments in the space below. You may wish to comment on general facilities for science teaching, the design of science rooms, or on the influence of science facilities on teaching methods.

Thank you for answering this questionnaire.
Please return it to ACER as soon as possible.

APPENDIX C

DETAILS OF SAMPLING AND WEIGHTING

The Sampling Design for the Survey

Details of the Sampling design, which was described in Chapter Three, have been included in Table C1. Four features of this design may be recalled:

1. Schools were selected with a probability proportional to size.
2. A stratified sampling frame was used.
3. The selection of schools was random within each stratum.
4. An oversample of non-government schools was drawn.

The Calculation of Weighting Variables

Weighting was necessary when estimating State and national values of various parameters because the sample was not a simple random sample. Three features of the sample needed to be considered when weighting. Firstly, the non-response, though very small, was different in different strata. Secondly, an oversample of non-government schools had been deliberately chosen to provide a more reliable indication of the standard of science facilities in those schools. Finally, even though equal size samples were drawn from each State, the total number of schools in each State was different.

A variable (State-weight) was calculated to allow for the between-State differences. It was based on the enrolments of 14-year-old students in each State (Table C2). A second variable (weight-factor) was calculated to allow for the differential non-response and oversampling. It was calculated from the number of 14-year-old students enrolled at schools in each stratum, and applied within States. These two variables were combined to give a weighting variable (total-weight) which was used in computing national values of various parameters. Values of the variables weight factor and total weight have been recorded in Table C3.

Table C1   Science Facilities in Australian Schools
Survey Sample Details

State	Sampling Fraction	Stratum	Number of 14-yr-olds	Theoretical Sample	Actual Basic Sample	Total Sample	Integral Multiplier
ACT		Govt	2329	13	13	13	1
		Cath	920	5	5	5	1
		Ind	3	3	3	3	1
		Total	3249	21	21	21	
New South Wales	.0006023	Govt Met	37424	22.5	23	23	1
		Govt NM	27398	16.5	16	16	1
		Cath Met	9198	5.5	5	11	2
		Cath NM	5438	3.3	4	6	2
		Ind Met	2861	1.7	2	12	7
		Ind NM	691	0.4	0	2	7
		Total	83010	49.9	50	70	
Victoria	.0007621	Govt Met	30970	23.5	24	24	1
		Govt NM	18581	14.2	14	14	1
		Cath Met	7699	5.9	6	12	2
		Cath NM	3125	2.4	2	5	2
		Ind Met	4305	3.3	3	13	4
		Ind NM	940	0.7	1	3	4
		Total	65620	50.0	50	71	
Queensland	.0013806	Govt Met	10845	15.0	15	15	1
		Govt NM	16964	23.4	23	23	1
		Cath Met	2765	3.8	4	8	2
		Cath NM	3139	4.3	4	8	2
		Ind Met	1351	1.9	2	8	4
		Ind NM	1152	1.6	2	6	4
		Total	32216	50.0	50	69	
South Australia	.002074	Govt Met	13715	28.4	25	25	1
		Govt NM	6854	14.2	14	14	1
		Cath Met	1796	3.7	3	11	3
		Cath NM	277	0.6	0	2	3
		Ind Met	1471	3.1	4	13	4
		Ind NM	000	0.0	0	0	4
		Total	24113	50.0	46	65	
Western Australia	.00195	Govt Met	11208	21.9	21	21	1
		Govt NM	4991	9.7	10	10	1
		Cath Met	2248	4.4	4	13	3
		Cath NM	688	1.3	1	4	3
		Ind Met	1312	2.6	2	12	5
		Ind NM	70	0.1	0	1	5
		Total	20517	40.0	38	61	
Tasmania	.004902	Govt Met	2152	10.6	10	10	1
		Govt NM	4672	22.1	21	21	1
		Cath Met	414	2.0	2	7	3
		Cath NM	428	2.1	2	5	3
		Ind Met	306	1.5	1	5	4
		Ind NM	188	0.9	1	4	4
		Total	8160	39.2	37	52	

Table C2 Calculation of State weights

State	Theoretical No. of Sample Schools	No. of 14-yr-olds	Proportionate No. of Schools	State-weight (S)
ACT	21	3249	4.0	0.193
New South Wales	50	83010	103.7	2.074
Victoria	50	65620	82.0	1.640
Queensland	50	36216	45.3	0.905
South Australia	50	24113	30.1	0.603
Western Australia	40	20517	25.6	0.641
Tasmania	40	8160	10.2	0.255
Total	301	240885	301.0	

Note : The number of 14-year-olds enrolled at schools in each state has been taken at June 1975.

Table C3   Calculation of Weights Applied to Each Stratum

State	Stratum	Theoretical No. of Schools (T)	Actual No. of Schools (A)	Weight Factor $(W=\frac{T}{A})$	Total Weight (T=SxW)
ACT	Govt	13	12	1.08	0.21
	Cath	5	4	1.25	0.24
	Indep	3	2	1.67	0.32
NSW	Govt	39.0	38	1.03	2.14
	Cath	8.8	15	0.59	1.22
	Indep	2.1	13	0.16	0.34
VIC	Govt	37.7	37	1.02	1.67
	Cath	8.3	15	0.55	0.90
	Indep	4.0	14	0.29	0.47
QLD	Govt	38.4	38	1.01	0.91
	Cath	8.1	15	0.54	0.50
	Indep	3.5	14	0.25	0.23
SA	Govt	42.6	38	1.12	0.68
	Cath	4.3	13	0.33	0.20
	Indep	3.1	13	0.24	0.14
WA	Govt	31.6	31	1.02	0.65
	Cath	5.7	17	0.33	0.21
	Indep	2.7	13	0.21	0.13
TAS	Govt	32.7	29	1.13	0.28
	Cath	4.1	10	0.41	0.10
	Indep	2.4	8	0.30	0.08

APPENDIX D

LETTERS TO SCHOOLS

Executive
S A Rayner MA MED EDD FACE (President)
W Wood MA BED FACE (Vice-President)
A H Webster BA BEC FACE (Vice-President)
Professor P H Partridge MA FACE
Professor R Selby Smith MA AM FACE
Director
W C Radford MBE MA MED PHD LLD(Hon) FACE
Associate Directors
M L Clark BA BED PHD MAPSS MACE AAIM
J P Keeves BSC DIPED MED PHD FILDR MACE

Australian Council for Educational Research
PO Box 210 Hawthorn
Victoria Australia 3122
Telephone 81 1271
Cables Aceres Melbourne

Table D1   The letter to School Principals

Dear Sir/Madam,

The Australian Council for Educational Research is conducting an evaluation of the educational effects and impact of the Australian Science Facilities Program. A grant to support the project has been made by the Australian Schools Commission. Advice on the project comes from an Advisory Committee chaired by Professor R. Selby Smith (University of Tasmania).

In each State there is a liaison officer for this project. This person will help maintain contact with the schools in that State and advise on particular features of the provision of science facilities.

It has been agreed that we should approach schools directly to seek their participation in the project. The Director General of Education has given his approval for this procedure in this project.

Your school has been selected by a random sampling technique to be one of those to be requested to participate in the first phase of the project, in which all that is required is that the teacher in charge of science complete a questionnaire and return it to ACER. We anticipate that this would take about one hour of that person's time. No other science staff would need to be involved. No students will be either tested or asked to complete questionnaires.

In the questionnaire for the teacher in charge of science, information is sought about science facilities in the school, the adequacy of those facilities for the science teaching program, the science teaching staff (qualifications and the number of years at the school) and student enrolments. All the information gathered will be confidential and no school will be identified in any report of the study.

.../2

In a subsequent phase of the project, to be conducted in 1976, we will approach a small number of schools selected as case studies. In these case studies we will seek, through interviews with science teachers, more information concerning the adequacy of science facilities and the effect of those facilities on science teaching. A separate approach to this small number of schools will be made at a later date to request their participation in the case study phase of the project.

We hope that the results of this project will provide evidence upon which judgments can be made about the educational effects and impact of the Australian Science Facilities Program. It may also reveal the effects of facilities upon science teaching and provide guidance for the future provision of science teaching facilities in secondary schools. A summary report of the results of the survey will be sent to all participating schools.

It is appreciated that your school may have been involved in the ASSP project conducted by ACER. However it is unlikely that that project would have involved science teachers.

May I request the co-operation and participation of your school in this project? Within the next two weeks the Project Officer, Mr John Ainley, will write to the teacher in charge of science enclosing the questionnaire. We would be grateful if this could be completed and returned as soon as possible. If you are unable to participate could you let Mr Ainley know as soon as possible? Other arrangements will need to be made and this will reduce the accuracy of the carefully chosen sample.

Thank you,

Yours sincerely,

Wm C. Radford
Director

Table D2   Letter to the School Science Co-ordinator

The Science Co-ordinator,

Dear Sir/Madam,

The Australian Council for Educational Research is conducting an evaluation of the educational effects and impact of the Australian Science Facilities Program. The evaluation is supported by a grant from the Australian Schools Commission. An outline of the project is contained in the attached document.

In this first phase of the project we are seeking, by means of a questionnaire sent to a sample of schools, information about the provision, adequacy and use of science facilities. All the information gathered will be confidential and no school or individual will be identified in any report of the study.

Your school has been selected by a random sampling technique to form part of the sample for the first phase of the project. A letter has been sent to the school Principal informing him/her of this and of the fact that we would be writing to you.

We would be grateful if you could complete the enclosed questionnaire and return it to ACER in the envelope provided by November 14.

We emphasise that no students need to be tested and that no other science teachers need to be involved. The questionnaire has been designed with the intention of its being completed in less than one hour.

Space is provided on the questionnaire for comments. If you wish to make any additional comments, please attach these to the questionnaire. If you have any questions whilst completing the questionnaire please either contact me directly or the Liaison Officer appointed for your state. A list of Liaison Officers is enclosed with this letter.

As part of a subsequent phase of the project, we will be making visits to a much smaller number of schools in each state. In these case-study visits we will seek more detailed information about the provision and effects of science facilities. Interviews with teachers will form part of the case studies and in these teachers will be able to elaborate upon the questions raised. They will be able to comment on the appropriateness of the design of the science rooms in which they work. An approach to schools selected for case study will be made in early 1976. It is mentioned here only to indicate that the survey questionnaire is but one aspect of the study.

.../2

The Science Co-ordinator

We hope that the project will provide information upon which judgments can be made about the Science Facilities Program. In addition it is hoped that the results of the study will be useful in guiding future policy for providing science facilities and be of value to science teachers when planning their laboratories.

In conclusion could I ask you to please return the completed questionnaire by 14 November 1975? This will greatly assist us.

Thank you,

Yours sincerely,

John Ainley

John Ainley
Project Officer
Science Facilities Project

Encl.

The Science Co-ordinator

Science Facilities Evaluation Project

LIST OF LIAISON OFFICERS

New South Wales	Mrs M.B.Roberts	Science Inspector 2 O'Mara Street Mayfield NSW 2304
Victoria	Mr J.G.Ainley	ACER PO Box 210 Hawthorn Vic. 3122
Queensland	Mr G.W.Robins	Staff Inspector (Secondary) Education Department PO Box 33 North Quay Qld 4000
South Australia	Dr E.Best	Senior Research Officer Research and Planning Division Education Department Box 1152 GPO Adelaide SA 5001
Western Australia	Mr K.Betjeman	Superintendent of Biological Science Education Department 35-37 Havelock Street West Perth WA 6005
Tasmania	Mr G.Fish	Supervisor of Science Mathematics/Science Resource Centre 2 Edward Street Glebe Tas. 7000
ACT	Mr F.Jones	c/o ACT Schools Authority 9th Floor Wales Centre London Circuit Canberra ACT 2600

AUSTRALIAN SCIENCE TEACHERS ASSOCIATION

Honorary Secretary, Malcolm J. Rosier
Australian Council for Educational Research
PO Box 210, Hawthorn, Victoria 3122
Telephone 811271   Cables ACERES

16 October 1975

A LETTER OF ENDORSEMENT TO SCHOOL SCIENCE CO-ORDINATORS

The accompanying letter from Mr John Ainley of the Australian Council for Educational Research sets out information about a project currently being carried out by ACER, which is concerned with aspects of the provision of science facilities in schools.

The results of the study, as well as being important for authorities making decisions about factors related to school science, should be most interesting and informative for science teachers, school administrators and others concerned with science teaching in schools.

The Australian Science Teachers Association endorses this investigation and urges you to complete and return the enclosed questionnaire which should take no longer than one hour of your time, and will help to make the study successful.

GREGOR RAMSEY

PRESIDENT - ASTA

Executive
S A Rayner MA MED EDD FACE (President)
W Wood MA BED FACE (Vice-President)
A H Webster BA BEC FACE (Vice-President)
Professor P H Partridge MA FACE
Professor R Selby Smith MA AM FACE

Director
W C Radford AO MBE MED PHD LLD(Hon) FACE

Associate Directors
J P Keeves BSC DIPED MED PHD FILDR MACE

Australian Council for Educational Research
PO Box 210 Hawthorn
Victoria Australia 3122
Telephone 81 1271
Cables Aceres Melbourne

Our ref. JA/JMR

Table D3   Letter to School Principals about Visits

In October last, the Australian Council for Educational Research wrote to you about a project concerned with the evaluation of the educational effects and impact of the Australian Science Facilities Program. Subsequently, the teacher in charge of science at your school completed a questionnaire concerned with the provision of science facilities at the school and the science teaching program for which those facilities were used.

This year we are visiting a much smaller number of schools in order to obtain more detailed information about the impact which provision of science facilities have upon a school. The schools have been chosen to represent a range of school types and level of facilities throughout Australia. We would be grateful if your school would be willing to participate in this program of follow-up visits.

We mentioned in the letter which was sent last year that advice on the project is obtained from an advisory committee chaired by Professor R. Selby Smith (University of Tasmania). The former chairman of the Commonwealth Advisory Committee on Standards for Science Facilities in the Independent Secondary Schools (Mr E.D. Gardiner) is a member of the committee. We repeat also our assurance that the information gathered will be confidential in that no school will be identified in any report of the study.

In each school visit it is envisaged that the Project Officer will:

(i) Interview the teacher in charge of Science (approx. 40 minutes) about the effects of facilities on the work of the Science Department.

(ii) Interview each teacher who teaches Science in Year 9 (approx. 30 minutes) about the effect of facilities on Science teaching.

(iii) Talk to the laboratory staff.

(iv) Talk to the Principal or Acting Principal.

(v) Look at the school's Science facilities with the teacher in charge of Science.

(vi) Arrange for a questionnaire 'Views of Science Classrooms' to be completed by approximately 100 students in Year 9 (i.e. three or four intact classes from Year 9). This questionnaire has been given a trial in about twelve Victorian schools and takes about twenty minutes to complete.

The program for each school visit has been so arranged that each activity would fit easily into the time normally allowed for one lesson. In this way we hope not to disrupt the normal work of the school.

It is hoped that you can participate in this phase of the project. The information gained from talking to this school staff is regarded as most valuable in a project of this type. If you agree to take part in this stage of the project the Project Officer, Mr J. Ainley, plans to visit your school on
If work remains to be done after those days he will be in the locality for one or two weeks and could return to your school to undertake any work which is outstanding.

We have attached to this letter a form on which we ask that you indicate whether or not you are willing to participate in this stage of the study. We would appreciate it if you could discuss the matter with the teacher in charge in Science and return the form to the Project Officer as soon as possible.

If you have any comments on the proposed activity for the visit, please feel free to add them to the form.

Thank you for your help.

Yours sincerely,

Wm C. Radford
Director

Encl.

APPENDIX E

THE STUDENT QUESTIONNAIRE

AUSTRALIAN COUNCIL FOR EDUCATIONAL RESEARCH

SCIENCE FACILITIES PROJECT

VIEWS OF SCIENCE CLASSROOMS

There are two sections to this questionnaire. Be sure to answer both section A and section B.

Section A

Section A contains statements which could possibly describe what your science classrooms and science classes are like.

Think about how well each statement describes your science classrooms or science classes. There is space alongside each statement to indicate your answer.

Draw a circle around

> SA   if you STRONGLY AGREE with the statement.
> A   if you AGREE with the statement.
> D   if you DISAGREE with the statement.
> SD   if you STRONGLY DISAGREE with the statement.
> N   if you have NO OPINION about the statement.

Practice Statement

47. It is hard to write things in science because the chairs are not comfortable.

    Suppose you agree with this statement. Then you would circle the A in space next to the statement like this

    SA   (A)   D   SD   N

Now continue with the statements in section A.

1. In our Science room it is hard to be involved in class discussion unless you sit near the front.   SA   A   D   SD   N

2. The Science store contains many interesting charts and models which we can examine.   SA   A   D   SD   N

3. We can't do many experiments with electricity because there aren't enough power points or batteries.   SA   A   D   SD   N

4. The Science room is well designed: we can change from class lessons to experimental work without wasting time.   SA   A   D   SD   N

5. I would learn more Science if I could do some of the experiments myself.   SA   A   D   SD   N

6. In Science we are sometimes able to grow things and study how they grow. SA A D SD N

7. The seats and benches in our Science room are so arranged that we can't have discussion groups. SA A D SD N

8. It is hard to form discussion groups in our Science room without making a lot of noise. SA A D SD N

9. Demonstration experiments are a waste of time because some of the class can't see what is happening. SA A D SD N

10. In our Science room we sometimes watch T.V. programs or video replays. SA A D SD N

11. The Science room is all right for practical work but it is not good for ordinary class lessons. SA A D SD N

12. When everyone is doing experiments the Science room is very noisy. SA A D SD N

13. In Science we have enough space and apparatus for students sometimes to carry out experiments or projects they choose themselves. SA A D SD N

14. In Science every group can easily get to a tap when they need water for an experiment. SA A D SD N

15. In the Science room it is hard to find a clear space in which to write an account of an experiment. SA A D SD N

16. In Science there is just not enough good apparatus to go around so some people cannot take part in the experiments. SA A D SD N

17. The Science room always seems to have enough space for everyone to work effectively. SA A D SD N

18. The Science room is too crowded when everyone is doing experiments. SA A D SD N

19. We rarely watch movie films and slides in Science. SA A D SD N

20. In Science no matter where you sit you can see everything clearly. SA A D SD N

21. Experiments in Science are difficult because apparatus is often broken or hard to find. SA A D SD N

22. In Science we often work from a number of books available in the science room or the library. SA A D SD N

23. When we work in groups in Science the groups are too large. SA A D SD N

24. The Science room is a good place for watching films and slides. SA A D SD N

25. In Science we have to have separate lessons for theory and practical work each week. SA A D SD N

Section B

The statements in this section are descriptions of the sort of science lessons students about your age have at school. They cover a range of types of science lessons.

For each statement indicate how often the statement has been true of the science lessons you have had this year.

Draw a circle around

    A   if the statement is ALWAYS true.
    B   if the statement is OFTEN true (about 3/4 of the time)
    C   if the statement is SOMETIMES true (about 1/2 of the time)
    D   if the statement is RARELY true (about 1/4 of the time)
    E   if the statement is NEVER true.

Now continue with the statements in section B.

	Always	Often	Sometimes	Rarely	Never
26. We learn most of our Science through practical work and experiments.	A	B	C	D	E
27. Our Science teacher tests us only on what is in the textbook.	A	B	C	D	E
28. Students are encouraged to read Science magazines and reference books to become familiar with all aspects of Science.	A	B	C	D	E
29. We have a textbook for Science.	A	B	C	D	E
30. For Science homework we write up our laboratory and practical work.	A	B	C	D	E
31. Our Science classes contain more theoretical work than practical work.	A	B	C	D	E
32. The main aim of our Science lessons is to understand our textbooks.	A	B	C	D	E
33. We are encouraged to take part in fieldwork and scientific research outside school.	A	B	C	D	E
34. Our Science lessons include laboratory experiments in which we all take part.	A	B	C	D	E
35. Our Science homework requires using a textbook.	A	B	C	D	E

	Always	Often	Sometimes	Rarely	Never
36. We make observations and do experiments during our Science lessons.	A	B	C	D	E
37. When we work in the laboratory we are given complete instructions from the teacher as to what to do.	A	B	C	D	E
38. We use a book which tells us how to do our experiments in the laboratory.	A	B	C	D	E
39. We usually make up our own problems and then the teacher helps us to solve them experimentally.	A	B	C	D	E
40. In class we are encouraged to devise our own projects and experiments, either individually or in groups.	A	B	C	D	E
41. Our Science teacher demonstrates how to carry out the experiments before we do them.	A	B	C	D	E
42. In our practical work our teacher gives us certain problems to solve and then leaves us to find our own methods and solutions.	A	B	C	D	E
43. The teacher gives us questions to answer while we do our experiments.	A	B	C	D	E
44. We do our practical work from laboratory cards or instructions which tell us how to carry out the experiment.	A	B	C	D	E

For statement no.45 indicate your answer by drawing a circle around the appropriate letter as in the list below the statement.

45. During our Science lessons the amount of time we spend reading our textbooks is: A   B   C   D   E

    A All the time.
    B About one quarter of the time.
    C About one half of the time.
    D About three quarters of the time.
    E None of the time.

*   *   *   *   *   *

Thank you for completing this questionnaire.

Published by Australian Council for Educational Research, Frederick St, Hawthorn, Victoria, 3122
March, 1976.

APPENDIX F

ITEMS USED IN SCALES FROM THE STUDENT QUESTIONNAIRE

I - <u>Involvement in purposeful activity in the science room</u>

1   In our Science room it is hard to be involved in class discussion unless you sit near the front.

5   I would learn more Science if I could do some of the experiments myself.

8   It is hard to form discussion groups in our Science room without making a lot of noise.

9   Demonstration experiments are a waste of time because some of the class can't see what is happening.

11   The Science room is all right for practical work but it is not good for ordinary class lessons.

12   When everyone is doing experiments the Science room is very noisy.

20   In Science no matter where you sit you can see everything clearly.

0 - <u>The organization of the room and materials is effective and conducive to learning</u>

3   We can't do many experiments with electricity because there aren't enough power points or batteries.

4   The Science room is well designed : we can change from class lessons to experimental work without wasting time.

14   In Science every group can easily get to a tap when they need water for an experiment.

15   In the Science room it is hard to find a clear space in which to write an account of an experiment.

16   In Science there is just not enough good apparatus to go around so some people cannot take part in the experiments.

17   The Science room always seems to have enough space for everyone to work effectively.

18   The Science room is too crowded when everyone is doing experiments.

V - **Variety in the learning experiences in science**

2   The Science stores contain many interesting charts and models which we can examine.

6   In Science we are sometimes able to grow things and study how they grow.

10 In our Science room we sometimes watch TV programs or video replays.

13 In Science we have enough space and apparatus for students sometimes to carry out experiments or projects they choose themselves.

19 We rarely watch movie films and slides in Science.

22 In Science we often work from a number of books available in the Science room or the library.

24 The Science room is a good place for watching films and slides.

E - **Encouragement to explore and take part in activity which extends beyond the classroom.**

28 Students are encouraged to read Science magazines and reference books to become familiar with all aspects of science.

30 For Science homework we write up our laboratory and practical work.

33 We are encouraged to take part in fieldwork and scientific research outside school.

34 Our Science lessons include laboratory experiments in which we all take part.

37 When we work in the laboratory we are given complete instructions from the teacher as to what to do.

39 We usually make up our own problems and then the teacher helps us to solve them experimentally.

40 In class we are encouraged to devise our own projects and experiments, either individually or in groups.

41 Our Science teacher demonstrates how to carry out the experiments before we do them.

42 In our practical work our teacher gives us certain problems to solve and then leaves us to find our own methods and solutions.

T - <u>Emphasis on learning Science based upon textbooks</u>

27 Our Science teacher tests us only on what is in the textbook.

29 We have a textbook for Science.

32 The main aim of our Science lessons is to understand our textbooks.

35 Our Science homework requires using a textbook.

38 We use a book which tells us how to do our experiments in the laboratory.

45 During our Science lessons the amount of time we spend reading our textbooks is:

P - <u>Emphasis placed upon structured practical work</u>

26 We learn most of our Science through practical work and experiments.

31 Our Science classes contain more theoretical work than practical work.

34 Our Science lessons include laboratory experiments in which we all take part.

36 We make observations and do experiments during our Science lessons.

38 We use a book which tells us how to do our experiments in the laboratory.

44 We do our practical work from laboratory cards or instructions which tell us how to carry out the experiment.

APPENDIX G

MEASURES OF SCIENCE FACILITIES

School Variables Obtained from the Survey Data

1. Science Room Availability (Q1)

2. Dual-Purpose Science Room Availability (Q2)

3. Science Room per 1000 Students (L1)

4. Dual-Purpose Science Rooms per 1000 Students (L2)

5. The average quality of school science rooms.

6. The proportion of school science rooms built under the Science Facilities Program.

7. The adequacy of the supply of expendable apparatus.

8. The adequacy of the supply of minor apparatus.

9. The adequacy of the supply of major apparatus.

10. The number of laboratory assistants per 1000 students.

11. The number of laboratory assistants per 10 teachers.

School Variables obtained from Visits

12. The design of the schools science rooms.

13. The location of science facilities relative to each other.

14. The quality of school science facilities as assessed by the Project Officer.

Class Variables obtained from Visits

15. The proportion of time spent in science rooms.

16. The number of different science rooms used each week.

17. The quality of the science room most often used,
    (a) as assessed by the science co-ordinator, and
    (b) as assessed by the Project Officer.

18. The proximity of the science room to the store room.

19. The type of design of the science room most often used.

APPENDIX H

EXPENDITURE UNDER THE AUSTRALIAN SCIENCE FACILITIES PROGRAM

Table H1 Expenditure between 1 July 1964 and 30 June 1971
(Amounts in dollars)

State	Government	Non-Government Catholic	Non-Government Independent	Non-Government Total	Total
New South Wales	18,892,000	8,350,500	2,579,900	10,930,400	29,822,400
Victoria	14,303,800	5,251,200	3,032,900	8,284,100	22,487,900
Queensland	7,357,700	2,604,100	1,660,770	4,264,800	11,622,500
South Australia	4,778,200	1,353,000	1,422,900	2,775,900	7,554,100
Western Australia	3,659,200	1,323,000	804,000	2,126,000	5,785,200
Tasmania	1,673,700	552,500	414,300	966,800	2,640,500
TOTAL	50,664,600	19,433,300	9,914,700	29,348,000	80,012,600

Table H2 Expenditure between 1 July 1971 and 30 June 1975

State	Government	Non-Government Catholic	Non-Government Independent	Non-Government Total	Total
New South Wales	9,471,780	4,120,230	1,221,310	5,341,540	14,813,320
Victoria	8,035,620	3,138,965	2,298,215	5,437,180	13,422,800
Queensland	3,072,780	2,411,520	911,500	3,323,020	6,395,800
South Australia	2,647,125	408,527	254,998	663,525	3,310,650
Western Australia	1,870,035	1,173,514	599,591	1,773,105	3,643,140
Tasmania	990,660	426,947	241,683	668,630	1,659,290
TOTAL	26,088,000	11,679,073	5,527,297	17,207,000	43,295,000

Source: Commonwealth Department of Education, 1975.

APPENDIX I

TEACHER ATTITUDE TO SCIENCE TEACHING SCALE

This scale was taken from IEA Study of Science Achievement (Comber and Keeves, 1973). To save space only the ten statements used have been reproduced here. Teachers were asked to indicate their response to each statement by means of five response categories.

       A. Disagree strongly
       B. Disagree
       C. No opinion
       D. Agree
       E. Agree strongly

Below are given ten statements on the teaching of Science. We are interested in obtaining information on how teachers regard the job of Science teaching. Will you therefore indicate against each item the extent to which you agree or disagree with each statement.

Please answer these questions by blackening in the appropriate space.

1. Open-ended investigations are possible, and desirable, from the very beginning of Science education.
2. Practical experience is not essential for the acquisition of scientific knowledge.
3. There is so much to learn about Science nowadays that it is better not to take up time with practical work.
4. A pupil may forget all he learned at school about the facts and principles of Science but the experience he gains in carrying out his own practical investigations will last him in good stead for ever.
5. A teacher's time is better employed in giving lectures and demonstrations than in preparing for laboratory work.
6. The difficulties of providing opportunities for practical work of an investigational nature are so great that teachers should be advised not to undertake such work.
7. A pupil's Science education is not complete unless he has had opportunities for carrying out investigations on his own.
8. However hard-pressed a Science teacher is, the top priority in his work should be to provide opportunities for his pupils to carry out their own original investigations.
9. At least half a pupil's time in Science should be spent on practical work, preferably in a laboratory or in the field.
10. Pupils gain little of value from carrying out their own investigations.